Diagnosing Individual Needs for Early Childhood Education

Jean K. Mowbray

Harcum Junior College

Helen H. Salisbury

Temple University

Charles E. Merrill Publishing Co.
A Bell & Howell Co.   Columbus, Ohio

Published by
Charles E. Merrill Publishing Co.
A Bell & Howell Co.
Columbus, Ohio 43216

This book was set in Times Roman and Helvetica.
The cover was designed by Will Chenoweth.
Cover photograph from the National Education Association.

International Standard Book Number: 0–675–8696–5

Library of Congress Catalog Card Number: 74–33616

1 2 3 4 5 6 7 8 9 10—79 78 77 76 75

Printed in the United States of America

Preface

The idea for this book originated several years ago when we team-taught a course entitled *Principles and Techniques of Guidance for Teachers of Young Children.* As we organized the course, we were dismayed by the scarcity of guidance materials available for early childhood teachers. Recognizing the crucial need for more sensitive guidance at the pre-primary level, we began to develop a manual of appropriate forms for collecting information about children.

As the manual took shape, we realized that the project involved a broader commitment than the mere compilation of forms. Each instrument reflects a philosophy of working with children. We believe that each child is special because he is unique: therefore, the instruments should focus on the *individuality* of the child. Inattention to the uniqueness of children, especially in the early years, has in too many cases resulted in emotional sores and in educational disabilities. If each child is treated as a *special* child, he is less likely to become an *exceptional* child.

We believe that each child, whether he is excelling, developing as expected, or lagging behind, needs individualized help to grow and to learn. Regardless of how he compares to his agemates, each child requires guidance to make the most of his potentialities and to overcome his limitations. Without this help a child may miss out on opportunities to develop his strengths and to use them wisely. Without individual attention a child's unique growth-trends may be overlooked, causing mild to serious complications later on in his developmental career.

Designed for use with all children, the forms described in this book are based on our belief that each child has his own pattern of developmental needs. Focusing on the uniqueness of the individual child, the materials help the teacher to identify where the child is developmentally. On the basis of this assessment, the teacher evolves ways to help the individual child grow to his optimum potential for successful living.

We want to express our gratitude to all those who have shown concern and interest in this project. Over the years countless students have experimented with the instruments and techniques. Their experiences and constructive criticism helped to refine the materials ultimately included in the book. Specialists in various fields have verified the accuracy and authorized certain sections involving unpublished data and theories. Demonstrating their interest in helping children, Dr. David Hamilton, lecturer in pediatric optometry, Pennsylvania College of Optometry; Mr. Richard C. Bevan, director, Child Study Department, Pennsylvania School for the Deaf; and Dr. Jay M. Yanoff, Coordinator of Staff Training and Evaluation, Pennsylvania Advancement School and Intensive Learning Center gave unsparingly of their time to review and criticize materials pertinent to their fields. We deeply appreciate the artistic contribution of Mrs. Suzanne Fredrikson deMilt. Capturing the behavior of children with insight and charm, her illustrations reflect the flavor of the ideas we are trying to express.

Jean K. Mowbray

Helen H. Salisbury

With love to our husbands,
Bill and Jack.
Their continuing support
and encouragement made
the project possible.

Contents

1 Introduction 1

2 Using the Records 7

3 The Importance of Preentrance Records 19

4 The Diagnostic Interview 47

5 The Case of Allan 59

6 Readiness 79

7 Diagnosing and Planning for Physical Development 89

8 Diagnosing and Planning for Emotional Development 109

9 Diagnosing and Planning for Mental Development 121

10 Diagnosing and Planning for Social Development 145

11 The Master Readiness Record 161

12 Progress and Permanent Records 223

Glossary 245

Selected Bibliography 251

Index 255

1

Introduction

Changing Emphases in Early Childhood Education

Early childhood education is undergoing a period of rapid and revolutionary change. One of the most basic factors contributing to such change has been the recognition that the preprimary years (ages two to six) are critical for intellectual development. There is mounting evidence that learning during this period has a profound influence on later school success. Both in the home and in more formal settings, the quality of education in the early years matters. With this insight early childhood education has achieved a new stature, commanding widespread and serious attention.

The preprimary years are now the focus of intensive inquiry. Traditional concepts about the nature of early childhood education have been challenged and new ideas have emerged with such momentum that those directly involved in the field can scarcely keep pace. Many of the questions relating to learning during this period are still controversial. The issues are comparatively new, and the studies too recent to settle conflicting ideas. There are, however, some areas of clear agreement. For example, it is accepted that the child's developmental status limits what he can learn and determines how he learns. It follows that learnings must be

1

specifically geared to what the child is developmentally ready to do. Understanding the young child as a learner begins with his developmental pattern—what he is like physically, mentally, socially, and emotionally.

Increasingly, research points to the crucial need to understand the *total* child in order to provide appropriate learning experiences for him. Physical, mental, social, and emotional growth systems interact to affect the child's learning potential. What happens in one system influences growth in the other areas. Irregularities erupting in any dimension of growth can potentially inhibit the use of learning capacities. In view of this interdependence, success in learning, often narrowly identified with mental growth, is more related to total developmental factors than to any single factor.

Implications for the Early Childhood Teacher

This emphasis on planning educational experiences based on the developmental pattern of the child implies complex responsibilities for the early childhood teacher. Not only should she know how the child of this age differs from his predecessor, the toddler, and his successor, the primary school child, she also should understand each child as a unique expression of the developmental program. Each child has his own roster of needs to be identified, interpreted, and fulfilled by a plan designed especially for him. In evolving her plans, the teacher needs to recognize that no developmental program unfolds smoothly. Each child develops some areas of strength and some areas of weakness in growing and learning. He needs help in developing his strong areas fully and in using them wisely. He also needs help in overcoming his limitations and, in some cases, in coming to terms and living with his shortcomings. Without an in-depth knowledge of every child in her care, even the most perceptive teacher may miss the cues which give her insight into the needs of each child.

Implications for Guidance at the Early Childhood Level

Understanding the child in this developmental context calls for quality controls at the guidance level. Practically defined, "guidance" is present whenever efforts are made to know and to help the child as an individual. In these terms guidance is not a new concept in early childhood education; in fact, the humanistic approach is the natural hallmark of teachers of young children. Planning activities appropriate in timing and sequence to the needs of the individual has been a basic objective of nursery-kindergarten practice.

The guidance procedures used in this planning are not necessarily organized into a system. Many teachers have relied on subjective evaluations to determine what a child is ready to do. Inadequate methods for gathering and organizing information have resulted in hazy impressions of the child. Intuitively, the teacher may feel that a child is more advanced in mental growth than in physical, and somewhat immature socially and emotionally. But what evidence has she to support these judgments? She needs reliable data to back up her assessment and to bring the developmental profile into sharper focus.

Precision Tool for Guidance: The Record System

The tasks of data collection and identification of developmental patterns must be as free of error as possible, for it is only on the basis of objective and trustworthy information that the teacher can plan, help, and guide effectively. The precision tool for guidance is the record system. Comprehensive, systematic records assure more complete, accurate, and organized information about individual children. The term *records* refers to the forms, inventories, charts, summary sheets, and other materials which structure the collection and recording of data about pupils. Placed in logical sequence these records become a "record system."

Because of the importance of a record system in education, there is a need to marshal what is currently known about records appropriate for use at the early childhood level. This book represents an effort to consolidate available records developed for nursery-kindergarten settings. Sample records proposed for sequential phases of the child's school career are explained in terms of their purpose, the directions for their use, and their contributions to understanding the child. When necessary for effective use of the record, the theoretical background underlying the construction and purpose of the record is given. For example, the use of records designed to identify readiness levels depends upon knowledge of readiness factors—what to look for, how to interpret and evaluate findings, and the implications of the data for planning.

One of the major emphases of this book is to simplify and streamline the record-keeping procedure. It is the authors' hope that explanations and directions are sufficiently clear for the book to qualify as a training manual for the procedure.

None of the records presented requires specific professional training for understanding or use. Even though specific records are geared for the nursery-kindergarten, the book is intended as a source of reference for all those who guide young children. The records can easily be adapted for use in other kinds of early childhood settings. Moreover, with slight modifications they can be used with older age groups.

GUIDANCE ASSUMPTIONS BASIC TO THE RECORD SYSTEM

The effective record system reflects the following assumptions underlying educational guidance: (1) Guidance is for the individual, (2) Guidance is for all children, (3) Guidance is continuous, (4) Guidance is planned. *Guidance is for the individual.* Guidance is based on an awareness of individual differences. Children cannot be cast in a single mold. Each child has a unique pattern of needs, potentialities, strengths, and limitations. No two children are endowed with the same maturational program; no two children exist in precisely the same environment; no two children have been modified by the same experiences. Varied cultural backgrounds create differences in values, motives, and life-styles. If the school is going to help each child to learn optimally, then provision must be made to know and to understand children as individuals. The record system helps to fulfill this responsibility by focusing on the individual child with all the variations that make him different.

Guidance Is for All Children. Affirming that each child is different from all others in some ways, guidance emphasizes the inherent worth and dignity of each. The value of the individual is recognized regardless of his achievement. No child is expendable. In the practical situation individual attention is often reserved for the child whose needs are obvious. The record system assures that all children—not just the exceptional few— receive help to realize the most from their educative experiences.

Guidance Is Continuous. Ideally guidance begins before the child enters school and continues beyond his period of formal schooling. Consequently, the records extend into the child's past experiences, his current home life, and his future academic career. Attention is given to developmental antecedents that shape and give meaning to what he is and what he can do. The records facilitate systematic contact with parents, promoting consistency between what goes on in the home and what goes on in the school. Finally, the system assures continuity of educational experience by articulating the child's progress to the next school level.

Guidance Is Planned. A school program set up to put all children in command of their powers to do and to become can scarcely proceed without careful planning. Yet in many early childhood settings guidance is an incidental thing, whereby help is given only as situations arise. There are those who contend that too many variables exist in the human situation to warrant guidance by plan. But more often than not, guidance by ear results in inappropriate help, after-the-fact help, or no help at all because significant clues have been overlooked.

Effective guidance evolves only when provision is made to anticipate situations requiring help and to plot ahead of time the nature of help to be given. The overall program is planned with the critical adjustments encountered by most children staked out in advance. Helping strategies are ready for use as cues are given. Moreover, the individualized program for each child, based on a continuing assessment of his developmental needs, is mapped out to provide direction for the next step. Of course, predictive powers are limited as developmental surprises can disrupt the most carefully conceived plan. However, more problem situations are identified and neutralized, in some cases, averted with planning.

Planned guidance is imperative at the nursery-kindergarten level because of the preventive measures that can be taken then. Many learning problems have their origins in these early school years. If recognized, these potential problems may be arrested rather than develop into full-blown disabilities. Physical, emotional, and behavioral difficulties are more responsive to correction or treatment when detected in their beginning stages. Guidance is legitimately concerned with both prevention and cure; however, it becomes increasingly apparent that more attention to the preventive aspects of guidance at these lower levels may obviate the need for remediation later on. This responsibility for early identification of problems is so crucial that it cannot be left to chance. Only by planning can the job be effectively done. Planning is based on the complete, accurate, and organized information yielded by an efficient record system.

Value of the Record System

The system of records gives shape and substance to the guidance aspect of the school program. Providing direction for the overall guidance plan, the record system follows a logical sequence beginning with the child's initial contact with the school and extending long after his association has terminated. As an information-getter, the system brings together all the important data about the child. As an information-organizer, the system integrates the data, enabling the school to know and understand the total child.

Understanding the child requires a detailed investigation into his past and current environment. Especially in dealing with young children, the background history is important. Sources of such data are preentrance records and parent-teacher conferences.

Readiness records permit continuing evaluation of each child's growth and development. These records not only reveal the child's maturity levels, but also determine the kinds of learning from which he can benefit with ease and interest at any given time. The records alert personnel to developmental subtleties that might be missed, or even dismissed, because their meaning is not recognized. The long-range picture brings to light behavioral patterns. In this context seemingly critical episodes assume perspective. Geared to pick up stumbling blocks, readiness records are sensitive to deviations from the normal that are potential problem areas.

The system facilitates communication with parents and others concerned with the development and adjustment of the child. Progress records serve as the basis for mutual planning at the parent-teacher conference. Moreover, evidence recorded over a period of time validates reports to parents and administrative personnel and supports recommendations for referral to resource agencies.

Since education is a continuous process, the transition from one level to the next is not sharp and complete. There is overlapping, unfinished business. The permanent record communicates information about the child's progress to the primary school teacher, helping to assure continuity of educational experiences based on the child's developmental pattern.

The record system is more than a procedural blueprint for guidance. The practical benefits are important in synthesizing guidance efforts, but the real value lies in the changing attitudes toward children brought about by the continuing use of the records. Daily work with the materials reorients thinking from what a child ought to be to what he is. Consistent reference to the records turns the focus of attention from what he ought to learn to what he is developmentally ready to learn. From these more realistic vantage points, behavioral expectations grow increasingly reasonable; learning experiences are more closely related to a child's needs.

Based on guidance assumptions, the records are designed to bring to light each child's pattern of needs. Using the records helps to assure that the individual child receives appropriate and timely attention, regardless of where he ranks along the developmental continuum. Emphasizing the uniqueness of each child, the records provide a guidance-oriented basis for working with *all* children. Use of the records ultimately encourages the guidance way of dealing with young children—an approach that results in more positive outcomes for the child and more gratifying experiences for those who guide him.

2

Using the Records

If values inherent in the record system are to be realized, then the records must be maintained and used in an organized manner. Some teachers shy away from records because of the time factor; they insist that they can be more productively engaged in direct interaction with the children. There is no question that record-keeping takes time, but this activity is an investment that pays compound interest in hours saved. The major value of efficient record-keeping is a more complete understanding of the child and a more valid basis for helping him. Without adequate records teachers must rely on memory and are faced with the job of preparing a report each time an incident occurs. A check-mark on a chart could have expedited the task. There are schools that develop elaborate systems and invest the effort to keep the entries up to date, but often the records stay in the file, consulted only when a problem occurs. This incidental use inevitably results from lack of a method to centralize and condense the materials. If the information collected in the records is brought together in a summary form providing an easy reference to the child's developmental history, the records may be used to make plans for the child that will prevent problems as well as to overcome existing problems.

A summary of the records for each child needs to be maintained, reviewed, and evaluated on a periodic basis in order to determine the developmental progress of the child physically, mentally, socially, and emotionally. The objective of the evaluation is diagnosis in order to provide a basis for helping the child. If an irregularity is identified and more information is needed to determine a plan of help for the child, then the "supporting" records should be examined. Each record has its specific diagnostic sensitivities; however, the overall use of the record rests on an understanding of the guidelines for diagnosing from recorded materials.

Diagnosing from Recorded Materials

CAN THE TEACHER DIAGNOSE?

The teacher's role in diagnosis has not been clearly established; consequently, there is confusion about whether or not the teacher should assume this responsibility. It is not unusual for teachers to back away from the task for fear of making a misjudgment which will affect the child. This conservative tendency on the part of teachers is supported by some educators who regard diagnosis as a "touch-me-not" area beyond the limits of a teacher's skills. On the other hand, there are teachers who feel compelled to diagnose even on the basis of isolated samples of behavior. In view of the uncertainties about the role of the teacher in diagnosing, it is essential to clarify the meaning of diagnosis, the procedure for diagnosis, and the ways in which the teacher may be involved appropriately in this task.

MEANING OF DIAGNOSIS

The generic origins of the term *diagnosis* are the Greek words *dia*—through and *gnosis*—to know. The diagnostician sifts *through* all the information in order to *know* the individual. Knowing involves more than information-collecting; it suggests delicate balancing and blending of data to arrive at a penetrating understanding of a person's total behavior. The key to diagnosis is knowing the individual in terms of this enriched perspective.

Simply defined, a diagnosis is made when a judgment is applied to the information. The quality of the judgment depends largely upon the completeness and accuracy of the information. Not until all the evidence is in, summarized, and evaluated should a judgment be made. In view of this definition, the question is not a matter of whether the teacher *can* diagnose, but *when* diagnosis can legitimately take place. Problems seem to arise when judgments are made too early in the data-processing sequence. The teacher should not begin to diagnose until information from a variety of sources has been collected and the findings weighed and analyzed. Even though two teachers have exactly the same information, the more complete the data are, the less chance there is for disparity between their judgments. In order to avoid the danger of premature judgment, the teacher should follow specific steps in carrying out the diagnostic task.

PROCEDURE FOR DIAGNOSIS

The procedure is initiated in carrying out routine evaluations of recorded data. In this instance, the diagnostic judgment concerns the developmental status of the individual. The same procedure is followed when the teacher identifies a "difference"—a behavioral or growth irregularity—and checks the information to see if there is a plausible explanation. In this context, the judgment concerns the cause of the behavior. In either case, the following procedure for diagnosis is observed:

1. Collect the data.
2. Summarize the pertinent data.
3. Evaluate the data.
4. Make the diagnosis.
5. State the diagnosis in objective terms.

1. *Collect the Data.* The record system is designed to provide a complete developmental profile of each child. Using the records assists adequate data collection and helps to avert the error of diagnosing from limited data or biased behavioral samples. The validity of the judgment will in all probability be proportional to the amount of pertinent data collected from various sources.

Many teachers support the need to collect ample information about children; however, they express a realistic concern for the time it takes to do the job. In order to make it possible to do this arduous task, the record system was developed. One of the primary purposes of the system is to put information in a condensed form at the fingertips of the teacher. The Master Readiness Record (Chapter 11) is a summary of the available data about the individual child. This record provides a quick reference, expediting the data-collection task.

2. *Summarize the Pertinent Data.* Whether the teacher is conducting a routine evaluation of a child's record or trying to trace out the cause of a developmental irregularity, *all* the information is reviewed. It is natural to first consult the sections of the Master Readiness Record most obviously related to the problem under investigation. Plausible reasons accounting for a behavior may turn up in these sections; however, a more compre-

hensive review of the record may yield either confirming or contradictory evidence. During the review of the Master Readiness Record the teacher culls factors pertinent to the problem. When identified, the factors are summarized.

3. *Evaluate the Data.*   Evaluation may be defined as estimating the value of the information in clarifying the specific situations or problem. What patterns do the data form? What are the meanings of the parts in terms of the whole? During this step the information is weighed, compared, put together in different combinations, and tested to see that all the variables have been considered. Occasionally, one entry will seem to be the key to explain the problem. When checked against other available data, however, the one item may be incongruous in terms of the overall behavioral pattern. Any datum, regardless of its strength of import, must always be examined for its functional relationship with other information accumulated over time. Diagnosis is made from a pattern of information, never from an isolated datum, no matter how dramatic. The information must combine to form a clear-cut pattern before a diagnosis is possible.

4. *Make the Diagnosis*   A diagnosis is made when a judgment is applied to the information. Once the pertinent data are examined in the context of the total child and a pattern is identified, the teacher makes a decision about the developmental status of the child. When an irregularity is identified, the information is reviewed to find an explanation. In this case the teacher hypothesizes (makes an educated guess) about the nature and cause of the problem. In either situation the judgment serves as a guide for setting up a program to help the child.

Two kinds of information are necessary in making the diagnosis: (1) Information about the specific child and (2) Information about human development. Knowing what to expect of a child of a given age provides a basis for diagnostic judgments about his levels of maturity. Without an understanding of how the child unfolds physically, mentally, socially, and emotionally, the teacher has no guidelines for making these judgments. Extreme departures from expected performance may be identified, but the less obvious problems may be overlooked.

Diagnosis is not an easy task. Sound judgments depend not only upon the completeness and accuracy of recorded information but also upon the know-how to recognize diagnostic meanings. The more informed the teacher about human development, the better equipped she is to apply valid judgments to information.

5. *State the Diagnosis in Objective Terms.*   The diagnostic judgment should be stated in language that means the same thing to everyone. There

is a tendency to use labels to describe judgments on the assumption that the problem has been cornered and resolved once a name has been found for it. Just a few of the popular labels are "hyperactive," "retarded," or the more elitist label, "learning disabled."

The label is a capsule-form method to transmit a mental image of certain behavioral characteristics exhibited by the child. The problem is that the image of behaviors implied by the label may be different for different people. As innocuous a label as "immature speech" may mean arrested vocabulary development, infantile pronunciation, limited concept of grammar, repetitions, hesitations, or a host of other possibilities. "Hyperactive" and "learning disabled" carry more complex associations; hence, greater latitude for misunderstanding.

Labeling is contrary to the developmental approach. Attempts to put children into categories dehumanizes them by taking away that which is most uniquely theirs—their individuality. Rarely does a label account for all the variations of a child's behavior and rarely does a child exhibit all the behaviors associated with the label. One of the most demeaning aspects of this pigeonholing tendency is that the label, meant to enlighten, actually closes off efforts to understand the individual child. Once classified, the label tends to stick, following the child in subsequent records and influencing future teachers.

REVISION OF THE DIAGNOSIS

The diagnosis is in all cases tentative and flexible enough to change in the face of new evidence. As more information about the child is available, the judgments may require adjustment in order to fit the more complete picture. Increasing maturity of the child is bound to influence the diagnosis. Yesterday's judgment may be obsolete because the child has grown, expanded, overcome the problem, made up the lack that characterized his behavior at an earlier period. Developmental patterns shift and assume new meanings. Moreover, there are instances when regressions invalidate a diagnosis. The child seems to turn back the clock and behave at a less mature level. Change calls for updated information, another evaluation, a revised diagnosis, and a modified plan of help.

The Case of Eric

The procedure for diagnosis is illustrated by the case of Eric. The case materials demonstrate how a child's problem was clarified and helped when the teacher took the necessary steps to arrive at a diagnostic judgment.

Eric was four years, two months old when he was enrolled in nursery school. Presumably he adjusted to the new experience easily. His teachers were concerned, however, because his speech was so rapid and inarticulate that he could barely make himself understood. The following is a phonetic reproduction of an excerpt of his recorded speech:

TEACHER: Do you have any brothers?

ERIC: Tilm (Tim). Cowun (Karen) don' hab (have) a burber (brother).

TEACHER: Do you have a dog?

ERIC: Er—er—er—Pudgy. Luk (lick) ar (ear) an' t'umbs (thumbs).

TEACHER: He licks you?

ERIC: Ya' He come—he come— he-ah (here) and then—and then—and then— he bit me in moy (my) ar (ear).

TEACHER: He bit you in the ear?

ERIC: He dinna (didn't)—dinna. I hadda (had to) to the hobsel (hospital).

A speech "difference" was suspected at the time of the preentrance interview. The interviewing teacher had recorded that Eric tended to speak in an indistinct manner. As support for this observation, she noted that during the visit Eric had explored the nursery school room and asked questions about various play materials. His speech was so indistinct that the teacher had been unable to understand him. Almost by reflex, Eric's mother repeated his questions. Anticipating the inquiry about models for developing speech, the teacher had noted on the interview form that the mother's speech was "rapid, but fluent and articulate."

Alerted to this "difference," Eric's teacher routinely *collected the data through the records.* In order to determine his developmental progress, she gathered data about his physical, emotional, mental, and social levels of maturity. This information was centralized on the Master Readiness Record.

The inventories in the Master Readiness Record were reviewed for information that might cast light on Eric's problem. Most entries indicated normal progress. A finding of apparent diagnostic significance appeared in the area of gross motor coordination. He could hop without support eight times on his right foot; however, he could not sustain a hopping movement on his left foot. Maneuvers on the walking beam showed a slight dragging of his left foot that upset his balance and decelerated both forward and backward movement. The suspicion that the left side of the body might not be functioning as well as the other was ruled out by other exercises that indicated both sides moving together in a coordinated way.

According to the Background Information Form Eric's health history was clear except for an allergy to milk products. Hearing and vision had been professionally checked and found normal. His Health Record indicated that his energy level tended to be high. A notation about his speech at the diagnostic interview appeared under "individual variations" in the speech section of the interview form.

Emotionally, Eric exercised reasonable self-control and ability to stick by a task or activity until completion according to the Master Readiness Record. He made positive references to his family. In the Special Problems section, the following comment had been transferred from the Background Information Form filled out by the parents:

> He may be confused during the first few weeks of school as his mother will be hospitalized and then convalescing. He has been told about what's going on, but we're not sure he understands. The situation is not serious.

According to the Mental Inventory of the Master Readiness Record, Eric could recognize, name, and manipulate colors, shapes, and numbers beyond average expectations. He could print his first name. During free play period he showed unusual capacity to focus on a project. When confronted with problem situations, he demonstrated ingenuity and self-direction. Curious about his surroundings, he experimented with objects, puzzles, and games on his own initiative. Infantile pronunciation was indicated in the speech section of the record. Also, the item "verbal output" was checked "high." In the Word Reproduction Exercise he satisfactorily reproduced both basic sounds and complex words.

A review of the Social Inventory of the Master Readiness Record indicated that he fit into the routines and entered into activities with enthusiasm. At circle time he was attentive and followed directions. Responsive to other children, he played cooperatively with them, assuming a leadership role among them.

The next step was to *summarize the pertinent data*. Not only did the teacher review the Master Readiness Record for items that would have bearing on his speech production, but she also investigated the pre-entrance records for information forecasting a speech problem. In response to the item about speech on the Background Information Form, the parents had checked "rapid," "clear," "talks constantly," "uses many words." The background history revealed that Eric's father was a lawyer; his mother was a doctoral candidate at a university. One older brother, now age seven, had formerly been enrolled at the nursery school. The brother's record attested to "high verbal output" and "advanced articulation." Despite demanding career schedules, both parents spent time with Eric. Leisure and vacation periods were devoted to outdoor activities and camping trips which included the children.

The teacher's summary was as follows: The recording of Eric's speech revealed a unique garbling of sound. The Physical Inventory indicated the problem of the sluggish left foot. Recent professional examinations ruled out vision and hearing as possible sources of the problem. Emotionally, a pertinent item was the notation that Eric might be confused because of his mother's hospitalization. The Mental Inventory contained a reference to his infantile pronunciation; yet he was successful in both the basic sounds and complex words sections of the Word Reproduction Exercise. His leadership role among the other children indicated that his speech "difference" had not interfered with his social development. A significant item was his ability to follow directions which implied that he was perceiving correctly what other people said.

The preentrance records revealed that the parents were apparently unaware of the speech "difference." The response to the item on the Background Information Form did not recognize a problem. The interview form indicated the mother's reflexive tendency to repeat Eric's questions so that the teacher could understand what he was saying. The description of the brother's speech seemed to be a pertinent item. The interviewing teacher had made the notation that the mother's speech was "rapid, but fluent and articulate."

The teacher *evaluated the data.* In clarifying Eric's speech problem, one explanation was that his unintelligible speech was related to the temporary disruption in the home. Anxiety about his mother's hospitalization, coupled with the new experience of nursery school, could step up the tempo of his speech. Regression to infantile pronunciation might be a natural reaction to the situation. The idea of transient difficulty would clarify the parents' response to items checked relating to his speech. He might not have exhibited the behavior at the time the Background Information Form was completed.

When examined for its functional relationship with other information, this explanation did not account for all of Eric's behavior. The sluggish left foot did not fit the pattern. His social adjustment, his positive reference to his family, his ability to focus, to attend, and to control did not support this explanation. Furthermore, there was the indisputable evidence that the interviewing teacher had picked up the "difference" in his speech at the time of the preentrance visit which had taken place before his mother was hospitalized.

The teacher was aware that persistent infantile pronunciation together with Eric's sluggish left foot might signify a perceptual-motor problem. An auditory perceptual problem severe enough to reflect in unintelligible speech would surely influence Eric's ability to reproduce sounds and words, yet he was successful in both basic sounds and complex words in the Word Reproduction Exercise. Also a problem in this area would influence his ability to follow directions. The left foot was still incongruous in terms of other findings about his motor coordination.

When all the items were weighed and compared, a pattern seemed to emerge. The accurate recording of Eric's speech revealed a unique garbling of sounds. On the interview form the teacher had identified a "difference" in his speech and had described the mother's speech as "rapid, but fluent and articulate." The records of Eric's brother had contained references to "high verbal output" and "advanced articulation." Originally viewed in a positive context, the descriptions of the speech of both the mother and brother assumed new meaning in light of *all* the information. What kind of speech was Eric hearing in the home? What models were available to imitate? Rapid and articulate speech, especially when people are talking almost at once, can be a blurred babble to a little boy who is not yet mature enough to sift out sounds accurately and spontaneously. This explanation seemed most compatible with the total pattern of information.

On the basis of her evaluation, the teacher *made the diagnosis.* She applied a judgment to the information and *stated the diagnosis in objective terms:* Eric was reproducing the indistinct impressions of the high-tempo speech heard in the home. Recognizing that the diagnosis was only an educated guess, the teacher checked further. At the fall parent-teacher conference Eric's progress, including his speech problem, was discussed with his mother. Careful questioning elicited from the mother the picture of a highly vocal family with accelerated speech tempo. She explained that she and her husband had been oblivious to Eric's problem because his speech was merely a "babyish rendition" of the older child's style of speaking. Although the family understood Eric, his mother realized that people outside the home sometimes had difficulty grasping what he was saying. She had not felt it was unusual for a child of Eric's age to be misunderstood.

The report about his left foot drew a confirming response from his mother. She had an hereditary foot defect that had been corrected by minor surgery when she was an adolescent. The possibility that Eric had fallen heir to the same problem was later verified by professional examination. Eric's mother was relieved that the foot problem had been identified at his young age. With prompt correction, he would be spared the difficulties she had experienced as a result of the handicap.

The values of the diagnostic· procedure are apparent in the case of Eric. In reviewing his records, the teacher recognized the need to look at the "whole child." Only as his physical, emotional, mental, and social progress were investigated did the total pattern come to light. On the basis of a more limited investigation, the first explanation about the influence of the mother's hospitalization might have been accepted as plausible. If the teacher had stopped with this solution, not bothering to find corroborative data, she may have decided to let time take care of the problem, missing the opportunity for early intervention. If the teacher had not been aware of the need for a pattern of information, the judgment about a perceptual-motor problem could have led to an inappropriate and circuitous plan of treatment. As a result of the teacher's thoroughness, a special benefit was the identification of the foot problem. Because of early detection, this developmental handicap was arrested. The objective of diagnosis is to provide a basis for evolving a plan of help. If the teacher had settled for either of the original possibilities, her decision would have deterred appropriate planning.

After the Diagnosis, What?

Diagnosis is only a beginning step. The procedure has no meaning except to provide a valid foundation for helping the child. The judgment serves as a guide for setting up a program specifically designed to strengthen areas of vulnerability or to correct or offset problems. The plan may consist of strategies worked out in advance to strengthen readiness or to improve skills in given areas. When the problem concerns an atypical behavior or growth pattern that requires professional attention, the plan may involve referral to a resource person or agency for further screening and treatment.

In the case of Eric, for example, when the diagnosis was validated by the interview with his mother, the next step was to outline a plan to help him to overcome his problem. Since his speech was his version of the high-tempo patterns heard in the home, the key to helping him was to provide models of slow, clearly enunciated speech. His teacher and mother agreed to concentrate on using slow, clear speech and to spend time talking with him on a one-to-one basis. A program of exercises to improve his understanding of spoken sounds and words was initiated and carried out by both teacher and mother. Recordings of his speech made after the plan was in progress for two months showed dramatic improvement over those made at the outset.

Confidentiality

The responsible care and use of recorded materials are basic to the professional handling of information about people. In developing a record system, the school must set up procedures to assure the physical safe-keeping of the materials. It is also imperative to establish policies to promote the prudent and selective use of the information.

Precautions must be taken to insure the security of the records against loss, misplacement, or accessibility to persons not authorized to use them. Obviously, a fundamental procedure for record maintenance is to house the materials in a *locked* file. The file should not be left unlocked except when the records are being used *in the immediate area.* Although there may be reason to remove sections of a child's records to other parts of the school, his individual folder should remain in the file. In the event that a record or sample of a behavior, e.g., a drawing, must accompany a report to a referral agency, a copy or duplicate, not the original, should be sent. Materials that leave the premises, as in the instance of a report to a referral agency, should be enclosed in a sealed envelope by the person sending the materials.

The guidelines governing the confidential use of information should be observed by all school personnel. Discussing the business of a child with or in the presence of those not parentally or professionally associated with the child violates the privacy of both the child and his family. Information about a child should never be shown to or discussed with anyone except his parents or those authorized to work with him. Those authorized to work with the child include teachers, ancillary personnel (e.g., consulting physician), persons or agencies to whom the child has been referred, and in some instances, auxiliary personnel.

Discussions about a child should never take place within the hearing of other children. Careless comments to a parent or to other staff members about a child in the presence of other children can be misinterpreted and generate anxieties. The assumption that children are not mature enough to understand what is being said has an inherent danger. Innocent repeating of information or misuse of what has been heard about another child may result.

Summary

The record system provides a convenient reference for summarized information about a child. To be useful, the Master Readiness Record for each child must be evaluated on a periodic basis. The objective of the evaluation is diagnosis. Simply defined, a diagnosis is made when a judgment is applied to the information. Only when data from a variety of sources have been collected, summarized, and evaluated can valid judgments be made about a child's developmental status or the cause of an irregularity. The purpose of diagnosis is not to label or pigeonhole, but to provide a basis for helping the child. When defined in these terms, the question is not whether a teacher *can* diagnose, but *when* diagnosis can take place. The problem of diagnosing too early in the data-processing sequence can be averted by following the procedure for diagnosis:

1. Collect the data.
2. Summarize the pertinent data.
3. Evaluate the data.
4. Make the diagnosis.
5. State the diagnosis in objective terms.

The case of Eric illustrates how the procedure for diagnosis helped the teacher to make an hypothesis (an educated guess) about a child's problem and evolve a plan for helping him. The thorough investigation afforded by the use of the record system not only made it possible to confirm the cause of Eric's speech problem, but also facilitated the identification of the more subtle problem of his left foot.

Diagnosis is a beginning step. The procedure has no meaning except to provide a basis for evolving a plan of help for the child. In using the records a basic consideration concerns the confidential care and use of the recorded materials.

3

The Importance of Preentrance Records

The primary purpose of the preentrance records is to establish a communication system between home and school. The term *communication* means exchange of information; *system* implies that the giving and receiving of information flows between two parties in an orderly way. As introductory instruments, the preentrance records set in motion a sequence of communication between home and school.

The immediate purpose of the records is to facilitate the exchange of information essential to an admissions decision. The records also provide developmental information necessary to ease the child's entrance into the program. The quality of this information depends upon the adequacy of the home-school communication.

Two forms, the brochure and the Entry Agreement, are included in the following discussion because of their importance in the home-school communication of the private nursery-kindergarten sector. The other records, and the philosophy underlying their construction, can be used in the public school, day care centers, or any special school.

The preentrance records include: (1) the brochure, (2) the Application Form, (3) the Diagnostic Interview Form, (4) the follow-up letter, (5) the Entry Agreement, and (6) the Background Information Form. Each of these instruments has a specific purpose in building constructive home-school relations. How the school handles these beginning communications sets the stage for successful use of the record system, creating the climate for active dialogue between home and school.

Home-School Communication

Efficient, open communication is of crucial importance at the preprimary level because of the nature of the relationship to be established between home and school. The child of this age is in the absolute sense a dependent. He neither makes the arrangements for enrollment nor negotiates the terms. This dependency adds another dimension to the parent-child-teacher relationship since business arrangements necessarily take place *between* the parent and the teacher *about* the child.

Communication can be disrupted at any point in the preentrance period. Problems in record construction can close off communication. In some cases, a potentially appropriate placement for a child is never consummated because of poorly constructed preentrance materials. Ineffective techniques of information-giving and getting may arouse feelings of doubt and mistrust on the part of the parent. A breakdown in communication not only blocks the passage of necessary information, but also results in the parent's lack of trust and confidence in the program. Without an open, honest basis in these critical beginning stages, the rapport essential to a successful parent-child-teacher relationship is not apt to develop.

Well-planned beginning steps lay the groundwork for the parent and teacher to become collaborators, promoting the best developmental interests of the child. Since communication during the preentrance period can foster or hinder the rapport necessary to these collaborative roles, the records and techniques used during this period must be carefully developed. Accurate, well-constructed records eliminate confusion and misunderstanding.

The contents of preentrance records will necessarily vary according to the needs and features of a specific program. The following descriptions and models of each record in the admissions sequence represent guidelines that can be *adapted* to a variety of programs. Each description is accompanied by a sample appropriate for the fictional PEMS Nursery-Kindergarten. In terms of the developmental emphasis, the philosophy of the school is reflected in its name. The PEMS Nursery-Kindergarten promotes the *P*hysical, *E*motional, *M*ental, and *S*ocial development of the child. Coventry Crossing where the school is located represents a fictitious city of about 30,000 population. Because of the size of the city and the location of the school, the program attracts a cross section of children representing a variety of cultures. The heterogeneity of the group makes it imperative to evolve a record system to help the teacher meet the diverse needs of individual children.

THE BROCHURE

The brochure may represent the parent's initial contact with the school. Developed for distribution to the parents of prospective enrollees, the brochure is a folder describing the program and staff. The contents include information about the type of school, location, philosophy, goals and objectives, curriculum, history, teaching staff, and quality of the school. A brief description of the school plant, including special facilities, tuition and schedule of payments, and special services (transportation, school psychologist) are included to answer immediate questions (see pp. 22–24).

The brochure should mirror what is, not what should be, or even what can be. The way the school and its staff are presented reflects the substance, organization, and integrity of the program. The brochure can encourage confidence in the program and staff or generate reservations about them depending upon the content and how it is presented.

Construction.   The purpose of the brochure is to inform the reader about the program in a concise, accurate manner. Educational jargon and such specialized terms as "gross motor coordination," "visual and auditory perception," and "left-right sequencing" should be avoided. These concepts can be expressed in general, simple, brief language. Terms from the educational idiom do not enhance the professional tone of the program if their meanings are not known to the reading public. Photographs or illustrations of the school, activities, the children, and teaching staff are appealing and often communicate more information at a glance than a full-page verbal description.

The brochure is organized in a logical sequence with the name, type, and location of the school and ages of the children served listed on the face page so that parents may know immediately whether the school is appropriate for their child in terms of age and type of program, and whether it is located within reasonable distance.

Philosophy.   The philosophy of the school is a practical, cogent statement of the staff's beliefs about children—how they grow and how they learn. A brief description of the curriculum gives specific information about the objectives and methods stemming from these beliefs. Whatever the philosophy, the statement must reflect what the staff actually believes and tries to do. If the philosophy expresses remote ideals that cannot possibly be implemented under the conditions that currently exist, then the statement is false. For the program to have integrity, there must be continuity from philosophy to objectives, from objectives to planning, and from planning to implementation. As McAfee pinpoints it, "The teacher who talks of individual differences, yet who has all the children making

PEMS
NURSERY-KINDERGARTEN

4 CIRCLE DRIVE
COVENTRY CROSSING,
PENNSYLVANIA 14850

ENROLLMENT
PROCEDURE

For further information
  write:
Miss Janice Murray
Director, PEMS N-K
PEMS Nursery-Kindergarten
Coventry Crossing, Pa.
14850

Or Call: 218–5256

HISTORY

PHILOSOPHY

STAFF

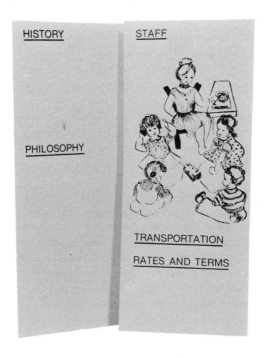

TRANSPORTATION

RATES AND TERMS

HISTORY   OBJECTIVES   PROGRAM

PHILOSOPHY

PEMS NURSERY-KINDERGARTEN
4 Circle Drive
Coventry Crossing, Pa.
14850

BROCHURE

History

The PEMS Nursery-Kindergarten has served the community since 1940 under the direction of a board of directors from the community. Over the years boys and girls from a variety of backgrounds have come together to live and learn in an atmosphere of acceptance and love.

Located in the center of the city, the Nursery-Kindergarten has accommodated the whole Coventry Crossing community including the university and outlying rural and industrial areas. The school provides a unique opportunity for the preprimary child to interact with different personalities, cultures, and situations that will help him grow to meet life's expectancies.

PEMS Nursery-Kindergarten is fully licensed by the State Department of Education and has been recognized as a full member of the regional accrediting agency.

Philosophy

The belief that all children should have the opportunity to grow and learn to their fullest potential has been the prevailing philosophy of the board of directors since the founding of the school. Each child is recognized as an individual with a different timetable for growing and learning. Each child brings to the school a unique pattern of strengths, weaknesses and experiences that affect his development. In order to help each child reach his fullest potential, the school subscribes to the philosophy reflected in its name: the child develops *P*hysically, *E*motionally, *M*entally, and *S*ocially.

the child is a grower..............physical development
a thinker..............intellectual development
an interactor..............social development
a feeler..............emotional development*

It is the work of the education team to know how each child grows, thinks, interacts, and feels in order to plan appropriate experiences for him. From this philosophy the following objectives evolved for the school.

Objectives

To create an atmosphere in which each child feels worthy, accepted, and secure.

To recognize what the child is like physically, emotionally, mentally, and socially in order to provide an appropriate program of activities for him.

To enrich the environment of the child so that he may gain strength as he grows physically, emotionally, mentally, and socially.

To supplement the experiences of the home and to help establish continuity in the child's learning experience.

To help the preprimary child to grow at his own rate in areas of muscular coordination, independence, emotional control, self-expression, intellectual curiosity, and social competence.

To develop a readiness for school and life experiences.

A child who has developed a readiness for reading, numbers, and social and emotional experiences will have developed a positive attitude toward learning new skills and interacting with a group. Readiness for reading includes developing a positive attitude toward learning to read, as well as toward life, proper handling of books, use of the spoken language, and the ability to observe, listen, and interpret his world.

---

*Evangeline Ward, Early Childhood Education (Danville, New York: F. A. Owen Publishing Co., 1968), p. 17.

Program

The program of the PEMS Nursery-Kindergarten, under the direction of competent teachers, provides periods of independent play, circle (directed activity), art, music, snack, rest, and outdoor play. Special field trips are planned to give emphasis to particular interests and areas of study.

The school is equipped to accommodate the needs of children three to five years of age. Furniture, bathroom facilities and playground equipment are scaled for the preprimary child. The school environment includes blocks for building, a dollhouse area, a workbench, puzzles, games designed to develop different areas of growth, a wide variety of art materials (including easel and vegetable painting), rhythm instruments, records, a library corner, flannel board stories and ingredients for making different kinds of dough. Yes, we actually work with real dough; cake dough, biscuit dough, cooky dough, and yeast dough. The children love to make the dough, work with it, bake it, and then enjoy it for snack. The school kitchen is especially designed to accommodate the young child and provides for a variety of experiences in science, language, social studies, math, and muscular development.

Parents are encouraged to visit the school, or to call, at any time, for an individual conference. Home and school must work together to enrich the total daily life of the child. Regular parent conferences are scheduled after the first month of school and at the end of school.

Staff

The teaching staff at PEMS Nursery-Kindergarten is certified by the State Department of Public Instruction. There is a certified teacher and an aide for each group of twelve children in the school. The aides and assisting parents allow flexibility in our program and make it possible to provide more individual attention for each child.

Transportation

Transportation service is available. The current rate is $_____ per month.

Rates and Terms

$_____for_____months
Payable: In full with 10% deduction
         By semester (no deduction)

General Information

The PEMS Nursery-Kindergarten is in session Monday through Friday. The morning session is from 9:00 A.M. to 11:45 A.M. The afternoon session is from 1:00 P.M. to 3:45 P.M. Holidays are announced at the beginning of each year.

All clothing, including overshoes, must be plainly marked with the child's name.

Please choose comfortable and durable clothing for your child to wear to school. Clothing should be suitable for outdoor play and for the day's weather. A smock is needed for painting and cooking.

If your child shows symptoms of a cold or other illness, please be fair to the other children and keep him at home. Please notify the school of the illness.

In case of snowstorms which make driving hazardous, school closing will be announced over all radio stations in the area.

Children should be picked up promptly from school. If someone other than a parent or regularly designated person is to pick up your child, please notify the school office on that day.

Enrollment Procedure

Parents are urged to fill in and mail, without delay, the enclosed Application Form. Upon its receipt the school will arrange for an interview with parent and child. Following the interview a letter concerning the child's admission will be sent to the parent. The child is enrolled after parents and teacher have carefully considered the suitability of the program for the child.

For Further Information, Write:

Miss Janice Murray, Director of PEMS Nursery-Kindergarten
PEMS Nursery-Kindergarten
4 Circle Drive
Coventry Crossing, Pa. 14850
or call: 218–5356

---

identical pictures within the same span of time will probably manifest this inconsistency elsewhere also."[1]

History.   The history of the school is an indication of the quality of the program. If the program has been a going concern for a period of years, this longevity suggests a viable institution with substantial support. Specific reporting of licensure, accreditation, or community support enhances the school's image of dependability.

Staff and Services.   The school's quality is expressed in the description of the members of the teaching staff, their qualifications, and the existing pupil-teacher ratio. Listing of such resource personnel as a consulting physician or a psychologist indicates the breadth of professional backing. Special services, e.g., routine eye examinations, should be mentioned. In some cases, for religious or other reasons, parents do not permit the child

---

[1] Oralee McAfee, "Planning the Preschool Program," in *Curriculum Is What Happens*, ed. Laura L. Dittman (Washington, D.C.: National Association for the Education of Young Children, 1970), p. 20.

to see resource personnel or to be exposed to special services. A statement in the brochure about these services alerts parents what to expect.

Type of School.   If the school is operated as a laboratory school under the aegis of a college, university, or teacher training institution, this fact should be noted. There are parents who prefer not to place their child in an experimental setting. If the school follows a specific methodology or if the school is for children of specific gifts or disabilities, these facts should also be noted.

Address, Telephone Number, Whom To Call.   The address and telephone number of the school should be set apart from the body of the brochure in a conspicuous place for easy reference. The person to be contacted for further information is given. The hours that the person is available to answer calls are noted. Parents may feel favorably disposed toward the school, but inability to reach the person in charge is not only frustrating, but can engender lack of confidence.

Enrollment Procedure.   In terms of the communication sequence, one of the critical items in the brochure appears in the section about the enrollment procedure. The statement, "The child is enrolled after parents and teacher have carefully considered the suitability of the program for the child," suggests the theme of cooperation. While informing the parent that the child is not automatically enrolled in the school when the application form is submitted, the preentrance emphasis is not on whether the child measures up, but whether the service is appropriate for the child.

THE APPLICATION FORM

In response to inquiries about the school, the brochure with the Application Form enclosed is mailed to the parent. The Application Form gives the parents the opportunity to make a formal inquiry regarding enrollment. Completion of the form and payment of the registration fee signify the parent's serious intention to investigate the program as a possible facility for the child (see pp. 28).

The Application Form is limited to items calling for information essential to communication between home and school for business purposes. Parents may develop resentment if it is too long and cumbersome and requires information that is irrelevant at this step of the procedure.

Upon receipt of the Application Form, the teacher telephones the parents to arrange for an interview with parent and child. At this time basic requirements of the school are discussed, such as the age of the child and whether or not he is toilet-trained. The teacher finds out when the

PEMS NURSERY-KINDERGARTEN
4 Circle Drive, Coventry Crossing, Pa. 14850
APPLICATION FORM

Date_____

Child's Full Name_____
           (last)   (first)   (middle)

Age_____Date of Birth_____
           (mo.)   (da.)   (yr.)

Home Address_____
         (no.)   (street)   (city)   (state)   (zip)

Home Phone_____

For Academic Year 19____ to 19____

Father or Guardian_____
         (last)   (first)   (middle)

Father or Guardian's Occupation_____

Business Address_____
         (no.)   (street)   (city)   (state)   (zip)

Business Phone_____

Mother_____
        (last)   (first)   (middle)

Mother's Occupation_____

Business Address_____
         (no.)   (street)   (city)   (state)   (zip)

Business Phone_____

Registration Fee: $25.00
Payable to PEMS Nursery-Kindergarten.
Fee will be applied to tuition or refundable prior to August 1st.

Mail with application form to:
Director, PEMS Nursery-Kindergarten
4 Circle Drive, Coventry Crossing, Pa. 14850
Phone: 218-5356

PEMS NURSERY-KINDERGARTEN
4 Circle Drive, Coventry Crossing, Pennsylvania 14850

(Date)

(Address)

Dear (Parent's name),

Thank you for your interest in the PEMS Nursery-Kindergarten. We are pleased that you and (Child's name) plan to visit our school.

Your interview has been scheduled with the teacher for (date) at (time) in (location) as planned.

We will look forward to meeting you and (Child's name) in the near future.

Sincerely,

Janice Murray, Director

child naps and schedules the interview accordingly. The telephone call is followed by a letter of confirmation (see p. 29). A written record of the time and place of the interview in the form of this letter helps to smooth relations between home and school.

THE DIAGNOSTIC INTERVIEW FORM

The overall purpose of the preentrance diagnostic interview is to determine the suitability of the program for the child. This determination can be made by accomplishing certain objectives. The objectives of the diagnostic interview are to estimate: (1) the readiness of the child for nursery-kindergarten; (2) parental attitudes, philosophy of education, involvement in family, work, and community affairs, and expectations of nursery-kindergarten for the child; and (3) the parent-child relationship. In addition, the interview functions to establish rapport among parent, child, and teacher. The Diagnostic Interview Form reflects these objectives (see pp. 31–34).

A detailed explanation of the techniques for planning, conducting, and recording the interview is given in Chapter 4. In terms of the communication sequence, the rationale underlying the design of the form needs to be clarified. It is of particular importance to note that the form is designed for use before and after, not during the interview. Prior to the interview, the teacher reviews the specific items listed under each section. In this way she is keyed to look for behaviors as they occur naturally and is prepared with activities to elicit certain responses. For instance, recognizing and naming colors is a specific item in Section II of the form. As the interview progresses, the child may or may not reveal his capacity to match and name colors. If he does not spontaneously indicate his color knowledge, the teacher guides him to the crayons or other materials to test his knowledge.

A persistent record-keeping problem concerns when and how to record what transpires during the interview. Consulting a form for reference or making notations on a form during the interview not only disrupts the continuity of discussion, but tends to depersonalize the interview. From the parent's viewpoint, the teacher's attention to the form may seem to shift the emphasis from warm concern to a businesslike exchange of information.

In order to avoid these problems, the teacher records what happened during the interview after the parent and child leave. The listing of items prompts the teacher's memory. Moreover, the task is not laborious since most of the items call for a check-mark rather than a written response.

THE FOLLOW-UP LETTER

Regardless of the outcome of the diagnostic interview, a letter confirming the decision is sent to the parents (see pp. 36–37). Even though the enrollment decision might have been discussed at the diagnostic interview, a follow-up letter provides closure. If the service is not acceptable for the child, the reasons should be given in the letter. A review of alternative measures helps the parents to adjust their plans and compile information about available resources.

The letter following a positive enrollment decision welcomes the child to the program and provides direction for the next step. Helpful suggestions and routines are briefly discussed. If developed early, a school calendar should be enclosed; if the calendar is scheduled to be sent at a later time, then the date and time of the opening session are given in the letter. Clear instructions about the person or persons to contact during the months leading to the enrollment are included. The letter also points out the significance of the enclosed Entry Agreement Form and the Background Information Form. Directions for the return of both forms should be given in the letter. A self-addressed envelope facilitates prompt return.

Whether a letter of acceptance or rejection, the tone should suggest warm, personal concern for the child and the parent. Even if the letter must be mimeographed, spaces are open for names to be inserted. "Dear

PEMS NURSERY-KINDERGARTEN

DIAGNOSTIC INTERVIEW FORM

Child's Name _____Date _____

Age____Yr.____Mo.____   Interviewer _____

Birth Date_____
              (mo.)   (da.)   (yr.)

I. INDIVIDUAL CHARACTERISTICS OF THE CHILD

A. Body Type   B. Complexion   C. Body Size

   slight____   pale____   large____
   well proportioned____ healthy____   medium____
   stocky____   flushed____   small____

D. Dress   E. Expression

   appropriate for play____   tense____   composed ____
   requires assistance____   bland____   happy____
   lends self-help____   masked____   troubled____

F. Personality

   shy____   nervous____
   confident____   aggressive____
   outgoing____   distractible____

   Other_____

II. READINESS FOR NURSERY-KINDERGARTEN

A. Physical
   1. Gross Motor (large muscle)
      runs rhythmically____
      maintains balance on beam____
      climbs with alternating feet____
      parts of body move independently____
      throws ball____
      throws ball with direction____

31

Individual variations_____

_____

2. Fine Motor (small muscle)
   picks up small objects____
   manipulates: scissors____ puzzles____ crayons____
             strings beads____
   manipulates toys with skill and direction____

   Individual Variations_____

   _____

B. Emotional
   accepts with ease: praise____ correction____
   free from tensional outlets (thumb-sucking, etc.)____
   responsive____ exhibits control of emotions____

C. Mental
   demonstrates ability to focus on one task____ curious____
   exhibits general knowledge____
   recognizes colors: red____ yellow____ blue____ green____
   demonstrates ability to organize____ counts 1–5____
   demonstrates knowledge of concept 1–5____
   willing to try unknown____
   stays with an activity

   Individual Variations_____

   _____

D. Social
   explores on his own____
   exhibits ability to solve problems____follows directions____
   willing to engage with teacher____ exhibits self-help____
   cooperates in suggested activities____

   Individual Variations_____

   _____

E. Speech

speaks in complete sentences____ rich vocabulary____
uses adjectives and adverbs____
speaks clearly____ speaks fluently____
listens to what others are saying and answers____

Individual Variations_____

_____

III. INTERESTS

trucks____blocks____ doll corner____ trains____ records____
art materials____ stories____ playground____ wheel toys____

Special Competencies or Interests_____

_____

IV. DESCRIPTION OF PARENT

outgoing____ shy____ directive____ receptive____ tense____
at ease____ relaxed____speech: controlled____ disorganized____

V. PARENT INVOLVEMENT

community involvement: heavy (3 or more days/wk.)____
                         moderate (1 day/wk.) ____
                         minimal (on occasion)____
willing and available to participate in school activities____
willing and able to attend school functions____
willing and able to extend training in home____

VI. PARENT'S REASONS FOR CONSIDERING ENROLLMENT FOR CHILD

new baby____ playmates____ intellectual development____
learning special skills____ working mother____ discipline____
single sex influence in home environment____

Other_____

_____

VII. PARENT-CHILD RELATIONSHIP

parent sets limits____ parent enforces limits____

child respects limits____ child ignores limits____

parent exhibits warmth toward the child: verbally____

physically____

child clings to parent____ child touches base with parent

regularly during interview____

child asks for help early in solving a problem or doing a task____

child perseveres before asking for help____

parent gives help early ____child resists help____

parent gives explanations clearly____

parent confuses child with explanations____

parent ignores child's questions____

parent uses criticism and coercive control____

parent uses tangible reward to motivate____

parent's role is supportive guide____

parent's role is authority figure____

child demands parent's attention____ waits for recognition____

relationship is: comfortable____ strained____ hostile____

indifferent____

Other observations_____

_____

VIII. ADMISSION DECISION

accept without reservation____

accept conditionally____ explanation_____

_____

did not accept due to:_____

_____

IX. RECOMMENDATIONS

A. Special Interest

B. Parent Involvement

C. Plan for Help

34

Parent" and "your child" are impersonal referents. In this particular letter the child and parent are referred to by name. (The impersonal referent may be acceptable in more routine communications, such as announcements of special events.) A teacher's offer to help to answer questions or be of further service during the interim period tends to keep the channel of communication open.

THE ENTRY AGREEMENT FORM

The Entry Agreement is a formal expression of the contractual terms agreed upon by home and school (see p. 38). Tuition rates and terms are clearly and specifically stated. Concealing exceptions in fine print creates distrust. The agreement clarifies rates and terms of payment for any special service; e.g., transportation. Policies regarding financial commitment in the event of withdrawal are clearly stated.

THE BACKGROUND INFORMATION FORM

The Background Information Form enlarges the developmental picture of the child (see pp. 39–44). With the exception of one section, most of the information elicited by this form is factual and objective. Many of the items are included because they call for information that is necessary but too routine to take up valuable interviewing time. The health history, for example, is more easily recorded on this form. Occasionally, routine items will turn up responses that require further investigation. For example, if the child has a history of heart disorder, this condition needs to be explored in terms of its potential influence.

The first part of the form concerns basic information about the structure of the immediate family. The isolated facts are not predictive of how the family functions; however, put together with other information, they may help to extend the teacher's understanding of the child. If he is a product of the smallest family conceivable—mother and child—then he is bound to be modified by a different set of experiences than the child who is a member of a large family.

The next section concerns the number of family members living in the community. The size of both the immediate and extended family influences the breadth of available support.

The information relating to family physician, persons to be called in case of emergency, and hospital represent preparatory measures in the event of emergencies ranging from a breakdown of the bus, to an accident, to a civil defense alert. The importance of the *immediate availability* of this information can scarcely be overemphasized. The home telephone

PEMS NURSERY-KINDERGARTEN
4 Circle Drive
Coventry Crossing, Pa. 14850

(Date)

(Address)

Dear (Parent's name),

It is with pleasure that we are reserving a place in PEMS Nursery-Kindergarten for (Child's name) during the coming year 19____ to 19____

Please find enclosed the Entry Agreement Form which explains the rates and terms regarding tuition and transportation. If you have any question, the Director will be glad to help you.

A Background Information Form is enclosed which should be completed and returned to the Director of the school. Your assistance in helping us to know your child will be very valuable in planning activities for a good educational experience.

The Entry Agreement Form and Background Information Form should be returned to the Director of the school by August 1.

A school calendar for the coming year is enclosed for your information.

(Child's name) will need the following items for school in the fall.

1. A smock for painting and cooking.
2. A pair of rubbers for rainy days.
3. A complete change of clothing packaged in a shoebox to be left at school.
   ** ALL POSSESSIONS SHOULD BE CLEARLY MARKED WITH THE CHILD'S NAME.

If you need to contact the school for any reason, please call Miss Murray (218–5356). We shall look forward to hearing from you.

Sincerely,

Janice Murray, Director

PEMS NURSERY-KINDERGARTEN
4 Circle Drive
Coventry Crossing, Pa. 14850

(Date)

(Address)

Dear (Parent's Name),

Thank you for visiting PEMS Nursery-Kindergarten. I hope (Child's name) had a pleasant time and will look forward to a future school experience.

As we agreed at the interview, a later enrollment would be more suitable for (Child's name). A school experience will be more beneficial to him if he has more time in the home environment.

Please come and visit the school again in the future. If we can be of further service, please contact us.

Sincerely,

Janice Murray, Director

number and the first person to be called in the case of an emergency is compiled from the Background Information Forms of the enrollees and posted beside the telephone.

The form next calls for specific information about the child's daily routines. Is he used to attending school as part of his routine? If the parent answers "Sunday school" to the item, this response may be evidence of a pattern of family life. The items relating to regular playmates not only reveal the child's opportunity to interact with his peers on a regular basis, but also provide the teacher with a point of departure for later investigation of his exposure to other children. Information about the child's self-care and his likes and dislikes helps the teacher to plan for the child and to avoid potential problem situations.

The only subjective part of the form concerns the child's interests, his behavior, and his speech. These items are necessarily answered in terms of

PEMS NURSERY-KINDERGARTEN
4 Circle Drive
Coventry Crossing, Pa. 14850

ENTRY AGREEMENT FORM

Please fill in and return to PEMS Nursery-Kindergarten, 4 Circle Drive, Coventry Crossing, Pa. 14850 by August 1.

I agree to pay the fees described on this form under section RATES AND TERMS. In the event of withdrawal for any reason the tuition will be adjusted.

RATES AND TERMS

RATES: TUITION FOR THE 8-MONTH SCHOOL YEAR $ _____

____TRANSPORTATION TO AND FROM SCHOOL PER MONTH $___
(please check if service is desired)

TERMS: Please check one

____Payment may be made in full by Oct. 1 with 10% deduction.

____Two Payments: first payment due Oct. 1 (1st semester)
                  second payment due Feb. 1 (2nd semester)

____Monthly payment plan is available at a slightly higher rate.
Contact Director of School for information.

****The $25.00 registration fee will be credited toward tuition. NOT refundable after August 1.

Date_____

Child's Full Name_____
                    (last)   (first)   (middle)

Age____ Date of Birth_____

Home Address_____
                  (no.) (street) (city) (state) (zip)

Home phone_____

For Academic Year 19____ to 19____

Parent or Guardian_____
    (signature)

38

PEMS NURSERY-KINDERGARTEN
4 Circle Drive
Coventry Crossing, Pa. 14850

BACKGROUND INFORMATION FORM

The school staff needs your help to understand and plan for your child. Please fill out the following form and return to the school in the enclosed self-addressed envelope by August 31.

Date _____

Child's Name _____
           (last)   (first)   (middle)

Child's Preferred Name _____
(first, middle, or nickname)

Address _____
     (no.)   (street)   (city)   (state)   (zip)

Phone Number _____

Birth Date _____ Age _____
    (mo.)   (da.)   (yr.)

Sex: male _____ female _____

Father's Name _____
(or guardian)   (last)   (first)   (middle)

Occupation _____

Business Address _____
          (street)   (city)   (state)   (zip)

Business Phone _____

Mother's Name _____
          (last)   (first)   (middle)

Occupation _____

Business Address _____
          (street)   (city)   (state)   (zip)

Business Phone _____

Is father living?_____ Is mother living?_____ Separated?_____
                                              Divorced?_____

Is there anyone whom you do not wish to pick up your child?_____

If so, please give name and relationship to child.

Name_____ Relationship_____

Other members of the family (brothers, sisters, grandparents, etc.)
living at home:

NAME	AGE	RELATIONSHIP	INDICATE NAME USED BY CHILD
_____	___	_____	_____
_____	___	_____	_____
_____	___	_____	_____
_____	___	_____	_____
_____	___	_____	_____

Other members of the family (grandparents, aunts, uncles, etc.)
living in the community:

NAME	AGE	RELATIONSHIP	INDICATE NAME USED BY CHILD
_____	___	_____	_____
_____	___	_____	_____
_____	___	_____	_____

Family Physician (or pediatrician)_____
                                  (last)   (first) (middle)

Office Address_____
               (street) (city) (state)   (zip)

Office Phone_____

Hospital to be called in case of emergency_____

Address_____
        (street)   (city)   (state)

Hospital Phone_____

Person to be called in case of an emergency (give 4 persons in order
of preference):

1._____ Phone_____

2._____ Phone_____

3._____ Phone_____

4._____ Phone_____

Has your child had any previous school experience?_____
If so, please give name and type of school.

_____ length of attendance_____

Does your child have regular playmates?____

Does your child take a nap?____ morning____ afternoon____

How many hours does your child sleep at night? (approx.)____

Is your child toilet-trained?____

Does your child use any special word for toileting?____
If so, please state_____

Describe your child's appetite: always hungry____ eats at mealtime____
snacks____ snacks all day____ never hungry____
has to be coaxed to eat____

Are there any foods your child may not or cannot eat?____
(due to allergies, religious customs, etc.)

If so, please list:_____

_____

_____

Are there any foods your child dislikes?____

If so, please list:_____

_____

What are your child's favorite foods? Please list: _____

_____

_____

Special interests: singing_____ painting_____ stories_____ trucks_____
pets_____ records_____ outside play_____ crayoning_____

Other_____

_____

_____

Is your child generally cooperative?_____ shy?_____ competitive?_____
aggressive?_____ sensitive?_____ submissive?_____
angry?_____ happy?_____ usually does what is asked of
him/her?_____ seldom does what is asked of him/her?_____
whines?_____

List other behaviors characteristic of your child.

_____

_____

_____

Does your child exhibit specific fears? If so, please list.

_____

Describe your child's speech: rapid_____ slow_____ moderate_____
clear_____ talks constantly_____ seldom speaks_____
uses many words_____ uses few words_____ talks only during play_____

Other characteristics_____

_____

Describe any special circumstances that will help us to understand your
child.

HEALTH RECORD

Physical description of child: body build_____ color hair_____
color eyes_____ height _____ weight_____

Is your child subject to colds?_____ allergies?_____ If so,
what kind?_____ fatigue?_____
nervousness?_____

Has your child had or does your child have:
any serious illness?_____ please state_____
any physical disabilities? (heart, eyes, ears, kidneys, etc.)

Please describe_____

_____

any mental disorders?_____ any speech problems?_____
any social problems?_____

Does your child receive any regular medication?_____ If so, for
what purpose?_____

Is your child allergic to any medicines to your knowledge?_____

If so, what medicines? _____

IMMUNIZATION RECORD: (please give date of last shot or booster)
Diphtheria_____ Tetanus_____ Polio_____
Whooping cough_____ Smallpox_____ Measles_____
Other_____
Tuberculin test: positive____ negative____ date____

CHILDHOOD DISEASES: (please check the ones your child has had)
Red measles_____(yr.) German measles_____(yr.)
Chicken pox_____(yr.) Mumps_____(yr.)
Other_____

OPERATIONS: _____(tonsillectomy, appendectomy, etc.)
operation_____ year_____
Any previous serious illnesses? (Rheumatic fever, etc.)_____

43

PEMS NURSERY-KINDERGARTEN
4 Circle Drive
Coventry Crossing, Pa. 14850

PHYSICIAN'S REPORT

A physical examination is required for admission to PEMS Nursery-Kindergarten. Please have your physician examine your child and return this form to the director of the school in the self-addressed envelope.

I have examined _____ and in my opinion he/she is in good physical condition and able to attend nursery school or kindergarten.

There are ____ are not ____ diagnosed conditions that will influence the child's school experience. Precautionary measures to be observed by the school are listed below.

Physician's Signature _____

Date _____

the parent's evaluation. Even though this information lacks objectivity and may represent misconceptions, it is valuable in terms of knowing the child through the eyes of the parent. Even if the answers conflict with the teacher's observations, they serve as a check and indicate the need for further investigation.

The Health Record can be detached from the Background Information Form for separate filing. If there is a health service associated with the kindergarten, as might be found in an elementary school, all of the child's health records may be maintained in the Health Office. The final page of the form may be detached and given to the physician facilitating his report. The examination should take place within three months prior to entrance.

The information on the Health Record enables the teacher to estimate the health trends characteristic of the child. The parent and nursery-kindergarten teacher are in key positions to identify changes in appearance, patterns of response, and functioning that are cues to illness or defect. Occasionally apparent changes are symptoms of existing conditions. Allergies, for example, may be more apt to flare up at certain times of the year. If a teacher is forewarned about the effects of physical conditions, she is better prepared to deal with these problems.

The immunization records and information about childhood diseases are necessary for the protection not only of the child, but of the other children in the school. In the event of any incidence of childhood diseases in the school, it is the teacher's responsibility to notify the parents of all the children. In cases where the record indicates that the child has not had the disease, the teacher may want to alert the parents even if an incidence is merely suspected.

As factual and routine as this information may seem, the Background Information Form often arouses apprehension in parents. A popular attitude is revealed in the following:

> When my oldest daughter received her Kindergarten registration form, I was surprised and a little apprehensive about answering all the personality and social development questions. Meeting a neighbor whose son was also registering, I asked her what she thought about the questionnaire. Her answer summed up my feelings completely. "I'm torn," she said, "between telling the truth or giving him a good start."[2]

As pointed out earlier, the questions referred to in this incident should not be asked in an application or registration form. Trust must develop before questions of this nature are introduced. If trust has not grown through the communication sequence, the parent may experience the doubt exhibited in the above incident.

Throughout the preentrance period it is the responsibility of the teacher to communicate the rationale for the inclusion of any of the items on the forms. The way the teacher explains the Background Information Form at the diagnostic interview can alleviate some of the fears associated with filling out a form of this kind. The parent must be assured of the potential value of honest answers. He should recognize that efforts to deemphasize, in some cases, to cover up apparent shortcomings are more likely to hinder the plan of help that leads to positive growth. Optimally the parent leaves the interview with the security that his child is worthy regardless of his developmental progress, and that the form provides a basis for *help,* not for *judgment.*

Summary

The preentrance records set in motion a system of communication between home and school. Accurate, carefully constructed instruments open

---

[2]Ruth Dinkel in the October 1968 *Reader's Digest.* Copyright 1968 by The Reader's Digest Assn., Inc. Used with permission.

communication channels and help to develop the trust and rapport essential to successful home-school relations.

Guidelines for construction and samples of the following instruments are provided: (1) the brochure, a folder describing the school program; (2) the Application Form, a formal expression of the parents' intention to consider the program for their child; (3) the Diagnostic Interview Form, a guide for planning the interviewing activities and a method for recording what transpired during the interview; (4) the follow-up letter, a confirmation of the enrollment decision; (5) the Entry Agreement, a statement of the contractual terms agreed upon by home and school; (6) the Background Information Form, a record of factual, objective developmental data, including the health history and status of the child.

4

The Diagnostic Interview

As the heart of the enrollment process, the diagnostic interview provides the setting for an exchange of information that will lead to an admissions decision. Some of the information results directly from consultation with the parent; other data are inferred from the responses of the child to the school setting, to his parent, and to the interviewer. Input from *both* sources is necessary to fulfill the primary objective of the interview: To determine the suitability of the program for the child.

In view of the many dimensions of behavior to be observed and discussed, the most productive interview is arranged with both parents and the child. Although the ideal situation involves both parents, usually the interview is arranged with the mother; therefore, the terms *parent* and *mother* are used interchangeably. When both the mother and child are present, the teacher can observe firsthand what the child is ready to learn and to do as well as acquire a feeling for the parent-child relationship. Optimally, the interview provides the basis for the parent's and child's constructive, trusting relations with the teacher and school.

The interview takes place at a time when school is not in session in order to avoid repeated interruptions and distractions which decrease the information flow and limit the exchange to superficial information. A visit during which the parent can observe the classroom operation of the school can be scheduled for another time.

Objectives of the Interview

The interview is planned to elicit practical information that will not only contribute to the admissions decision, but prove helpful in planning for the child when he enters school. The kinds of information relevant to the decision and future planning are reflected in the objectives. The objectives of the interview are to estimate: (1) the child's unique characteristics and readiness for nursery-kindergarten; (2) parental attitudes, involvement in family, work, and community affairs, and expectations of nursery-kindergarten for the child; and (3) the parent-child relationship. A fourth objective is to establish rapport among parent, child, and teacher.

Noting the unique characteristics of the child begins the focus on his individuality. There are two reasons for estimating his readiness: (1) to get a general view of his maturity to benefit from the nursery-kindergarten experience and (2) to provide a temporary guide for individualized planning when the child enters school. The teacher must be aware of parental attitudes, philosophy of education, and expectations of nursery-kindergarten for the child in order to appreciate the parent's role in the educational experience of the child. A general impression of how the parent and child relate enables the teacher to build constructively on the child's home experience.

The interviewing process—*how* the teacher carries out the activities and relates to both parent and child—sets the tone for a mutually supportive working relationship. The most significant outcome of the interview is the developing sense of trust between home and school.

Information collection is facilitated by the Diagnostic Interview Form which structures the specific and critical items to be observed during the interview. The following sections illustrate how the form can be instrumental in helping the teacher to achieve the objectives of the interview.

Knowing the Child

The Diagnostic Interview Form is designed to help the teacher estimate the child's unique characteristics and his readiness for nursery-kindergarten. The impression of the child provides a basis for planning in terms of special activities and staff assignments. The amount and kind of attention he needs can be estimated and provided for, easing the transition from home to school experience. The form includes items relating to the child's progress physically, emotionally, mentally, and socially. Of course, on the basis of a single encounter, the picture is not sharply etched; more refined data can be acquired only through working with the child over a period of time.

Since the interview is scheduled at a time when school is not in session, the whole facility becomes a laboratory in which the child can move freely. His capacities are revealed through his actions. His spontaneous responses to equipment and materials are the most valid indications of his readiness for nursery-kindergarten. In preparing for the interview, the teacher sets up the environment to encourage the child to reveal what he is able to do. The child's responses to the interview activities and the setting enable the teacher to observe his readiness for nursery-kindergarten physically, emotionally, mentally, and socially.

In terms of physical development, an impression of the child's gross motor coordination (control of large muscles) can be inferred from his behavior in the outdoor playground area. Running, jumping, climbing, and balancing show the degree of mobility and control of the body. The child's approach to the swings, the slide, and the climber reveals his degree of coordination. If weather conditions do not permit outdoor play, the balance beam and indoor climber can be used. It must be noted that some children may hesitate to approach this less familiar equipment and consequently require more time and guidance to demonstrate what they can do.

Ball play is a familiar and routine activity which reveals the level of body movement. As the child throws the ball, does his body move as a unit with his legs and torso involved? Or can he move his arms freely without moving his torso? If he can move his legs and arms without moving his torso, then he is demonstrating independence and mobility in movement of body parts. His level of proficiency also indicates how much he has practiced the skill.

The child's emotional and mental development are revealed in his approach to concentration equipment. In preparing for the interview, the teacher selects and sets out for use an assortment of familiar concentration and problem-solving items. These materials will vary somewhat with the age of the child; however, a typical assortment would include a puzzle, a block design kit, beads and a string, and an item requiring the child to stack blocks or rings in graduated sizes. Crayons, both right- and left-handed scissors, and paper should be on hand.

The way a child copes with these materials may reveal his emotional development. Is he responsive, attentive to tasks and suggestions? Is he well enough organized to follow through and try to do what is requested? Does he respond to or back off from praise? Does he resist correction? As she watches the child play, the teacher may observe the extent of his emotional control. What is his reaction to unsuccessful problem solving? What is his frustration tolerance? How does he deal with failure and miscalculation? Does he show acceptance of failure and/or a willingness to start over again? Or does he show anger verbally? Does he act out against the material by throwing the pieces or pushing them aside? Does he ignore the material and teacher or parental encouragement to try again?

In terms of mental development, working with these materials gives an indication of his problem-solving techniques, his attention span, his language skill, and his knowledge of colors and numbers. The way the child works with the equipment shows his capacity to organize and his ability to conceptualize a task or, on the other hand, to use a haphazard trial-and-error approach to problem solving. It also reveals his determination to stay with the task until completion or his recognition that he needs help. In addition, while the child works with the equipment, the teacher can observe whether he has a tendency to concentrate on a single item or to flit from one to the other.

The child's social development is indicated by his response to directions, his cooperation, his independence to leave his mother's side, and his security to explore the school environment. Willingness to engage in ball play with the teacher may give a hint of his progress toward cooperative play as well as his reaction to engaging in a game with a stranger. A significant observation is his willingness to interact with the teacher. A child may touch base with his mother at regular intervals; however, if he constantly clings to his parent for rescue from interaction with the teacher, this response is a doubtful sign of social readiness for nursery-kindergarten.

The child's speech patterns are reflected in his spontaneous conversations with his mother and the teacher. Does he speak in complete sentences? Does he use specific words to name and to describe the things and events of his environment? Is his speech clear and organized, or is he difficult to understand? Does he demonstrate that he comprehends what others are saying by appropriate responses?

During the interviewing activities the teacher can also observe the child's special interests and competencies. What kinds of activities attract his attention? Does he seem to derive the most satisfaction from play materials that keep him on the move, vigorously involved? Or does he appear to gravitate toward more sedentary activities? Does he demonstrate unusual abilities in any area? This information can aid in planning the child's initial program in terms of selecting activities and materials which reflect his interests, give him security, and assure his success.

Knowing the Parent

During the interview the teacher forms an impression of what the parent is like. Does she tend to be outgoing or shy? Does she seem to be more directive or receptive? Is her speech deliberate and controlled or disorganized? Does she tend to be relaxed or tense? Is she someone who can be called upon to help with school activities; for example, the room-mother role?

In the course of discussion, the interviewer listens for answers to the following questions: What are the parent's reasons for considering enrollment of the child in a preprimary program? What is the extent of her community participation? What is her reaction to her employment responsibilities? Is she a devoted career woman, or is she working just to supplement the family income? All of this information contributes to a picture of the parent and the role she will fulfill in the child's educational experience.

Parents consider nursery-kindergarten for the child for a wide variety of reasons ranging from the imminence of a new baby and the need to provide continuing security for the child during the mother's confinement to an urgency for the child to learn to read, regardless of his readiness. Social exposure is still a commonly cited reason for enrolling a child. If the child is an only child, or if he lives in a neighborhood where there is limited opportunity to play with agemates, a preprimary program can fill out and enrich his social experience. Some parents are concerned about too much single-sex influence on their child's social development; they want to balance a predominantly female or predominantly male play community with members of the opposite sex.

With the growing emphasis on intellectual development in the early years, parents increasingly mention the child's need for greater mental stimulation than is provided in the home environment. Parents may fear that if the child is not enrolled in school, he will miss out on the optimal time to learn certain skills, perhaps even fall behind in mental development. Sometimes this concern is accompanied by urgent concerns about how quickly the school can teach specific skills, such as reading. An explanation of how intellectual development is handled in the program may be all that is needed to relieve the parents and to bring their expectations into harmony with the goals of the school.

In some cases parental expectations conflict with the philosophy of the school. These differences, most often rooted in child-rearing convictions, must surface; otherwise, a false contract may be established. For example, parents may earnestly believe that structure of any kind at this early level inhibits the child's growth toward creative self-direction. Therefore, such parents would be unable to support a curriculum including planned, teacher-guided activities. To the extent that the parents adhere to these convictions in the home, the teacher would find it difficult to support the parental role.

Some parents envision the controlled environment of the school as the means to fulfill a child's need for limits which cannot be met in the home situation. Casting the school in a disciplinary role is almost bound to result in the child's negative perception of the teacher which may be generalized to the school, influencing attitudes toward future learning. The situation invites the child to manipulate adults in both home and school creating cleavages difficult to bridge

The Parent-Child Relationship

One of the advantages of an interview involving both parent and child is that the pattern of their interaction may be observed. The relationship that exists between mother and child provides an indication of the kind of relationship the teacher will be able to develop with the child. The child tends to bring to the nursery-kindergarten the responses that have been reinforced in the home; consequently, his plan of help will vary according to the behaviors he has learned in the home setting.

In order to acquire a feeling for the parent-child relationship, the teacher needs to be attuned to specific interactions that may transpire during the interview. As a rule, mother and child have evolved ways of behaving with each other that are sufficiently consistent and stable to be detected under normal interviewing conditions. Discussion with the mother may cast further light on the relationship.

The way the mother sets limits during the interview affords clues to the relationship. Does she give directions for behavior? If so, how? Does she guide the child by negative deterrents: "Don't," "Stop," "Not now"? Does she use reason to help the child to understand the direction? Does she make use of opportunities for him to choose? When the mother does set limits, does she follow through? Does she expect compliance or does she exhibit permissiveness, ranging from easy tolerance to pampering?

The responses of the child may indicate how effectively limits are enforced. Doing as his mother asks, either promptly or after questioning, shows a respect for limits. The child who uses delaying tactics, or argues to the point that the mother gives in and rescinds the limit, may be revealing that he can ignore limits without reprisal.

During the interview the teacher may inquire about sleep and rest patterns as well as breakfast and lunch habits. She listens for clues to whether the child is accustomed to strict or lax routines in the home. Information about consistency of routines helps to round out the picture of whether the child tends to follow his own inclinations or has been accustomed to respecting parental direction and a schedule of activities.

As the mother interacts with the child, regardless of what she says, her manner and tone of voice carry nonverbal cues that have stronger meanings than the words spoken. When the mother is *nurturant,* she exhibits a warm, caring, protective concern for the child. Occasionally, the mother tends to be overly nurturant, protective to the point where she anticipates every need and shields the child from the responsibility of doing for himself and solving his own problems.

The child who is accustomed to warm acceptance is apt to be more responsive to his mother and to other adults. Not only is he more likely to respond to affectional contact, but he may initiate closeness, touching, reaching for a hand, climbing onto his mother's lap which are just some of the ways the child has of touching his security base. There is apt to be more distance between the nonnurturant mother and her child. Physical contact may be at a minimum.

The mother's concern for the child is evidenced in her support of his activities. For example, when he is working with the concentration toys, does she display interest in what he is doing? Does she encourage his efforts and praise him for success? Or does the mother communicate disinterest by apparently being oblivious to his efforts?

Related to the mother's support of the child's activities is the timing of her intervention in buttoning a coat, working the mechanism of a toy dump truck, or in other problem-solving tasks. Does she rush to help the child at the first signs of frustration? Or does she delay until the child obviously cannot manage the task? Does the child accept her help, or does he resist her intervention? On the other hand, how long does the child persevere before seeking help from the parent? Does he give up without asking for help? Does he seek help after only minimal efforts to solve the problem? Or does he delay in seeking help until he realizes that he does not have the skills to solve the problem?

The mother's concern and guidance with specific tasks give an indication of her potential participation in the child's school experience. Her ability to give clear explanations in an organized manner will influence her effectiveness in helping the child. If the mother does not regard the child's activities as important, it is doubtful that she will be willing and able to extend training in the home. Moreover, her lack of interest may stifle the child's motivation to be engaged in certain tasks. The interplay of help-giving and help-seeking gives a clue to the child's self-reliance. The child who has been rewarded for help-seeking in the home may be confused if he is immediately expected to do for himself in another setting.

Observing specific interactions, the teacher acquires a feeling for the quality of the parent-child relationship. Are mother and child comfortable with one another? Do they like and accept one another? Do they communicate with ease and understanding? A strained relationship may evidence some communication breakdowns. Inappropriate responses may stem from occasional misreadings of verbal and nonverbal messages. Tension is indicated when the mother apologizes for the child or explains his behavior.

In a hostile relationship mother and child tend to operate at cross-purposes. Efforts to communicate result in annoyance, impatience, or exasperation. When the parent-child relationship reflects indifference, the bond is broken. There is a lack of mutual commitment, and mother and child scarcely seem aware of one another.

Any human relationship evolves from complex interactions that can hardly be understood on the basis of one encounter. Even the most tentative notion of the quality of the parent-child relationship, however, can help the teacher to individualize her plan for dealing with the child. She is better prepared to support the positive aspects of the pattern of interaction rather than inadvertently deepen the negative aspects.

Establishing Rapport

How the teacher carries out the planned activities and relates to both parent and child sets the climate for the establishment of rapport. Discussion of the admissions procedure has underscored the importance of involvement of the parent in the enrollment process so that parent and teacher can work toward a mutually determined decision. This cooperative approach is promoted by acceptance of the parent's opinions and feelings.

To create an accepting atmosphere, the interviewer expresses interest in the ideas, observations, and opinions of the parent. There is emphasis on what the parent thinks: "What do you think about this?" or "How do you think we can best handle this matter?" Acceptance connotes recognition of the legitimacy of human feelings, negative as well as positive. Response to an emotional expression by "I see" or "I understand" communicates concern for the parent's attitudes and feelings. The reflexive, "You shouldn't worry about that" tends to be perceived, "Don't worry *me* about that." The response, "We'll take care of that when he comes to school," or any reference to the effect that the school will accomplish or cure whatever the home has failed to do, scarcely relieves feelings and tends to be judgmental. Threat of judgment not only blocks communication, but this discomfiture in the beginning contact may result in a strained parent-child-teacher relationship which inhibits the development of mutual support.

Deemphasis of the judgmental aspects of the interview requires concentrated effort. Parents may come with the preconceived idea that the teacher will perceive the child as inadequate. If this idea persists, the parent is on the defensive. Assuming the position of defending his child and his own worth as a parent, he is apt to withhold information that might cast the child or himself in an unfavorable light. An area in which the school can be potentially helpful may go unrecognized because of the parent's fear of criticism or belittlement.

One of the most effective measures for initiating a positive parent-child-teacher relationship is the recognition of the primary importance of the parental role in the ongoing experience of the child. During the course of the interview the teacher takes advantage of opportunities to express support of the parent.

The way the teacher greets the child is a primary and significant step in gaining his trust, and coincidentally, the confidence of the parent. If the teacher immediately focuses on the parent, giving the child a mere token greeting or ignoring him, his reaction to being overlooked is inevitable. He senses that he is unimportant, not quite a person. To avoid this reaction the teacher focuses on the child from the beginning. The only instance in which the teacher devotes more attention to the parent is in the case of the shy child who cowers and pulls away from her approach. Observing the teacher's manner with the child gives the parent assurance that the child is liked, worthy of respect, accepted as he is. Furthermore, the teacher's attention to the child suggests that if the child enrolls, he will be well cared for and treated with concern and dignity.

Under normal circumstances a successful preentrance experience not only facilitates the child's transition from home to school, but plays a significant role in preparing him for school. The child tends to hold on to the initial impression formed during the interview. He reflects on the experience during the intervening period. Parents report that children incorporate in their play the images of the school building, the physical layout, the teacher, the equipment, and the toys. Also, children verbalize this concrete experience to family and peers. A favorable orientation provides security when he actually enters school because he knows what to anticipate. Familiar with surroundings that have pleasurable associations, he expects nice things to happen in the context of the school. The child's active expression of positive feelings toward the school gives the parent the satisfaction that his decision to enroll the child is an appropriate one.

The Admissions Decision

The most satisfactory decision is the one that seems apparent to all concerned. Preliminary home-school communications emphasize that the enrollment decision will evolve from mutual consideration between parent and teacher. From the first contact with the school, the parent is prepared for involvement in the decision-making process. This emphasis on mutual weighing and evaluation of the information begins a productive working relationship. If the bases upon which the enrollment decision is to be made are understood and shared during the course of the interview, the parent will feel a controlling part of the process.

The nursery-kindergarten may not be suitable for a particular child for any number of reasons. Causes for a decision against enrollment range from the child's immaturity to parental expectations of preprimary schooling that cannot be met by the type of program. The question most basic to the decision is the child's readiness to benefit from a nursery-kindergarten experience. The diagnostic judgment about readiness is more valid if the teacher relies on the data about the child's physical, emotional, mental, and social maturity as indicated on the Diagnostic Interview Form. If the profile indicates lack of readiness in over half the items, then the child's readiness to benefit from nursery-kindergarten is doubtful.

The child may be mature enough to profit by experience in a preprimary setting; however, the particular program may not be geared to meet his needs. The school may lack the personnel to give very immature children, or children with arrested development in some areas, the care and attention they require. Physical immaturities in terms of self-care skills may imply the need for a more demanding one-to-one relationship with a staff member. Occasionally a child will show behavioral disorganization evidenced by pronounced distractibility, destructive tendencies in handling physical property, or inability to play productively with the equipment and materials. Such a child needs individualized help to achieve maturity in terms of self-care, control, and adaptability. The school may not be set up to provide this care on a consistent basis. Even if the school is sufficiently staffed to give considerable individual attention, the suitability of the program for a child with these problems may be in question.

Awareness of the parent's attitudes, his philosophy of education, his involvement in family, work, and community affairs, and his expectations of nursery-kindergarten for the child contributes to the enrollment decision. Practical considerations come to the fore. In terms of the parent's home, work, and community responsibilities, incompatibility of schedules may disrupt the child's experience and create unreasonable inconvenience for parent and school. The terms of the contract, what the parents can expect of the school and what the school can expect of the parents, need to be fully clarified. The meaning of the school experience in terms of how it will modify the child's role as a family member must be understood. The teacher helps the parent to recognize that school influences will not always be positive. The child's experiences will include some negative exposures ranging from inappropriate speech to childhood diseases.

The parental expectations need to be carefully reviewed. The parent who is not sympathetic with the philosophy of the program can scarcely be counted on to support the school experience of the child. If the parent persists with the conviction that the role of the school should be other than what it is, expectations could not be met without compromising some aspect of the program. In this case enrollment of the child is not advisable. He would be more appropriately placed in a setting in which parental and school beliefs are compatible.

If the school is not a suitable service for the child, the teacher can alert the parent to available facilities in the community. For example, if the nursery-kindergarten offers a five-day program, and parent and teacher agree that a three-day program would be more appropriate for the child, then the teacher should be able to recommend a suitable program in the community. In view of the importance of appropriate placement in the initial school experience, one of the ongoing responsibilities of the teacher is to establish close, cooperative relations with community preprimary agencies and programs.

Occasionally, an acceptance will be conditional. There may be deterrents that can be overcome or cleared up in the interim months between the interview and school entrance. Incompatibility of home and school schedules or incomplete toilet-training are examples of these conditions. In the event that the child is not admitted, the reason should be noted for future reference.

Section IX of the Diagnostic Interview Form consists of recommendations concerning special interests, parent involvement, and a plan for help. Notations of special interests provide a ready source of information about the materials that should be available and the activities to be planned when the child enters school. Regarding parent involvement, arrangements for early or delayed parent participation are noted. If school entrance represents the child's first experience away from home, early involvement may be in order. The parent who is unsure about the potential benefits of nursery-kindergarten for the child may be another candidate for early participation.

The plan for help varies with the needs of the individual child. Readiness data are transferred to the Master Readiness Record. A beginning plan of activities for developing readiness is based on these data. Individual variations may suggest special recommendations about developmental areas to be alert to or precautionary measures to be taken. Information relating to the child's responses to limits, to cooperative interactions with adults, to problem-solving, and to help-giving and help-seeking determine helping strategies that recognize and build upon his previous experiences.

Summary

The most productive interview is arranged with both the parent and child during a time when school is not in session. Prior to the interview, the teacher sets up equipment and materials designed to encourage the child to reveal what he is able to do.

The objectives of the interview are to estimate: (1) the child's unique characteristics and readiness for nursery-kindergarten; (2) parental attitudes, involvement in family, work and community affairs, and expectations of nursery-kindergarten for the child; and (3) the parent-child relationship. A fourth objective is to establish rapport among parent, child, and teacher. Observing the child's responses to the school environment and the interviewing activities, the teacher estimates his readiness physically, emotionally, mentally, and socially. She also identifies his special interests and competencies to serve as a guide for individualized planning when he enters school.

Knowledge of the parent, particularly in terms of his expectations of nursery-kindergarten for the child, influences the terms of the contract between the home and school. The teacher acquires a feeling for the parent-child relationship. Since the child tends to bring to the nursery-kindergarten the behaviors he has learned in the home, his responses to limits, to interaction with adults, to problem-solving, and to help-giving and help-seeking help the teacher to individualize her plan for dealing with the child. The fourth objective, to establish rapport among parent, child, and teacher, is fulfilled in terms of how the teacher implements the interviewing process and relates to both parent and child. Sensitive handling of interpersonal aspects during the interview results in a supportive relationship which facilitates the child's transition from home to school. The enrollment decision, emphasizing the suitability of the program for the particular child, is based on an evaluation of all the information.

5

The Case of Allan

This chapter begins the story of Allan Norwood's career in nursery-kindergarten. Tracing the child's progress from the preentrance period through the parent-teacher conference, the case illustrates how the teacher used the record system to collect, summarize, and evaluate initial information about Allan and to evolve a plan of help.

Allan Norwood's application form for entrance into nursery school for the following September was sent in May, shortly before the school session closed for the summer. The information on the form was routine. Allan's age was listed as four; his birthday was in April. His father's occupation was noted, "Self-employed. Restaurant manager." The response to the item about the mother's occupation was: "Housewife and mother—former dietician." The diagnostic interview was scheduled for the afternoon of May 25.

When Miss Murray approached Allan and his mother at the diagnostic interview, Allan slipped behind his mother, peering around her skirt. He did not respond to the teacher's greeting. Mrs. Norwood tried to dislodge him from this clinging position, saying, "Can't you say 'hello' to Miss Murray?" Allan said nothing and remained behind his mother.

Since Miss Murray deliberately delayed making contact with Allan, waiting to gain his confidence, she suggested a tour of the facility. Mrs. Norwood responded, "We'd like that, wouldn't we, Allan?" and she put her hand on his shoulder. At the playground Allan stood close to his mother, holding her hand. He made no voluntary move to leave her side and did not respond to the teacher's encouragement to try the equipment. Finally Mrs. Norwood said, "Come on. I'll be right with you." She guided him to the slide and helped him to the first rung. From that point Allan scrambled up the ladder and slid down three times, then ran to the swings. His mother helped him on and pushed the swing. When Miss Murray introduced ball play, he ignored her. His mother took the ball, "Here! Show how nicely you can catch the ball," and threw the ball to Allan. He caught it easily and returned it to his mother with focus and direction. During this phase of the interview the teacher noted that he was slight in build and well coordinated. His deft handling of the ball suggested practice.

During the indoor tour Allan stayed by his mother's side, looking at the materials and equipment with a masked expression. In response to his mother's comments, "Aren't these toys nice? Won't it be fun to be here?" he said nothing. Then he spotted the toy cars. He sank to his knees, picked up a truck, examined it, then began to push it back and forth on the floor. "He loves cars," Mrs. Norwood pointed out.

Allan's Special Interest

With Allan engaged with the truck, the conversation turned to the Norwoods' reasons for exploring a nursery-kindergarten experience for Allan. Mrs. Norwood explained that enrollment had not been her idea. She had felt, "They're young such a short time. They have to go to school soon enough." She added that Allan was an only child, and that she was unable to have more children. Her husband, however, felt that she babied Allan too much, that it would do him good to be with other children and learn how to take his own part. She had delayed sending in the application form until she talked to other mothers who had sent their children to nursery school. They had convinced her that there were many things the child could learn in this setting that could not be taught in the home.

Mrs. Norwood explained that she and Allan were always together, except for once a week when she volunteered in the dietary department of the hospital. She was fortunate to have a reliable baby sitter with whom to leave Allan. He did not want to play with the neighborhood children because they were either too young or too old. One of her friends had a four-year-old son. On occasion they brought the children together. There were no quarrels, but the two boys never really played together. Each was occupied with his own toys.

Asked how Allan and she spent their time when they were together, Mrs. Norwood answered that she taught him to do things. He knew the alphabet, he could count to fifty, he could print his name. "Come here, Allan. Print your name for Miss Murray," his mother said kindly. Allan looked up, then turned his attention to the truck. "Don't you want to show Miss Murray?" Allan shook his head and began to suck his thumb. "Oh, come on, dear," Mrs. Norwood persisted in a gentle tone of voice, then turned to the teacher, "I don't know why he's acting this way. He must be tired."

Miss Murray smiled, nodded, and waited before asking, "Does Allan like puzzles?" When his mother acknowledged that he did very well with puzzles, the teacher took a puzzle depicting a traffic scene from the shelf. "Maybe he would like this one." She knelt and said to Allan, "Did you see this? This truck is just like the one you're playing with." Allan looked at the puzzle, but made no move to touch it. Miss Murray left the puzzle beside him, moved away, and began to talk to his mother. After a few moments Allan started to examine the puzzle, trying to lift the truck out of the picture. When he found he could not lift the truck, he dumped the pieces on the floor and began to reassemble the puzzle.

"There's the stoplight," he said as he worked, and he began to accurately designate colors. "See the *wed* light, See the gween light. See the yellow light."

"What do the red and green mean?" asked his mother.

"*Wed* means 'stop' and gween means 'go.' "

"That's right," praised Miss Murray, "what does the yellow one mean?"

Allan answered, "Be careful." As Allan continued with the puzzle, his mood began to brighten. He inserted a piece, naming it, "Here's a stason (station wagon)."

"Yes, it is," said Miss Murray. "Who do you know who has one?"

"Bompa," answered Allan.

"That's his grand-daddy," explained his mother.

"Tell me about Bompa," continued Miss Murray.

"He-he-he-he *plays* with me. He gave me a twuck for my birthday."

Allan was having difficulty fitting a small piece into the puzzle.

His mother said, "Look, here's where it fits."

Allan remarked, "It's a headlight." He picked up the car windows and started to insert them. "Here's one window, two windows, three windows. The big one goes back here." He completed the puzzle and handed it to Miss Murray. "There. It's done."

"You did a good job, Allan," said Miss Murray. "Let me show you where to put it." She guided him to the puzzle box on the shelf. "That's where it goes," He slid the puzzle into the box.

Allan looked at the stuffed squirrel on the shelf. "Is it real?"

Miss Murray answered, "It's real, but it isn't alive."

"Does it bite?" Allan asked.

"No it couldn't bite you. This squirrel has a name. The children call him 'Fluffy.' Would you like to touch him?"

Allan nodded, cautiously touched the back of the squirrel with one finger, and smiled. Miss Murray asked, "Do you have a pet?"

"Yeah," responded Allan, "two dogs."

"Two? What are their names?"

"Tag and Winnie da Pooh," he answered.

"He's a real *Winnie the Pooh* fan," put in his mother. "He just loves the stories. And of course, when Bompa gave him a new puppy for his birthday, Winnie the Pooh just had to be the name." She smiled and added, "To tell you the truth, I enjoy the Pooh stories, too."

"So do I," agreed Miss Murray. She showed Allan a sheet of paper with sketches of a bird, a dog, and a cat sitting on a bench. "Can you find the dog?"

He looked at the pictures for a moment, then said, "He's in the middle."

"Very good," said Miss Murray, "he most certainly is in the middle. Let's see if you can cut the paper up to where the dog is sitting. Be sure to stop when you reach the top of the bench." Allan took the scissors gingerly and began to cut. The scissors slid out of position. On the second try he started to make a deep slash to the left.

His mother cautioned, "No, Allan, toward the dog, not the bird," and guided his hand.

"No," said Allan, pushing her hand away. On the third attempt he directed a jagged slash toward the dog.

"That's fine," said Miss Murray. Allan smiled, put down the scissors, and started toward the trucks.

Miss Murray asked his mother if Allan still napped. Mrs. Norwood reported that he did not because he usually got up so late. "I think children should be able to enjoy being children," she explained, "instead of making them toe the same mark that adults do." She added, "I know

Diagnostic Test

there are a lot of people who don't agree with me." When asked how her husband felt about this, she admitted that he considered her too lax with Allan.

Miss Murray inquired, "Under the circumstances do you think the afternoon session is better suited to Allan's needs?"

"Yes, I think that would be best for him," answered his mother decisively. When asked about lunchtime, Mrs. Norwood responded that he didn't have a regular lunchtime. It just depended on when he had breakfast. She went on to explain that she and her husband had breakfast together. Allan was fed later. He did not have a good appetite, and he tended to be slow. Her husband prodded Allan to hurry up when they did have meals together. She felt her husband didn't understand children. It was just easier for all concerned if Allan had his meals alone.

"Perhaps you would like to visit our afternoon program," suggested Miss Murray. "It might be helpful for you to see what Allan will be doing."

"I would like that very much," said his mother. "Come to think of it, I really don't know what goes on in nursery school. People are pretty vague about it."

"That's exactly why we encourage our parents to come on a regular basis and see what their children are doing," pointed out Miss Murray. "Only through this understanding can home and school work together. There is no better way to understand the meaning of Allan's experience than to see him in action."

"It would mean a great deal to me to be able to come and visit," said the mother.

"Maybe you would like to help out sometimes with field trips or at special occasions," suggested Miss Murray.

"Any time," responded Mrs. Norwood eagerly. "I love to do things like that." She looked at her watch. "Oh Allan, we told Daddy we would meet him at the restaurant." Allan did not look up. He continued to push the truck back and forth. His mother urged, "Come on, dear. We're going to be late."

"No," said Allan, sucking his thumb, and looking around.

Miss Murray caught his eye, "I have something you might like to take home with you." She showed him mimeographed outlines of animals to color. Allan selected three. "Do you like to color?"

"Uh-uh," he answered through his thumb.

"Isn't that nice?" commented Mrs. Norwood. "We'll show it to Daddy. We'll have lots of things to tell Daddy, won't we?"

Allan took his thumb out of his mouth and nodded. He showed his mother one of the outlines. "Look! A lamb."

His mother took his hand, and turning to Miss Murray, "What's the next step?"

"I'll be sending you a letter with all the information you need," explained Miss Murray. "If you would like to come and observe, just call me."

"Oh, I wonder if my husband could come, too," asked Mrs. Norwood.

"By all means. We feel daddies are very special here."

Allan Leaving the Interview

Filling Out the Form

After Mrs. Norwood and Allan left, Miss Murray began to check the Diagnostic Interview Form. (see pp. 68–71). She noted that Allan was slight, medium in size, and pale. He was dressed in overalls buttoned at the shoulders. Getting these overalls on and off would require assistance. Since his expression was first masked, then brightened as the interview progressed, she checked both "masked" and "happy." Even though he warmed up, his initial behavior was shy.

Under the Physical Readiness Section, she checked all the items under "gross motor," and all but two under "fine motor." In terms of his emotional status, he accepted Miss Murray's praise as he worked with the puzzle and the cutting. Despite his shyness in the beginning, he was responsive to all activities. At no point in the interview did he express feelings inappropriately (crying, stamping his feet, hitting, defacing materials); however, he relied on his thumb during tense moments.

Most of the items under Mental Readiness were checked. He demonstrated his ability to focus on one task by completing the puzzle and persevering with the cutting until he was at least reasonably successful. His curiosity was indicated in his question about the stuffed squirrel. His general knowledge was exhibited in his conversation about cars, traffic lights, and animals, as well as by his mother's statement about his interest in *Winnie the Pooh*. Color recognition and naming were revealed spontaneously as he described the stoplight. When he touched the squirrel, he gave a tentative indication of his willingness to try the unknown. He counted the three windows in the station wagon in the puzzle.

Under Social Development the teacher did not check "explores on his own," because in the beginning he responded only to his mother's encouragement. He did not seek help with either the puzzle or the cutting. When Miss Murray began to build on his interests, he was willing to engage with her in activities and conversation. He cooperated with suggested activities and followed her directions in putting the puzzle away and cutting. There was no information about his ability to take care of his own needs; however, the overalls he was wearing suggested that he would need assistance. Under Speech Miss Murray checked "speaks in complete sentences" and "listens to what others are saying and answers," as evidenced in the puzzle and squirrel episodes.

Allan demonstrated a persistent interest in trucks and cars. His mother's report of his fondness for *Winnie the Pooh* was evidence of his interest in stories. He responded positively to the mimeographed outlines and acknowledged that he liked to color. He seemed to enjoy the playground.

Under Description of the Parent, Miss Murray checked "outgoing." Mrs. Norwood had been friendly and responsive during the interview. With little prompting she had volunteered considerable information about Allan, her husband and herself, and the relationships that existed among them. She tended to be directive, taking the lead in the playground and ball-play activities. This quality was indirectly revealed by her report that Allan had his meals alone. There was the hint that in order to avert what she perceived to be a problem situation, she made a decision on her own about Allan's mealtime and expedited it.

Mrs. Norwood's report about naptime and lunchtime indicated that Allan was not accustomed to a particular schedule in the home. He prolonged response to his mother's efforts to terminate the interview, and he never did comply with her request that he print his name. Lack of consistent enforcement of limits was evidenced in both of these incidents.

Mrs. Norwood's interaction with Allan reflected free overt affection. Her description of their relationship as well as her attitude toward enrolling him in nursery school suggested an unwillingness to let him go. Her explanation of why no particular schedule existed in the home hinted at her need to keep Allan young. She intervened early in problem solving in both the puzzle and cutting activities. His response to his mother's intervention in the cutting activity indicated strain in their relationship. His thumb-sucking was usually associated with a maternal directive. When Allan did not comply in printing his name, his mother excused his behavior, almost always a sign of tension.

Under the Parent's Reasons for Considering Enrollment, Miss Murray checked "playmates" and "intellectual development." She noted that the father had insisted on enrollment to provide Allan with the opportunity to play with other children; his mother had conceded because of friends' reports of the advantages in intellectual development. Although Mrs. Norwood had indicated willingness to become involved with school activities and functions, her willingness to extend training in the home was questionable.

In reviewing the summarized data about Allan, Miss Murray considered and weighed all the factors involved in enrollment. His slight, almost frail build and pallor raised a question about his stamina to meet the demands of the routines and activities. There was no question about his readiness for a nursery-kindergarten experience; he exhibited readiness in almost all the items. Also, no practical problems, such as schedule incompatibility between home and school, were apparent. The only questionable area was Mrs. Norwood's attitude toward nursery-kindergarten for Allan. Even though she appeared to go along with the idea of enrollment, she seemed to have reservations. To what extent could she be actively supportive of his school experience? Would enrollment intensify or neutralize the conflicting points of view between mother and father? If the problems would become more intense, then enrollment might not be beneficial for Allan. The tendency for home conflicts to become more severe would have been more likely if Mrs. Norwood had tried to establish distance during the interview. But she had been receptive and cooperative, willing to be convinced that nursery school would be in Allan's best interests. Since rapport and trust had begun to develop, Miss Murray decided that the evolving parent-child-teacher relationship would probably support the positive aspects of the home situation. She checked "accept without reservation."

Under Recommendations, Miss Murray entered Allan's special interests—trucks, *Winnie the Pooh,* ball play. She noted that Mrs. Norwood would probably appreciate early involvement. The recommended plan for help included a notation to examine the Health Record of the Background Information Form for an explanation of Allan's apparent frailty.

It was Miss Murray's opinion that Allan would have particular need for familiar objects and activities. In view of his mother's tendency to be overnurturant, he would probably feel abandoned in school. She noted that personnel working with Allan should not coax him to participate in activities and routines; rather, he should be allowed to come on his own terms. She considered her own role. Since Allan had invested his trust in her, he would need the continuity of Miss Murray's support when he entered the program.

Miss Murray sent the letter of Allan's acceptance to the Norwoods. The Entry Agreement and Background Information Form (see pp. 72–77) were eventually returned to the school. Miss Murray reviewed the Background Information Form and noted with interest Mrs. Norwood's positive response to the item "usually does what he is asked." She was also interested in the item relating to the recent tonsillectomy. Allan's condition leading to the operation might be an explanation for his apparent frailty at the preentrance interview. More information would be needed to support such a conclusion, however the tonsillectomy was a clue that Allan's frailty would be found in the physical inventory rather than the social or emotional inventories. A pattern of information was beginning to form which would help Miss Murray to know Allan and to plan for him.

PEMS NURSERY-KINDERGARTEN

Diagnostic Interview

Child's Name _allan Norwood_   Date _May 25, 19_

Age _4_ Yr. _1_ Mo.   Interviewer _J. Murray_

Birth Date _April 27, 1971_
            (Mo.)   (Da.)   (Yr.)

I. Individual characteristics of the Child

A. Body Type
slight _✔_
well proportioned____
stocky____

B. Complexion
pale _✔_
healthy____
flushed____

C. Body Size
large____
medium _✔_
small____

D. Dress
Appropriate for play____
Requires assistance _✔_
Lends self-help____

E. Expression
tense____
bland _✔_
masked _✔_

composed____
happy _✔_
troubled____

F. Personality
shy _✔_
confident____
outgoing____

nervous____
aggressive____
distractible____

Other_____

II. READINESS FOR NURSERY-KINDERGARTEN

A. Physical
1. Gross Motor (large muscle)
runs rhythmically _✔_
maintains balance on beam _✔_
climbs with alternating feet _✔_
parts of body move independently _✔_
throws ball _✔_
throws ball with direction _✔_

Individual variations_____

_____

2. Fine Motor (small muscles)
Picks up small objects _✔_
Manipulates: scissors _✔_ puzzles _✔_ crayons____
           strings beads____
Manipulates toys with skill and direction _✔_

68

Individual Variations_____

B. Emotional
Accepts with ease: praise **✓** correction____
Free from tensional outlets (thumb sucking, etc.)____
Responsive **✓** Exhibits control of emotions **✓**

C. Mental
Demonstrates ability to focus on one task **✓** curious **✓**

Exhibits general knowledge **✓**

Recognizes colors: red **✓** yellow **✓** blue **✓** green **✓**

Demonstrates ability to organize____ Counts 1-5 **✓** *(1-3)*

Demonstrates knowledge of concept 1-5____

Willing to try unknown **✓**

Stays with an activity **✓**

Individual Variations_____

D. Social
Explores on his own____

Exhibits ability to solve problems____ Follows directions **✓**

Willing to engage with teacher **✓** Exhibits self-help____

Cooperates with suggested activities **✓**

Individual Variations_____

E. Speech
speaks in complete sentences **✓** rich vocabulary____

uses adjectives and adverbs____

speaks clearly____ speaks fluently____

listens to what others are saying and answers **✓**

Individual Variations *Had difficulty in pronouncing*
r, th.

III. INTERESTS

Trucks ✓ blocks____ doll corner____ trains____ records____

art materials ✓ stories ✓ playground ✓ wheel toys____

Special Competencies or Interests _____

IV. DESCRIPTION OF PARENT

outgoing ✓ shy____ directive ✓ receptive____ tense____

at ease____ relaxed____ speech: controlled____ disorganized____

V. PARENT INVOLVEMENT

community involvement: very (3 or more days/wk.) ✓

moderately (1 day/wk.) ____

minimally (on occasion) ____

willing and available to participate in school activities ✓

willing and able to attend school functions____

willing and able to extend training in home **?**

VI. PARENT'S REASONS FOR CONSIDERING ENROLLMENT FOR CHILD

new baby____ playmates ✓ intellectual development ✓

learning special skills____ working mother____ discipline____

single sex influence in home environment____

Other _Playmates (father's reason) ~~Intellectual~~ development (mother's reason)_

VII. PARENT-CHILD RELATIONSHIP

parent sets limits____ parent enforces limits____

child respects limits____ child ignores limits____

parent exhibits warmth toward the child: verbally ✓

physically ✓

Child clings to parent____ child touches base with parent regularly during interview____

child asks for help early in solving a problem or doing a task____

child perseveres before asking for help ✓ parent gives help early ✓

70

VII. PARENT-CHILD RELATIONSHIP (con't)

child resists help ✓___

parent gives explanations clearly___

parent confuses child with explanations___

parent ignores child's questions___

parent uses criticism and coercive control___

parent uses tangible reward to motivate___

parent's role is supportive guide___

parent's role is authority figure___

child demands parent's attention___waits for recognition___

relationship is: comfortable___strained ✓ hostile___indifferent___

Other observations_____

VIII. ADMISSION DECISION

Accept without reservation ✓___

accept conditionally___explanation_____

did not accept due to:_____

IX. RECOMMENDATIONS

A. Special Interest *Trucks, Winnie-the-Pooh, ball play*

B. Parent involvement *Early involvement*

C. Plan for help

Examine health record for explanation of frailty.
Build on special interests - will have particular
need for familiar objects and activities.
Will probably feel abandoned in school - advise
staff not to coax him to participate in
activities and routines.
Allow him to come on his own terms.

71

PEMS NURSERY-KINDERGARTEN
4 Circle Drive
Coventry Crossing, Pa.
14850

BACKGROUND INFORMATION FORM

The school staff needs your help to understand and plan for your child.
Please fill out the following form and return to the school in the enclosed
self-addressed envelope by August 31.

Date _July 27, 19-_

Child's Name _Norwood_ _Allan_ _Paul_
             (last)   (first)   (middle)

Child's Preferred Name _Allan_
(first, middle, or nickname)

Address _731_ _Lakeside Dr._ _Coventry Crossing,_ _Pa._ _14850_
      (number) (street)   (city)   (state) (zip)

Phone Number _218-9588_

Birth Date _April_ _27_ _19-_   Age _4 yr. 1 mo._
       (mo.)   (da.)   (yr.)

Sex: ✓ male   _____ female

Father's Name _Norwood_ _John_ _Paul_
(or guardian)   (last)   (first)   (middle)

Occupation _Self-employed - Restaurant Manager_
Business Address _Lakeside Dr._ _Coventry Crossing,_ _Pa._ _14850_
        Lakeside Inn
       (street)   (city)   (state) (zip)

Business Phone _218-1030_

Mother's Name _Norwood_ _Janet_ _Allan_ (maiden name)
       (last)   (first)   (middle)

Occupation _Jack of all trades - housewife, former dietician,_
volunteer hospital worker, teacher of Sunday School, hobbyist
Business Address _____
       (street)   (city)   (state) (zip)

Business Phone _____

72

Is father living? _yes_ Is mother living _yes_ Separated? _no_

Divorced? _no_

Is there anyone whom you do not wish to pick up your child? _a stranger_

I trust any relative I have.

If so, please give name and relationship to child.

Name_____ Relationship_____

Other members of the family: (brothers, sisters, grandparents, etc.) living at home

NAME	AGE	RELATIONSHIP	INDICATE NAME USED BY CHILD

Other Members of the Family: (grandparents, aunts, uncles, etc.) living in the community

NAME	AGE	RELATIONSHIP	INDICATE NAME USED BY CHILD
Mrs. J. P. Norwood, Sr.	60?	Grandmother	Mimi
Mr. J. P. Norwood, Sr.	60?	Grandfather	Bompa
Robert Norwood	32	Uncle	"Uncle Bob"
Mrs. Geraldine Taylor	29	Aunt	"Aunt Gerrie"

Family Physician (or pediatrician) _Holland_ _Richard_ _Stanton_

(last)　　　(first)　　　(middle)

Office Address _888 Main St._ _Coventry Crossing,_ _Pa._ _14850_

(street)　　(city)　　(state)　　(zip)

Office Phone _218-1043_

Hospital to be called in case of emergency _Closest one_

Address_____

(street)　　(city)　　(state)

Hospital Phone_____

Person to be called in case of an emergency: (give 4 persons in order
of preference)

1. _Janet Norwood (mother)_ Phone _218-9588_
2. _John Norwood (father)_ Phone _218-1030_
3. _Mrs. J. P. Norwood, Sr._ Phone _218-9480_
4. _Rev. Lester A. Cole_ Phone _218-1962_

Has your child had any previous school experience? _no_
If so, please give name and type of school.

_____ length of attendance _____

Does your child have regular playmates? _no_

Does your child take a nap? _no_ morning_____ afternoon_____

How many hours does your child sleep at night? (approx.) _11 hrs._

Is your child toilet trained? _yes_ _at 22 months_

Does your child use any special word for toileting?_____

If so, please state _TT until age 3, then bathroom_

Describe your child's appetite: always hungry_____ eats at mealtime _small amounts_

snacks_____ snacks all day _✓_ never hungry_____

has to be coaxed to eat _sometimes_

Are there any foods your child may not or cannot eat? _yes_
(due to allergies, religious customs, etc.)

If so, please list: _strawberries - allergic reaction_
slight rash or red blotch

_____

Are there any foods your child dislikes? _yes_
If so, please list: _broccoli, stewed tomatoes,_
lettuce, asparagus, fish of any kind (inc. tuna)
does not care for pies.

What are your child's favorite foods?   Please list: _hamburger,_
french fries, Coke are only foods he eats out.
fresh fruits (any) carrots, peas, green beans, corn,
raisins, cereals (both hot & cold) bananas.

74

Special interests: singing _during bath_ ✓   painting ____   stories ✓

trucks ✓   pets ✓   records ✓   outside play ____

crayoning ____

Other _trains, machines used on farms_
(tractor, combines, trucks)

_____

Is your child generally cooperative? _yes_ shy? _yes_ competitive? ____

aggressive? ____   sensitive? _yes_ submissive? ____ angry? ____

happy? _yes_ usually does what is asked of him/her? _yes_ seldom

does what is asked of him/her? ____ whines? ____

List other behaviors characteristic of your child.

_____

_____

_____

Does your child exhibit specific fears? If so, please list.

_____

Describe your child's speech: rapid ____   slow ____   moderate ✓

clear ✓   talks constantly ____   seldom speaks ____

uses many words ✓   uses few words ____   talks only during play ____

Other characteristics _curious as to what a new_
word means.

Describe any special circumstances that will help us to understand
your child.

Recent Tonsillectomy, July 15. His eating habits
have changed considerably — intake has increased —
there should be a noticeable change in wt.,
from slightly underwt., to normal within
the next 6 months.

75

HEALTH RECORD

Physical description of child: body build _slight_   color hair _blonde_

color eyes _blue_ height _40"_ weight _34½ lb._

Is your child subject to colds? _yes_ allergies? _yes_ if so,

what kind? _undetermined_ fatigue?_____

Doctors told us he was a highly allergic child in June.

nervousness? _only when rushed._

Has your child had or does your child have:

any serious illness? _no_ Please state_____

any physical disabilities? (heart, eyes, ears, kidneys, etc.)

Please describe_____

_____

any mental disorders? _no_   any speech problems? _no_

any social problems? _not any that I am aware of._

Does your child receive any regular medication? _no_ If so, for
what purpose?_____

Is your child allergic to any medicines to your knowledge? _no_
If so, what medicines?_____

IMMUNIZATION RECORD: (please give date of last shot or booster)

Diptheria _April, 19-_ Tetanus _April, 19-_ Polio _Sept, 19-_____

Whooping cough _April, 19-_ Smallpox _Jan., 19-_ Measles _May, 19-_

Other _Mumps July, 19-_ _Retested April, 19-_

Tuberculin test: positive____ negative _✓_ date _Sept., 19-_____

CHILDHOOD DISEASES: (please check the ones your child has had)

Red measles_____(yr.)   German measles_____(yr.)

Chicken pox _✓ 19-_ (yr.)   Mumps_____(yr.)

Other_____

OPERATIONS:_____(tonsillectomy, appendectomy, etc.)

operation _tonsillectomy_ year _July 15, 19-_

Any previous serious illnesses?   (Rheumatic fever, etc.)_____

76

PEMS NURSERY-KINDERGARTEN
4 Circle Drive
Coventry Crossing, Pa.
14850

PHYSICIAN'S REPORT

A physical examination is required for admission to PEMS Nursery-Kindergarten. Please have your physician examine your child and return this form to the Director of the school in the self-addressed envelope.

I have examined _Allan Norwood_ and

in my opinion he is in good physical condition and able to attend nursery

school or kindergarten.

There are _____ are no _____ diagnosed conditions that will

influence the child's school experience. Precautionary measures to be

observed by the school are listed below.

Physician's Signature _R. S. Holland, M.D._

Date _July 15_

6

Readiness

Introduction

From the time the child enrolls in the nursery-kindergarten, information about his development should be recorded so that the staff can assess his readiness profile from an objective point of view. The Master Readiness Record has been developed to aid the staff in the task of recording the child's behavior and assessing his level of development.

The record consists of four sections: (1) Physical Inventory, (2) Emotional Inventory, (3) Mental Inventory, and (4) Social Inventory. Each inventory is organized according to developmental areas that are important in diagnosing readiness. Specific behaviors that reveal a child's sequential development in a given area are listed under each heading. Because the behaviors derive from developmental theory, the record can be understood and used effectively only in light of the theory and definitions of behavior explained in the succeeding chapters. These chapters also emphasize that a plan for help always follows a diagnosis. Suggested guidelines are given to develop appropriate activities that meet the individual needs of children.

THE DEVELOPMENTAL VIEWPOINT

One of the basic assumptions underlying developmental theory is that development occurs along a continuum. Regardless of the direction it takes, the process does not stop and start. There are no sharp transitions from one period to another. The growth sequences of one period are rooted in what has gone before and influence the events that will occur in the future.

Developmental Patterns

The developmental process follows patterns: (1) Development unfolds according to a predictable sequence, (2) Development proceeds from general to specific responses, (3) Development occurs according to varied rates of growth. It is important to clarify that despite similarities, each child goes through these patterns at his own rate. What each child brings into the world with him and what happens to him once he is here result in enormous individual variations in rate, rhythm, and quality of response.

GROWTH SEQUENCE

Most children follow an essentially similar order of growth. For example, motor developments are programmed according to a predictable sequence. The child sits up before he can stand. The muscles of the upper arm support a reaching movement before his hands can grasp an object. Loco-motion movement—crawling, creeping, walking, running—appear in an orderly sequence. Each event sets the foundations for succeeding steps. If a child has not learned to control his large muscles, then he will encounter difficulty with skills involving the small muscles. In terms of play behavior, the child follows a familiar sequence. Initially he plays by himself, gradually he moves near other children and plays beside them but not with them. Later he plays with other children. Emotional and mental development also follow a defined sequence.

GENERAL TO SPECIFIC RESPONSES

In motor, mental, and emotional development, the child's responses are first general and nondifferentiated. With maturation and experience, his responses become more refined and specific. In early motor activity the child's body tends to move as a unit. Later in his development, he acquires more mobility and independent movement of body parts. In terms of mental development, the child initially perceives the main characteristics of an object, but fails to notice details. He may refer to all four-legged, furry animals as "dogs." Emotionally, the neonate expresses one generalized reaction of excitement. A little later he experiences delight and distress. His response pattern soon differentiates into more specific expressions of fear, anger, and joy, revealing the beginning states of the mature spectrum of emotions.

VARIED RATES OF GROWTH

Even though development is continuous, the rate of the process is not steady and consistent. Development tends to be most rapid at its starting point and to slow down with the passage of time. The greatest increase in height, for example, takes place from conception up to two years, then levels off. At puberty there is a second growth spurt. By the same token, mental growth is most rapid at the beginning of development. Benjamin Bloom estimates that growth in this area unfolds as follows:

> . . . data suggest that in terms of intelligence measured at age 17, about 50% of the development takes place between conception and age 4. About 30% between ages 4 and 8, and about 20% between ages 8 and 17.[1]

Varied Rates of Growth

---

[1] Benjamin Bloom, *Stability and Change in Human Characteristics* (New York: John Wiley & Sons, 1964), p. 88.

Growth tends to involve spurts, lags, and regressions. When spurts occur, such as the rapid increase in height in the first two years, the growth curve shows a sharp upturn. A lag is a period in growth or learning when there appears to be little or no progress. For example, the child begins to walk, and it seems that he wobbles along unsteadily for a long period of time before suddenly acquiring grace and rhythm. Regressions, periods when a child reverts to more immature behavior, are also common. When a child faces a new experience, such as entrance into school, he may have accidents even though toilet-training has been well established.

Optimal Times for Certain Developments

As development unfolds, there are optimal times for certain developmental events to take place. If the event does not take place, or there are problems associated with its onset, the individual may encounter difficulty in making up the deficit as development progresses. Even though the organism has a tendency to compensate for what was missed earlier, there will be deviancies or disruptions as a result of this lack of preparation. The earlier the lack is identified and remediated, the greater are the chances to allay harmful effects.

For example, in terms of the rapid growth of intelligence during the early years, Bloom estimates that the preprimary period is the optimal time for the development of general learning patterns.[2] Unless environmental influences are conducive to appropriate learnings, there can be developmental deficits. Both stimulation before a child is ready and lack of stimulation when the child is ready can result in problems later on. It is therefore imperative that those who guide young children be aware of where the child is developmentally in order to provide for his needs.

Interdependence of the Four Dimensions of Growth

Knowing where a child is developmentally involves estimates of how far he has progressed in the physical, emotional, mental, and social dimensions of growth. One of the cardinal concepts of developmental theory is the interrelatedness of these growth areas. What happens in one area can make an impression on or profoundly affect growth progress in other areas. The full meaning of a child's progress can be understood only in the context of his total developmental picture.

The influence of physical incapacities and immaturities on emotional, mental, and social development have been well documented. An under-

[2]Bloom, p. 110.

nourished child, for example, not only lags behind in mental development, but loses ground in emotional and social development as well. He is more vulnerable to loss of emotional control, and he may lack the stamina to participate in activities with other children. Less well understood are the effects of emotional problems on physical growth. Studies have shown that emotional problems, or "psychologic malnutrition," can impede linear growth; in some cases, can even result in "deprivation dwarfism."[3] In light of this interdependence of the four dimensions of growth, an understanding of the child's needs is based on an estimate of his total developmental progress.

A DEVELOPMENTAL CONCEPT OF READINESS

The following concept of readiness evolves from these basic assumptions of the developmental viewpoint. Generally defined, readiness refers to a child's developmental preparation to acquire new behaviors. While there appears to be some agreement about this definition, the specific meaning of readiness and its implications for nursery-kindergarten practice differ widely among early childhood personnel. In view of the varied meanings attached to readiness, there is a need to clarify the particular concept underlying the readiness records. Specifically defined, readiness is the level of total development that enables a child to learn a behavior, comprehend a concept, or perform in a given way with ease. Since development occurs along a continuum, readiness is an emerging process. As a child grows and experiences, he acquires maturities that open his capacities to learn and to do. *Maturity* refers to the maximum level of developmental progress achieved by the child at a given time physically, emotionally, mentally, and socially. Since growth proceeds from general to specific responses, it follows that these emergent maturity levels qualify the child for progressively complex and differentiated functioning. At any point the maturity levels for each dimension of growth are determined by the interaction of maturation and experience.

Influence of Maturation

As the child develops, his body undergoes changes that stimulate and enable him to learn and to do. *Maturation* refers to this process of biological changes that ripen a child's capacities. Maturation prepares the body for learning to take place. It must be noted that maturation is the *process;* maturity is the *level* of developmental progress. Genetically con-

---

[3] Irving J. Olshin, "Problems in Growth," in *The Pediatric Clinics of North America* 15, no. 2, ed. Robert L. Brent, M.D. and Irving L. Olshin, M.D. (Philadelphia, Pa.: W. B. Saunders Company, 1968), p. 442.

trolled, the maturation program involves progressive changes in the skeletal, muscular, and neurological systems, permitting higher levels of functioning in all areas of experience.

The maturation process is most obvious in terms of physical development. Each step in the motor sequence depends on timed changes in bone, muscle, and neural structures. A child will be unable to walk, for example, until his leg musculature and bone development permit control of his legs and support of his body. Development of the brain and nervous system is essential for increasingly complex movements and coordinations. At any stage a child's anatomic and physiologic status influences not only the quality of response he can make, but reflects in his endurance, strength, and energy resources.

Programmed by maturation, certain biological changes must occur before various mental capacities appear. Changes in the cortical tissues of the brain develop the visual and auditory perceptual systems. These developments must take place before the child is able to identify marks on the page as letters, recognize letters in sequence as words, or relate the experiences he has had to the pictures and words he sees. Maturation also relates to social and emotional growth. Until certain neural changes take place, the child tends to be egocentric, unable to view a situation from the perspective of another person. In the early developmental stages, his social behavior reflects a lack of concern for the needs and wishes of others. "The ability to respond emotionally is dependent upon neural and endocrine development."[4]

The task of estimating readiness is complicated by the tendency of the maturation process to unfold unevenly in the four areas of growth. The maximum level of developmental progress at any given time may not be the same for each dimension. Maturation may have made the child physically ready to master certain skills. His eye-hand coordination as well as fine-muscle development may enable him to manipulate a crayon. He may seem ready to learn to print his name. In terms of mental development, however, maturation may not have sufficiently progressed to enable him to catch the meaning of letters appearing in configuration. The opposite maturational combination is common. Mentally a child may be advanced, but at the same time lag behind in physical, emotional, and social maturation.

Influence of Experience

Maturation alone is not sufficient to bring the child to the level necessary to learn a behavior, comprehend a concept, or perform a given task with

---

[4]Elizabeth B. Hurlock, *Child Development*, 4th ed. (New York: McGraw-Hill Book Co., 1964), p. 267.

ease. A child may be maturationally ready to engage in an activity, but lack the background experience to use his capacity. Piaget suggests that maturation opens up possibilities, but never is sufficient in itself to actualize these possibilities. Actualization requires both social and physical environment.[5]

An enriched environment contributes to a child's general readiness to respond to learning challenges. As he experiments and plays with the things in his environment, he learns their shapes and sizes, colors and names. By manipulating them, he finds out how they feel and how heavy they are. He learns their functions and how they fit with other things. These experiences give him a basis for interpreting his world and coping with its problems.

The multisensory stimulation of an enriched environment is of paramount value; however, it is not enough to guarantee the development of readiness in specific areas. The child acquires the experience necessary to use his developing capacities through planned and guided activities. As he indicates maturational readiness to learn certain skills, he needs to participate in experiences geared to strengthen his background for that learning.

At a basic level a child may have undergone the cerebral changes necessary to comprehend the meaning of letters and to discern differences and similarities among symbols. To actualize these capacities, he needs exposure to letters in a variety of directed and spontaneous learning situations. He needs to make letters, copy them, cut them, hear them, see them, say them, touch them. He needs to connect the letter he hears with the letter he sees.

A recent research project illustrates the value of specific, structured activities in developing readiness. The study was set up to determine the relative effectiveness of two different kindergarten experiences in raising predicted reading levels of kindergarten children. Four experimental groups consisting of randomly selected children from low-income, urban areas were assigned to the Kindergarten Diagnostic Prereading Program (Kidi-Prep). Four control groups consisting also of children from low-income, urban areas were assigned to classes following the traditional kindergarten curriculum. The experiences of the experimental and control groups varied only in that the children in the Kidi-Prep program participated in activities at designated "learning centers":

> Four learning centers were established in the Kidi-Prep classrooms. The instructional period of one hour was divided into units of 15 minutes. Instructional groups of from six to eight children moved through these four centers during the Kidi-Prep period each day, spending from 10–15 minutes at each center. In this manner, all children in the Kidi-

---

[5]Millie Almy with Edward Chittenden and Paul Miller, *Young Children's Thinking* (New York: Teachers College, Columbia University, 1966), p. v.

Prep curriculum participated in every activity planned for the learning centers . . . .

Each of the learning centers focused upon activities involving specific areas of cognitive skills. One center stressed activities requiring visual motor association and several conceptual competencies such as categorizing, classifying, and identification of similarities. At this center, a child might be asked to find pictures of household items in a magazine, cut them out, and then categorize them on the basis of various criteria such as function, color, or shape. The next center required visual decoding and sequencing on the part of the child. A typical activity at this center would be following a pattern and stringing beads in the proper sequence of shape and color represented in the pattern. At the third center, both auditory and visual activities took place. The children were provided with an array of items and played guessing games which required a child to verbally describe an item to the other children in his or her group and then have them select the item described from all the visible items. The fourth, teacher-directed, learning center focused upon intersensory integration involving auditory and visual reception and perception with verbal interaction. The teacher might show the children a picture of everyday objects in which some of the objects were pictured correctly and others were not. (A banana might be colored blue; a car would have square wheels, etc.) The children were asked to decide which items were pictured incorrectly and in what feature they were incorrect, color, shape, or use. The children were also asked how the item could be changed to make it correct . . . .

The activities at the other three learning centers were structured to extend the skills and concepts introduced at the teacher-directed station. The materials used at these three centers were the kinds of materials found in most kindergarten classrooms.[6]

The results indicated that the Kidi-Prep program was significantly more effective in raising the predicted reading levels of kindergarten children than was the traditional program. The outcomes showed that "kindergarten experiences do affect the cognitive skills and conceptual competencies related to future reading achievement."[7] The following recommendations were made:

A kindergarten curriculum should include a definite period of time each day for planned, diagnostic, structured learning experiences. This daily instructional period should involve both small group, independent activity and teacher-directed activities planned so that each child participates in every activity. Activities planned for small group instruc-

---

[6] Peggy L. Stank, *Kidi-Prep: A Kindergarten Diagnostic Prereading Program* (Harrisburg, Pennsylvania: Bureau of Educational Research, Pennsylvania Department of Education, 1973), p. 3.

[7] Stank, p. 4.

tion should be extensions of the teacher-directed activities and should focus on specific areas of cognitive skill and conceptual competencies . . . .

First grade reading readiness materials should not be used in kindergarten. The kindergarten curriculum should provide activities and experiences which build skills and competencies children need to function adequately when they begin the first grade readiness program. Children need experiences which will help them discern, identify and associate objects and concepts. Such experiences should also help children see cause and effect relationships. These kindergarten experiences must be at their level.[8]

Influence of Experience on the Maturational Process

One of the crucial problems concerns the timing of the experience. Since environmental stimulation has its greatest effect during the beginning stages of development, the optimal time to provide experience is when the child first reveals his maturational readiness to cope with a certain behavior.

The question is often raised: Will introduction of the experience of training in a certain task prior to biological readiness speed up the maturational program? Research evidence is forcibly clear and consistent on this point. In its simplest terms, forcing of learning is useless. A child is neither superior in the task nor more firmly grounded because of premature training; moreover, there may be harmful side effects. Inducing a child to learn before he is ready may result in attitudinal problems. Premature training may generate negative feelings toward the task that will interfere with the learning later on. A practice instituted to give the child a head start may, in the long run, cause a major setback.

Regarding the optimal time to intervene, Havighurst's concept of "The Teachable Moment" has relevance:

> When the body is ripe, and society requires, and the self is ready to achieve a certain task, the teachable moment has come. Efforts at teaching which would have been largely wasted if they had come earlier, give gratifying results when they come at the *teachable moment*, when the task should be learned. For example, the best times to teach reading, the care of children, and adjustment to retirement from one's job can be discovered by studying human development, and finding out when conditions are most favorable for learning these tasks.[9]

---

[8] Stank, pp. 4–5.

[9] Robert J. Havighurst, *Human Development and Education* (New York: David McKay Co., 1965), p. 5.

Summary

The concept of readiness underlying the Master Readiness Record derives from basic assumptions of the developmental viewpoint. Occurring along a continuum, development follows patterns: (1)Development unfolds according to a predictable sequence, (2) Development proceeds from general to specific responses, (3) Development occurs according to varied rates of growth. These developmental patterns are similar for all children; however, each child unfolds at his own rate.

There are optimal times for certain developments to take place. If a development does not take place, or if irregularities occur in its beginning stages, the individual may have problems in compensating for this deficit later on. In view of the interdependence of the physical, emotional, mental, and social dimensions of growth, a child's progress is estimated on the basis of his total developmental picture.

Readiness is defined as the level of total development that enables a child to learn a behavior, comprehend a concept, or perform in a given way with ease. A child's readiness to acquire a new behavior is indicated by his progressive levels of maturity for the four growth dimensions. Maturity levels of each dimension result from the interaction of maturation and experience. As the process of biological changes that makes the body ready to function at increasingly higher levels, maturation activates capacities to learn and to do physically, emotionally, mentally, and socially. Unfolding capacities need to be nurtured by planned and guided experiences. Introduction of experience prior to maturational readiness is not only useless but may be harmful to the child's developing capacity.

7

Diagnosing and Planning for Physical Development

The child's physical development is a sensitive index to his readiness to acquire new behaviors. The child uses his body to learn. He responds, experiences, reads, writes, speaks, listens, performs, and practices by means of his bodily systems and organs. The body provides the basic equipment for learning.

In order for the body parts to function optimally, they must be in good running order; otherwise, problems affecting readiness may emerge in one or several dimensions of growth. Immaturities or impairments of any organ or system not only influence the accuracy and durability of the learning, but control whether the behavior can be acquired at all.

In the preprimary years the body may not be ready to function in certain ways because the mechanisms are not yet fully developed. Since developmental changes carry behavioral correlates, the teacher needs to understand how the child's body works and how it changes in order to help him learn. The child's body gives clues to his condition and stages of development. The observer must be able to recognize and interpret these clues. If the teacher is not aware of the child's physical status, then there is the danger of introducing the wrong activities for his developmental level. For example, during the preprimary period the visual apparatus is developing. One of the messages that the eyes may be sending is that they are not ready for too much exposure to near-point visual activities (workbooks, printing). If the child is required to spend extended time on activities for which he is not visually ready, then the eyes compensate in ways that may prove detrimental later on.

On the other hand, if the teacher is alert to what the child's body is saying and how it is functioning, then she is in a position to detect "differences" that may develop into problems. If the condition is identified early, measures may be taken to offset or prevent a potential learning disability. Physical factors play such a decisive role in the child's capacity to learn and to do that attention to health and developmental progress is a major responsibility of the teacher.

The child's physical condition and developmental status are revealed in terms of the following areas: (1) physical health, (2) motor coordination, (3) right-left orientation, and (4) self-care skills. The major sections of the Physical Inventory of the Master Readiness Record comprise these areas.

Physical Health

Health is defined as a state of wholesome well-being. It suggests that the body capacities have full strength for optimal functioning. Ill health, on the other hand, implies the presence of indisposition, disease, or defect that affects the child's learning and growing in various degrees.

In the early years of nursery-kindergarten practice, emphasis was on the physical health of the child. Later on, social and emotional development received more attention. In recent years early childhood education has focused on the mental development of the child, and his physical condition has not been given high priority in the teacher's list of concerns. However, in view of the importance of the body's role in learning, one of the foremost concerns of the teacher should be close observation of the physical condition of the child. Not only must she be aware of "differences," but also she must note changes in patterns of response and functioning.

COMPLEXION AND ENERGY LEVEL

The child's complexion and energy level reflect his general condition. Although appearance and energy resources may vary somewhat during these years of rapid growth, pronounced changes may be diagnostically significant and should be recorded as they are observed. A child of high color who suddenly becomes pale or a vigorous youngster who winds down to a lethargic pace exhibit pronounced changes in pattern.

VISION

In identifying signs of visual problems, the teacher needs to be aware of the difference between *sight* and *vision*. *Sight* is the mere ability to see; it is the eye's response to light shining into it. *Vision* is the capacity of the eyes and brain to receive and interpret accurate sense impressions from an illuminated environment. Vision encompasses not only sight, but eye-movement skills, eye-teaming skills, and eye-hand coordination. Many children can demonstrate 20/20 sight, but still have a critical and interfering vision problem.

Overt symptoms (e.g., appearance of the eyes) or behaviors (e.g., difficulty staying in the lines while coloring) that indicate the possibility of a problem are listed under "vision" in the Physical Inventory of the Master Readiness Record. It must be recognized that children without vision problems occasionally evidence these symptoms and behaviors. If the child exhibits any of the symptoms on a consistent basis, his parents should be informed and a vision examination recommended. The behaviors may or may not be evidence of vision impairment or physical eye defect. All of these behavioral signs may be indications of visual developmental problems.

Thrusting the head forward or backward while looking at distant objects represents a difficulty in identifying objects, probably blurring. Frowning or scowling during near work may indicate focusing fatigue. The tendency to rub eyes may be a reaction to physiological visual stress. Difficulty in staying inside lines in coloring is evidence of immature eye-hand coordination. The tendency to move closer to the television set may indicate a developmental lag in eye-movement skills. Touching and fingering things constantly may evidence a developmental lag in vision and touch association. Turning and tilting the head to use one eye usually indicates that one eye is seeing things differently from the other eye. The head movement is an attempt to block off one eye.

Dr. David Hamilton states that if a child exhibits one or more of these behaviors consistently over a two-week period, this behavior may be evidence of too much exposure to near-point visual activities (workbook activities, printing) before he is visually ready. He recommends a complete cessation of near-point visual activities for a month, followed by resumption of these activities on a limited basis. If the child continues to experience too much exposure to these activities before he is ready, he will learn compensations that will prove detrimental later on in life. In the event that one or more of these behaviors is still evident even with the program of reduced activity, the child's eyes should be professionally examined.[1]

---

[1]David Hamilton, OD, FAAO, lecturer in pediatric optometry, Pennsylvania College of Optometry.

When a child indicates a problem in visual processing of information (not just seeing clearly), he should be checked by a vision specialist who is interested in functional visual analysis with special reference to the near-point vision problems of children. The specialist may be an ophthalmologist or optometrist. In each profession there are some who are interested in functional visual care and some who are not.

There is a need to identify many kinds of visual defects in the early stages if treatment is to be effective. Delaying corrective measures too long may mean that the child will never develop adequate vision. In some cases observation will not screen the problem. Amblyopia, "lazy eye blindness," which must be treated before the child's eyes are fully developed to restore vision, is a prime example of a condition that can be identified only through professional examination. On the basis of the importance of early detection, there is ample evidence to support the adoption of the policy that the vision of all children be professionally checked.

HEARING

Hearing is the faculty of the ears to receive sound impressions. *Listening* is the capacity of the ears and brain to receive and interpret accurate sound impressions. A hearing defect is an impairment of the outer, middle, or inner ear that interferes with sound reception. The impairment may range from mild hearing loss that results in faintness or blurring of sounds to profound deafness—no sound reception at all. Hearing problems are difficult to detect. Almost all the behaviors symptomatic of a hearing defect may be manifested by normal children at one time or another because of immature listening skills or compensatory "tuning out" skills. A major hindrance to early identification is the tendency to misinterpret symptoms. Lack of attention or misbehavior may result from inability to hear. Consistent repetition of the symptoms listed under "hearing" in the Master Readiness Record is evidence of the need for professional examination. Whether the behavior represents a hearing or listening problem the ears should be checked for the possibility of impairment by a qualified otologist (medical doctor who specializes in disorders of ear, nose, and throat) and a certified audiologist (specialist in measurement and remediation of hearing loss).[2]

ILLNESSES

The record of absences due to illness not only reveals health trends characteristic of the child, but also may be diagnostically significant in tracing the beginnings of a physical problem.

---

[2]Richard C. Bevan, Director Child Study Department, The Pennsylvania School for the Deaf, Philadelphia, Pennsylvania.

A record of the child's illnesses, height and weight, and existing conditions is maintained for ready reference in the Health section of the Physical Inventory.

HEIGHT AND WEIGHT

The height and weight of each child should be measured and recorded on a monthly basis. Any deviation from the child's pattern should be noted. Excessive loss or gain in weight or a plateau in height increase may be signaling an organic or emotional problem; however, any change, no matter how slight, should be noted and reported to the parent.

EXISTING CONDITIONS

The Health section of the Background Information Form indicates the child's health history and status at the time of entrance. A review of these data helps the teacher to understand the health trends characteristic of the child. This section brings to light physical problems, such as a defect which is not responsive to correction and treatment. In the case of chronic illness or defect, the teacher lists the limitations imposed by the condition and the recommended precautionary measures in order to provide special consideration.

PLAN FOR HELP

The child's plan for help begins with his individual health needs. Information about his characteristic health patterns revealed in the Background Information Form provides a basis for the plan. Additional information is derived from observations and examinations arranged by the school or by the parents. These observations and examinations are crucial in assessing general health as well as identifying vision and hearing problems. Depending upon the information the teacher plans appropriate and supportive activities. The plan for help may include referrals to or recommendations from professional sources.

The following examples are some indications of how the teacher might individualize a plan for help. If the child has been prone to illness, then he may not be as hardy as the child with a more stable health background. What may be a normal gross motor workout for the majority of children may be an overexertion for him. He needs to be watched and protected against expending his energies to the point of exhaustion. If a child has had a history of hospitalizations, he may have developed possible negative attitudes toward health personnel. Positive experiences with health personnel during nursery-kindergarten can help to overcome these feelings. In order to individualize the child's plan, the teacher takes into account specific differences, such as allergies; for example, an allergy to milk products.

In order to help *all* children to develop sound habits, the nursery-kindergarten should be a model promoting healthy routines. For example, nutrition can be incorporated into the program by teaching about foods that make up a balanced diet and by encouraging good eating habits. The teaching of good eating habits and of cleanliness practices such as washing hands can be incorporated into the program. The preprimary years, represent a time of rapid growth physically, emotionally, mentally, and socially. Growth requires energies that need frequent regeneration. Children of this age are resilient; their depleted energy reserves can be restored in a relatively short time. Rest period has significance not only in replenishing energies, but in helping the child learn how to relax. The key to optimal functioning of the body is frequent periods of complete and quiet relaxation when the child stretches out, releases tensions, and allows the body to rebuild it resources for further activity. Children who are not accustomed to these periods of relaxation need to be guided in how to rest. Sometimes this guidance requires the teacher to provide a model by resting with the children. The importance of learning to relax during these formative years can scarcely be overemphasized. The habits developed during this period tend to become fixed and carry over into later life.

Motor Coordination

Motor coordination is defined as body movement involving control of the voluntary muscles. The physical, emotional, and social importance of motor activities has long been recognized. Less emphasized is the role of body movement as an index to a child's mental readiness to learn and to do. How motor functioning and learning are related can be understood in light of the sequence of neuromuscular development.

The following developmental sequence, and its implications for readiness, was excerpted from a workshop conducted by Dr. Jay M. Yanoff. This theory represents a small part of Dr. Yanoff's comprehensive work in education. He is Coordinator of Staff Training and Education, Pennsylvania Advancement School and Intensive Learning in Philadelphia. He is also co-author of *The Psychology of Open Teaching and Learning* (Little, Brown and Co., 1972).

SEQUENCE OF NEUROMUSCULAR DEVELOPMENT

Yanoff states that motorically the newborn operates at a bilateral level. *Bilaterality* is defined as the stage of neuromuscular development in which the child uses both sides of his body equally to accomplish a task. In the newborn both sides function simultaneously. If one leg is lifted, the other comes up. He grasps the bottle or breast with both hands. In this initial stage the infant is incapable of dividing activity between the two sides. Both sides of the body operate as a single unit. This capacity to coordinate both sides of the body at one time is normally present at birth and continues through life.

In order to assess the child's bilateral competence, the teacher can observe coordinations which require equal use of both sides of the body. "Angels in the Snow," an appropriate activity for preprimary children, reveals ability to coordinate at the bilateral level. In this activity, the child lies on the floor and as his legs spread out, both arms drag along the ground until they touch overhead. He then returns to his starting position. When the child becomes proficient in jumping late in the preprimary period, the "Jumping Jack" activity also reveals his bilateral coordination: The child jumps as his arms swing overhead, hands touching, and then jumps back to his starting position. The same coordinations are demonstrated in both activities; however, for "Angels in the Snow" the child does not have to fight gravity for bilateral movement. "Jumping Jacks" are introduced when a child is able to move in space and against gravity.

Later in the first year the infant's motor activity shows more differentiated responses. He can now use one side at a time. He extends one arm while the other remains prone. He reaches out with one hand and grasps. When the child begins to use one side of the body without the involvement of the other to accomplish a task, he is demonstrating *alternating laterality.* This capacity normally continues through life. Skills involving the use of one side of the body increase in complexity as the child moves through the preprimary period. The child gradually learns to shift his movements from one side to the other. As he does this, he begins to maintain balance in walking and running. *Balance* is the distribution of energy used to control weight on both sides of the body. When balanced, the body parts function harmoniously and the body moves rhythmically. As the child acquires more refined postural control, he can stand on one foot with support, then without support. Gradually he learns to hop four to six steps in a forward movement. Later he can sustain a hopping movement for ten to twelve steps in a forward line, then in a circle, then in a backward line, and finally in a backward circle. Other activities indicating a child's capacity at the alternating laterality level are his progress in climbing and descending stairs using alternating feet to lead and his increasing skill in balance-beam maneuvers.

The stage of *integrated laterality* is reached by girls near the end of the preprimary period and by boys at a slightly later age, according to Yanoff. At this level one side of the body does one task while the other side

Integrated Laterality

does another task, a capacity that, again, normally continues through life. The child can use one side of his body to throw a ball and the other side to maintain balance. He can write with one hand while the auxiliary hand holds the paper. Ability to skip smoothly, shifting from side to side with cross-patterned (right foot forward while left hand is forward; left foot forward while right hand is forward) hand and leg movement is an indication of motor functioning at this level. When a child can perform in this manner, he is usually capable of complex and highly coordinated motor activities.

Motor coordinations become more precise and refined as the child moves through the sequence from bilaterality to integrated laterality. Gross motor coordination (control of the large muscles) precedes fine motor coordination (control of the small muscles). Each development in the motor sequence lays the groundwork for succeeding coordinations. When the large muscles are adequately developed, the child will fatigue less with coordinations involving the use of the small muscles. Efforts to train such specific skills as handwriting before adequate development of the large muscles result in fatigue and frustration for the child. Insufficient attention has been paid to the role of fatigue; indeed, it is now believed to be the greatest hindrance to a child's learning.

If there are problems associated with early coordinations, more advanced developments will show the effects. For example, irregularities at the bilateral level influence activities associated with alternating laterality and, ultimately, with integrated laterality. A child may develop the tendency to rely on the right (or left) side to the extent that the opposite side is less active, not keeping pace with the development of the right (or left) side. His motor activities become *monolateral.* He tends to use one side to the exclusion of the other. Body energy is unequally distributed, interrupting balance. Activities involving alternating use of the sides will show a weakness of the inoperative side. His walking and running will show a lack of balance and rhythm. He will be able to hop on the active side, but will have difficulty in sustaining a hopping movement on the inactive side. If the child carries a tray, it will tilt, because of his difficulty in balancing. Wheelbarrow activity will result in circular tilting and dumping of the contents.

PLAN FOR HELP

A child's progress along the developmental sequence has implications for helping him in terms of gross motor coordinations, fine motor coordinations, and mental readiness.

Gross Motor Coordination.   In view of the time and experience required for the child to reach the level of integrated laterality, the preprimary years represent the optimal school time for improving skills involving the large muscles. There should be less emphasis on skills involving the use of the small muscles. The child needs activities to strengthen bilateral coordination, such as jumping, lifting with both hands, pushing a wheelbarrow, drawing circles on a chalkboard with both arms and hands simultaneously, guiding a saw, rowing, pushing a baby buggy, carrying a tray full of cups, gathering up paper or leaves with both arms, and returning the puzzles to the puzzle box. The child also needs activities to strengthen coordinations at the alternating laterality level, such as walking, running, climbing, crawling, creeping, hopping, tricycling, maneuvering on the balance beam, bouncing a ball with each hand, and any other activity in which only one side of the body is used.

As the child masters gross motor skills, he should have opportunities to advance to more complex activities. Innovative variations and stunting often indicate mastery of a skill. When the child learns to ride the tricycle, he displays proficiency by riding with no hands. If irregularities show up at the bilateral or alternating laterality levels, as indicated by inability to perform certain motor coordination activities listed in the Physical Inventory of the Master Readiness Record, then a concentrated program of help is in order. For example, if the child cannot do "Angels in the Snow" or if he can hop on one foot but not on the other, then he needs activities to strengthen bilateral functioning. If he indicates lack of balance in walking or running or in other alternating laterality activities, then he needs activities to help him to strengthen use of one side of the body at a time. If the

Balance Beam Activity

child does not improve motorically, so that he can operate efficiently at these levels, he will fatigue and break down on more finite motor movements later on in his development.

Fine Motor Coordination.   Activities based more on gross motor than on fine motor coordination of the arm, wrist, hand, and fingers help to strengthen both large and fine muscles. The child needs the support of the large muscles to manipulate the smaller muscles with ease. Emphasis should be on *kinesthesia,* the sensation of movement of the fine muscles. Important movements to encourage are pounding, squeezing, rolling, twisting, and hammering. Workbench activities involve pounding, hammering, and sawing. Work with clay, Pla-Doh, papier mâché, plasticene, biscuit dough—materials that are pliable but resistant—involve these movements. Drawing or painting on large paper (15 by 18 inches for drawing; 18 by 24 inches for painting) on a flat surface or at the easel enables the child to move his hands freely with the support of his arms. Chalkboards at the child's eye-level should be provided for gross motor scribbling with large pieces of chalk or paintbrushes dipped in water.

The effects of fingerpainting in developing the fine muscles seem to be minimal because of the lack of resistance of the material; however, as Yanoff points out, fingerpainting has diagnostic value since the teacher can see which muscles the child is using by examining his artwork. She can tell whether the child is using one finger, representing the small muscles, or covering the page, demonstrating the use of the whole arm.

Close, fine work requiring restricted hand-finger movements and synchronization of hand and eye should be introduced sparingly, if at all, while the child is functioning at the alternating laterality level. At this stage too much activity involving small muscles and precise eye-hand coordination can have harmful effects on the child's visual development. He will be ready for longer periods of confined use of muscles when he reaches the level of integrated laterality. Tracing, cutting, coloring within lines, copying, pasting, and folding have their place in a program developing readiness for printing, writing, sewing, and other such complex skills.

Mental Readiness.   Yanoff contends that the child's level of motor functioning gives a clue to his mental readiness. The body and mind act as one. Until a child reaches the level of integrated laterality, his perceptual powers will be limited. Functioning at the more advanced level helps him discriminate likenesses and differences and reproduce his perceptions accurately. He will have greater facility in organizing his thinking into rules, conceptualizing, and comprehending abstract ideas. When total motor functioning becomes sophisticated, the child is able to bring meaning to the printed symbols he sees on a page. It must be recognized that all children do not learn to read simply because they have reached the integrated level of motor proficiency. On the other hand, there are some children who demonstrate ability to read prior to this level of motor development. Yanoff contends that in order to continue to read well with little fatigue, these early readers should also be encouraged in motor development.

Right-Left Orientation

Right-left orientation refers to the ability to distinguish between the right and left sides of the body. The child must establish awareness of his own right and left before he is able to identify position and direction of objects in space.

DEVELOPMENTAL SEQUENCE

During the preprimary years the child is functioning primarily at the bilateral and alternating laterality levels. As he experiments with natural movements, he feels the different roles of the two halves of his body. Gross motor activities, such as walking, running, jumping, climbing, and hopping require balanced coordination of right and left areas. As the child acquires and practices these skills involving the large muscles, he kinesthetically internalizes the differences between the two sides. He gradually develops an internal awareness of the right and left sides of his own body.

When the child is oriented to the sides of his own body internally, he can use his awareness of right and left to make judgments about the direction and position of objects (directionality) outside his own body. He is now able to determine his relationship to objects in his environment. He can establish abstract relationships of top, bottom, inside, outside, up, down, behind, left, and right. Later he can make judgments about the direction and position of objects in space without direct reference to himself. He can identify the chair on the right-hand side of the table, the door to the left of the cubbies, the picture on the right-hand side of the page, the letter *A* to the left of the *B*, and the letter *C* to the right of the *B*. It must be remembered that judgements about the direction and position of objects in space are always in relation to something, but generally in relation to the self.

The child's maturity level in terms of right-left orientation must be inferred from his behavior over a period of time. The development of right-left orientation, as all development, is characterized by lags and regressions. The child who responds accurately in exercises involving the right and left parts of his own body for some time may suddenly reverse his responses. Right becomes left, and left right. He may exhibit this confusion for a while, then suddenly begin to respond accurately again. This is a natural occurrence in early development; therefore, observations on a long-term basis are required.

Lateral Dominance.   The child's dominance provides a clue to his progress in establishing right-left orientation. *Lateral dominance* is defined as the preferred use and dominant functioning of one side of the body over the other. A person who uses his right hand in preference to his left shows right-hand dominance. A person who relies on his left hand shows left-hand dominance. Some children show nearly equal use of both sides. In the early stages the youngster tends to use both sides equally; however, during the period of alternating laterality, the child begins to experiment with each side to determine which works more comfortably. A dominant preference for one hand is one of the last alternating laterality developments to take place; therefore, Yanoff suggests that handwriting not be begun with children until they have fully developed integrated laterality, or reached approximately the third grade. Again, the emphasis is on development, not on age or grade level. Individual differences in reaching integrated laterality must be taken into account.

Lateral dominance should not be confused with monolaterality. When the child develops a leading side, this side does one part of the task, and the other side functions in an auxiliary and complementary manner.

The little boy who claimed that he was getting very "growed up" because he knew his right hand from his wrong was reflecting a societal attitude that used to prevail. Left-handedness was considered to be a handicap, primarily because the world is set up for right-handed people. At one time it was the vogue to try to change left-handed children to right. A later modification of this practice was to encourage right-handedness by presenting objects to the child's right side, but once dominance was established, not to try to change it. Current thinking cautions teachers not to encourage or try to change a child's dominance; rather, to let him operate with his better side. Developing a leading side happens neurologically; dominance cannot be forced. The teacher presents objects at midline, allowing the child to decide the hand easier for him to use. Activities are provided for both sides so that he can experiment in order to determine which side is more comfortable for him. Left-handed scissors, for example, should be standard equipment in the classroom. When repeated observations evidence that dominance has been established, this development is an indication that the child is aware of his right and left.

Reversal Error.   The *reversal error,* i.e., the tendency to mirror letters, words, and numbers, is also a clue to the child's progress in establishing right-left orientation. The error may be a horizontal reversal. For example, letters p, d, b, or q may be misperceived and confused for one another. Any nonsymmetrical letter may be perceived and reproduced as if reflected in a mirror; however, common reversals are B, E, J, N, P, and S. Vertical reversals may also occur. M and W, b and p may be confused. As the child begins to blend letters into words, pairs of words such as *on* and *no, pot* and *top, saw* and *was* may be reversed. The child's number renditions frequently reflect the reversal error. The numbers 3, 6, 7, and 9 are particularly prone to reversal, but again, any nonsymmetrical number is vulnerable (see p. 102).

Reversal errors are identified in the child's letter, word, and number renditions. A child may not consistently reverse; therefore, it is important to collect samples over a period of time. This tendency may also be evidenced in activities requiring the child to place or to match letters, words, or numbers. The presence of the error may be a symptom of confusion about sidedness. The child may not have developed internal awareness of right and left, and consequently, may project this confusion in his written symbols.

PLAN FOR HELP

Repeated observations of the child's inability to differentiate right and left as well as persistence of the reversal error and incomplete dominance

Reversal

indicate that internal awareness of right and left has probably not been established. If the child is not aware of his sides, he may experience confusion in the direction of eye movements, loss of orientation, and difficulties in letter, word, and number recognition. Following the sequence of printed symbols from left to right may not be stabilized.

In order to develop internal awareness of self, leftness and rightness included, the child needs experiences that will help him to "feel" how the two halves of his body function. A program of physical development emphasizing motor skills that involve control of the large muscles not only improves motor coordination, but the requisite postural balance helps the child to realize the roles of the right and left sides. Balance-beam exercises help develop the "feel" for the functioning of the two sides, and at the same time help the child's vision. At all times, when a child uses the balance beam, he should fixate the eyes on a target in front of him. A person's balance is not only related to large muscles, but also to the finest muscles of all, the eyes. Initially, the child walks forward and backward with his arms extended to help him to maintain balance. When this exercise is mastered, he can try to walk forward and backward, swinging his arms in a cross-patterned fashion. Any activity that involves large muscles helps the child to develop this internal awareness of right and left.

While the child is internalizing his own right and left awareness, he can engage in the background experiences that prepare him for the next step. Identifying the position and direction of objects in space requires not only the knowledge of right and left, but also the relational concepts—up, down, in, out, under, over, beside. Activities in which the child steps in and out of a circle on the floor, jumps over things, crawls under things, or places things beside him help him to learn kinesthetically how the positions of objects relate to him and to other objects.

A particular experience in identifying objects in space concerns the progression of printed symbols from left to right in English as well as in other languages. In order to help the child to become accustomed to this sequence, activities with concrete objects, such as bead-stringing, provide background experience for later reading and writing.

Exercises involving the naming of the parts of his body are appropriate for the child internalizing awareness of left and right. Verbal commands to name the right and left parts of his own body begin simply. For example, at first he points to his right leg, then his left hand. Later, at the integrated level, he is required to pull his left ear with his right hand, touch his left knee with his right elbow. When the speed of the directions is accelerated, the activity becomes more demanding. In exercises requiring the child to name the position and direction of objects, he first names the position of objects in relation to himself: "Is the red or blue block on your right side?" Gradually, as the need for reference to self drops out, more exercises not related to his position in space can be introduced: "Which block is on the right side of the yellow block, the red or the blue?" At this stage the child moves outside himself and is able to recognize the position and direction of objects in space with relation to one another.

It is important to remember that before a child can be aware of what is happening outside his body, he must first be aware of what is occurring inside. When repeated observations seem to indicate that internal awareness of right and left has been established, the child can operate in a confident manner with his body. Confidence with body reflects a strong self-image. Leftness and rightness are one sign of internal control of body and mind. It must be recognized that rightness and leftness cannot be taught. The most effective way to develop this confidence is to set up an environment that recognizes and is responsive to these needs of children.

As emphasized throughout the text, each child is an individual with a unique pattern of physical development. It is the responsibility of the teacher to know and understand the developmental pattern of each child in order to plan appropriate learning experiences for him.

Self-care Skills

The preprimary years are characterized by increasing independence in caring for physical needs. At the beginning of this developmental period the child has acquired the skills basic to dressing, handwashing, bathing, feeding, and toileting; however, he may still require help in taking care of

Self-care

these needs. The less mature child will need considerable assistance not only to accomplish self-care tasks, but to refine the skills and develop the habits necessary for independent personal care. The child who has moved further along the self-care continuum will require only minimal adult help.

IDENTIFYING PROGRESS IN SELF-CARE

In the early stages of this sequence the child's skills tend to lack smoothness and precision. He puts on his clothes, washes himself, and manipulates eating utensils with awkward, painstaking movements. Because of wasted motion and inadequate control of his arms and hands, he is apt to be slow in carrying out learned activities. Occasionally it takes him so long to dress or to eat that his attention span runs out. He will dawdle with dressing or get up from the table and do something else before returning to finish his meal.

Despite the time expended, the child's efforts are not always thorough. Clothes may be put on wrong side out, hands may not be entirely clean, and food may be spilled around his plate or down the front of his clothes. There may be aspects of skills he is unable to manage. Fasteners, back buttons, zippers, and laces may be too difficult for him to manipulate. He may not have mastered the skill of cutting his meat with a knife.

If a child exhibits these tendencies in caring for his needs, not only is he dependent upon others for active assistance in carrying out and learning skills, but he may rely on adults for reminders to initiate care. The less mature child often seeks help inappropriately or avoids seeking help when it is really necessary. His judgments about when he needs help and when he can manage by himself are not always reliable.

As the child advances along the sequence, his skills reflect refinement, speed, and economy of motion. He can carry out activities with more ease and flexibility. As he gains control of his arms and hands, there are fewer mishaps—dropping the soap, spilling, getting caught in his clothes. He may still experience problems with intricate coordination, involving fasteners and buttons in the back of his garments. He needs the eye to guide the hand. Pulling boots on and off depends upon integrated skills that are not usually acquired in the preprimary years.

The more independent child no longer needs to be told to take care of his physical needs. He understands and accepts the responsibility for washing his hands before snacks, hanging up his coat, and putting his possessions where they belong. Furthermore, he *seeks help appropriately*, recognizing when he needs assistance. The child who has achieved this level of independence requires only minimal help and attention.

FACTORS INFLUENCING SELF-CARE PROGRESS

The child's independence in self-care skills is determined by maturation, adult guidance, and experience. Maturation, the process of bodily changes that ripens the child's capacities to do and to learn, sets the time when the child will be physically and mentally ready to master certain skills. *Precision* in these activities depends upon complex coordinations involving control of both the large and small muscles. Certain neurological changes precede the child's understanding concepts of cleanliness and neatness as well as the social and hygienic reasons for following certain routines. He will probably not be capable of true self-responsibility until he has internalized these concerns.

There are instances when the child is maturationally capable to care for his needs to a much greater extent than he demonstrates in daily behavior. He may manifest immaturity in self-care because of the lack of opportunity to take charge of himself personally. His needs have been anticipated and met by the parent before he has had the chance to try to do for himself. When the child is dressed and bathed, his hands washed, his hair combed, and his food cut by another person, he is denied practice in these skills. His proficiency level may be similar to that of the child who lacks maturational readiness.

Parents may not encourage children to be independent in self-care or in other activities for a variety of reasons. Some parents may miscalculate the child's readiness. Observing how the child takes care of his needs in the initial stages, they may interpret his fumbling efforts as lack of readiness to do for himself. They do not recognize these attempts as tentative, beginning steps that will improve only with practice. The overly nurturant parent represents a different kind of problem. He may be reluctant to give up the close, attentive role. In order to delay the separation process, he may help the child, sometimes completely care for the child, rather then support his struggle to do for himself. There are parents who profess practical reasons for doing for the child. When time is at a premium, it is the line of least resistance to bathe the child, dress him, fix his hair, and prepare his food. Guiding a child to accomplish these skills takes time and patience which the parent may not be able or willing to give when it is needed, even though it will save time later on.

There are parents who, by default, make the child self-reliant. In some environments children are forced to do for themselves because adults are not available to help them. Under these circumstances a child may learn to care for his needs, but not necessarily in skillful and socially acceptable ways. For example, he may not have learned the routine of handwashing before meals and after toileting. Although he feeds himself, he may use his fingers, exhibiting limited facility with eating utensils.

PLAN FOR HELP

If the teacher follows guidelines for identifying progress in self-care, she can estimate the amount of help each child requires. The independent child poses few problems. It is more difficult to evolve a plan of help for the more dependent child. The kind of plan, the way she guides him to self-responsibility, depends upon the reasons for the dependency needs. If he is limited by maturation, then she encourages him to do what he can, but gives close guidance and assistance with activities he is not yet able to accomplish or complete. When the child tires or loses interest in a task, then the teacher is ready to give him the help he needs. If his problem is lack of experience and practice, she supports the use of his own powers to follow through to completion. This support may involve doing with him in the beginning. One of the keys to helping the child acquire independence in self-care is sensitivity to the appropriate time to intervene. The teacher anticipates the child's need for help. She provides the experiences for him to make judgments about needing help, but she is prepared to step in if he needs help to achieve success. One of the perplexing problems facing the teacher is to trace out the cause underlying a child's dependency. She is likely to make a more valid judgment if she follows the procedure for diagnosis with its emphasis on patterns.

Summary

In order to diagnose and plan for physical development, the teacher must be alert to the condition and developmental status of the child's body.

Awareness of what the body is indicating it is ready to learn and to do helps her to provide appropriate activities and to identify conditions that may develop into problems. Areas to be observed are physical health, motor coordination, right-left orientation, and self-care skills.

One of the foremost concerns of the teacher is close observation of the child's health. She must note the child's appearance and characteristic patterns of functioning in terms of complexion, energy level, vision, and hearing. Records of the child's illnesses, height and weight, and existing conditions are maintained. The child's plan for help is based on his individual health needs as well as on the routines that help him to develop sound habits.

The teacher needs to be aware of the role of motor coordination (body movement involving control of the voluntary muscles) as an index to the child's readiness to learn and to do. Motor development unfolds according to a sequence that permits increasing differentiation and complexity of body movement. During the preprimary years, physical activities should focus on developing the large muscles. There should be less emphasis on close work requiring restricted hand-finger movements. A record of the child's progress along the motor sequence not only helps the teacher to identify his level of functioning, but also provides evidence of any irregularities that need special attention.

During the preprimary years the child learns to distinguish between the right and left sides of the body. When he develops an internal awareness of right and left, he can make judgments about the position and direction of objects (directionality) outside his body. The child's orientation to right and left must be inferred from observations of his behavior over a period of time. The establishment of lateral dominance and absence of the reversal error are clues that internal awareness of right and left has developed. A progressive program of activities helps the child to "feel" his own right and left sides, then to project this awareness to objects in space.

By the preprimary period the child has usually acquired the basic self-care skills; however, he may need help in taking care of his physical needs. On the basis of the child's maturity in terms of self-care, the teacher estimates the amount and kind of help he requires. The child's independence in self-care skills is influenced by maturation, adult guidance, and experience. In evolving a plan to guide the child toward greater self-responsibility, the teacher needs to determine whether his dependency is based on lack of maturational readiness or on lack of experience and practice.

8

Diagnosing and Planning
for Emotional Development

In diagnosing and planning for emotional development, the teacher must first of all be aware of its importance in terms of the child's *total* readiness to learn and to do. Emotional immaturities may influence physical, mental, and social growth. Development in one or more areas is often impeded or diverted into a deviant course because of emotional roadblocks. Bentley, Washington, and Young point out,

> In the process of planning an educational program, the basic needs of young children must be given priority, beginning with a child's emotional development. If children's emotional needs have not been met, any attempt to provide learning experiences to foster their cognitive development could be futile. When a child is emotionally secure and stable, he is then ready to engage in a variety of learning experiences.[1]

What Is Emotion?

There is no generally agreed upon definition of emotion. Intricately related to the whole system of human behavior, emotions are difficult to isolate, to observe, and to describe. Practically defined, an *emotion* is a

---

[1]Robert J. Bentley, Ernest D. Washington, and James C. Young, "Judging the Educational Progress of Young Children: Some Cautions," *Young Children* 29, no. 1 (November 1973): 8.

feeling, an affective reaction experienced by an individual. The emotions that are experienced by a person affect and in turn are affected by the way he feels toward himself and others, and toward the things and events of his environment. Woven into the texture of his personality, these feelings influence his attitudes, his moods, his ability to cope with stress, and his motivation to learn and to do.

In order to diagnose and plan for emotional development, the teacher needs to understand how the emotions evolve in terms of the developmental sequence. She must also be aware of how emotional growth may be fostered or hindered in the life of the individual child.

THE SEQUENCE OF EMOTIONAL DEVELOPMENT

Emotional development is characterized by increased capacity to experience and to express feelings. As a newborn, the infant's feelings are probably limited to sensations of pleasure and pain. He responds to arousal by one generalized expression of excitement. As the maturation process unfolds, his capacities for feeling begin to deepen and differentiate.

By the preprimary years the child has matured to the point where he can feel and express the full range of human emotions to some degree. During this period he is learning to master such emotions as fear, anger, hate, and jealousy. His emotional expressions tend to be intense, uninhibited, and fleeting. He is apt to love one minute and hate the next; he may like an activity one day and dislike it the next. Whatever appeals at the moment may be passionately treasured, then discarded with indifference when something new lures his interest. Although emotional fluctuation is typical of the preprimary child, individual children differ in the amount of unevenness they exhibit.

Even though he may not always have the power to cope with his emotions, the child begins to understand that there are acceptable and unacceptable ways of expressing feelings. The preprimary period is the optimal time for the child to learn to bring his emotions under control. With guidance, he begins to internalize controls and direct his emotional energies into constructive channels. The way he responds to his environment begins to be more consistent as he moves along the continuum. A pattern of responding starts to form.

PSYCHOLOGICAL NEEDS

A child's characteristic way of responding to his environment reflects how his needs have been satisfied in the course of his day-by-day experiences. An emotional reaction is brought about by the satisfaction or frustration of a basic need. If the basic need is fulfilled, there tends to be a positive response towards whatever or whoever satisfied the need. A thwarted need, on the other hand, tends to generate negative feelings toward whatever or whoever was responsible for the frustration.

Early in life the following psychological needs develop: (1) need for gregariousness, (2) need for security, (3) need for mastery, (4) need for independence, and (5) need for relaxation.

Need for Gregariousness.   The child has a need to be with other people. In order to satisfy this need he has to develop positive relationships with those in his environment. His beginning relationship with his mother sets the direction for his later abilities to interact with others. The newborn has a native need for stimulation—to be held, to be cuddled, and fondled. As this need is satisfied in the early maternal-child interaction, the child develops a specific affectional attachment to his mother (or to the one who provides nurturing care). Gradually, he generalizes responses learned within this relationship to other people.

If his need to be with other people, to be liked, to be approved, to belong, to be accepted as a worthy human being is satisfied in his early associations, the child develops a positive self-image. A child's *self-image* mirrors what others have told him he is. During the preprimary years the child is establishing a separate identity. At this time he is more dependent upon the approval of significant adults to assure his worthiness and adequacy than will be the case later on. He is not yet capable of evaluating his own worth. The self-image is a pivotal consideration in evolving a plan of help for the child whose needs have been inadequately met.

Need for Security.   The child needs to feel safe and protected. He has to be able to make reasonable predictions about what the future will hold. Routine helps to provide the security that his basic physical needs will be met. And consistency on the part of significant adults in their attitudes towards him helps him to feel psychologically secure. The guesswork must be taken out of what he can and cannot do to be approved by adults and to get along successfully in his environment. He needs the support of positive limits set consistently by caring persons. As he matures he becomes able to set limits for himself.

Need for Mastery.   The child needs to have accomplishments. He needs to develop competence and have success experiences with skills and tasks appropriate for his developmental level. Early in life this need for mastery is fulfilled in terms of learned motor skills. Later, his mastery needs expand to include emotional, mental, and social accomplishments.

Need for Independence.   As the child develops, he needs to separate from significant adults to become an individual in his own right. Gradually, he

Need for Security

can tolerate longer and longer periods away from his mother or caretaker. In order to develop an identity of his own, he needs to do for himself, to manage his own emotions, to think for himself, to solve problems appropriate for his developmental level, and to behave as an individual separate from, but cooperatively and responsibly related to others.

Need for Relaxation.   During the course of his daily experience the child needs intervals of rest. Not only his physical energies, but his emotional, mental, and social resources need to be replenished by change-of-pace activities. In the beginning stages he is expending enormous growth energy. He wears down quickly. Even though he has ready revival powers, he requires frequent periods of time out to gather his strength. If rest periods are not provided, stress may develop. *Stress* is fatigue that results from unrelenting strain or stimulation. Upsetting the child's equilibrium, stress compels him to rely on compensatory behaviors to relieve tension and keep his emotions intact. Some stress is inevitable; however, its depressing effects can be neutralized by sensible pacing, a frequent "letting up" to relieve the pressure and restore energy.

NEED-SATISFACTION AND SELF-ESTEEM

When a child's needs are satisfied, he tends to develop healthy feelings of *self-esteem.* Cox interprets self-esteem as follows:

Independence

> During early childhood one psychological characteristic, perhaps more than any other, helps a child to grow emotionally and feel self-sufficient . . . . Self-esteem. It may be called self-confidence, but it is more, because self-esteem is constant. It gives the individual a sense of worth for his own sake—for his own capabilities, and for himself as a human being with unique qualities . . . .
>
> [Self-esteem is] a necessary part of the total package of health called "well-being." It means we accept ourselves and our limitations but trust ourselves to cope with most situations that occur.[2]

No child's needs are satisfied in every respect. There are bound to be disappointments and failures and defeats. However, if a child experiences more satisfactions than thwartings, he is likely to feel good about himself. To the extent that frustrations outweigh satisfactions, feelings of self-esteem tend to be diminished.

The child's level of self-esteem influences the number and intensity of his anxieties. Berger defines *anxiety* as "the affect or feeling that follows upon the perception of danger, be it real or imagined."[3] It is the anticipation of an unpleasant event. Berger explains that

> anxiety is not in itself pathological. It is indeed necessary for survival, for it stimulates ways, defenses if you will, of dealing with life's dangers, both

[2] James J. Cox, "Help Your Child to Self-Esteem," *Today's Health* 46, no. 2 (February 1968): 24, 27.

[3] Allan S. Berger, "Anxiety in Young Children," *Young Children* 32, no. 1 (October 1971): 5.

the real ones of the outer world and the make-believe ones of our inner world . . . . [It] is as inevitable a part of our life as our breathing and our heartbeat . . . . What counts with anxiety is how much of it there is and what we do with it.[1]

    The child with healthy feelings of self-esteem, including a positive self-image, tends to have few anxieties and knows constructive ways to work through them. The child who feels worthy, well-received, and capable is not as likely to have had experiences that lead him to anticipate unpleasant outcomes. He does not need to allay anxious feelings with behaviors that tend to alienate others. He continues to behave in ways that have proved effective in meeting his needs in the past, keeping in motion a cycle of positive emotional growth.

    The child whose history of unsatisfied needs has left him fearful about what the future will bring is more apt to anticipate unpleasant outcomes. In dealing with these uncomfortable feelings, he tends to behave in less socially acceptable ways. More often than not, such behavior leads to further thwarting of his needs, keeping in motion a negative cycle of emotional growth.

    The interrelationship of needs, feelings of self-esteem, and anxiety is shown graphically by the following diagram:

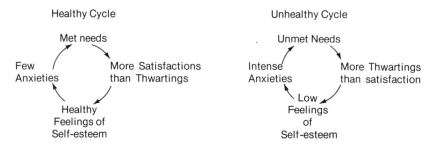

Identifying the Child's Pattern of Emotional Development

The concept of *pattern* is of particular importance to the teacher in diagnosing what the child is like in terms of emotional development. There is no instrument available to measure with precision the child's degree of need-satisfaction, his feelings of self-esteem, and anxiety. Inferences must be made from his behavior, specifically his overt reactions to a variety of situations. No single reaction is evidence of a child's emotional development; in their emergent stages the emotions of children are not stable. Negative feelings and inappropriate responses are exhibited by all children at one time or another. To be significant a behavior must be

---

[4]Berger, p. 6.

repeated consistently over a period of time. Only on the basis of evidence of habitual behaviors that have become a pattern can a diagnosis be made.

BEHAVIORS REFLECTING EMOTIONAL DEVELOPMENT

A child's characteristic ways of behaving are reflected in his attitudes, his moods, his level of self-control, and his signs of stress and fatigue. The major sections of the Emotional Inventory of the Master Readiness Record comprise these areas.

Attitudes.   A child's attitudes represent his prevailing feelings about himself and other people, and about the things and events of his environment. His attitude toward himself is based on his perception of himself as well as on his self-image, his perception of how others view him. What he perceives himself to be may or may not be the same as what he perceives others think he is. Differences can create conflicts that the teacher must take into account.

How the child feels about himself is revealed in his reactions to others and to daily activities. He may be enthusiastic, receptive, indifferent, resigned, resistant, or hostile in his behavior.

The child who is *enthusiastic* characteristically exhibits warmth and overt affection in relating to adults and other children. He is eager to participate in both routine and new experiences. The *receptive* child may be less demonstrative, but he too shows a willingness to interact with others and to participate in activities. The *indifferent* child may go along, but his responses are characterized by an absence of interest and concern. He is not willing to invest too much of himself in activities that might hurt him. The child whose attitude is *resigned* is submissive, but his behavior is characterized by apathy and weariness. He may not really want to interact or participate, but it is the line of least resistance to go along. The *resistant* child is unwilling to interact or participate. He may withdraw from overt affection. The more he is coaxed, the more he tends to refuse by actively moving away or by not listening. The child whose attitude is *hostile* demonstrates antagonism toward others and toward activities. His behavior is characterized by anger, brimming within or openly expressed.

Moods.   A child's mood reflects his emotional state or outlook at a particular moment. The child whose mood is *serene* tends to be at peace. He moves through his daily interactions and activities with ease and composure. The child whose mood is *even* tends to accept the people, things, and events in his life. He may have problems, but is able to cope with his daily interactions and activities. The *troubled* child tends to be upset. His interactions and activities are characterized by tension. The *sullen* child has built a wall around himself based on distrust. He relates to others and participates in activities with resentment.

Self-control. The child's progress in regulating his emotions indicates his maturing capacity to deal with emotion-arousing situations. His maturity is revealed in how often and with what intensity his emotions are aroused. When a child regulates his emotions, the intensity of his expression is in proportion to the stimulus. An emotional display out of proportion to the provocation indicates immaturity in regulating his emotions. The child's frustration tolerance when he is denied an object or activity also indicates his maturity. Self-control is evidenced in the ability to delay gratification of impulses; the child is willing to wait for attention, food, toys. The less controlled child may react with an emotional display if his impulses are not gratified the moment he expresses them. Ability to maintain focus is additional evidence of emotional control; ready distraction from tasks suggests lack of control.

Signs of Stress and Fatigue. When children experience tensions, conflicts, and emotional fatigue, they tend to express their feelings in a variety of ways. Some children use their bodies to provide solace (crying, nailbiting, crossing eyes, nose-picking, thumb-sucking). Other children relieve stress by acting out against adults, other children, or the environment (kicking, stamping feet, bullying, destroying property, hitting, talking loudly, responding irritably). Pointing out the shortcomings of others or blaming others for their own mishaps or wrongdoing is common with children under stress. Daydreaming or regressing to an earlier and more comfortable developmental period are other common reactions. A child may exhibit stress and fatigue by a strained or masked expression or rigid posture. A whining, demanding, or strained tone of voice is also a sign. It must be emphasized that in the beginning stages of learning to master the emotions, overt behaviors that serve to release tensions are expected. These behaviors are diagnostically significant only when they occur so frequently that they are a consistent characteristic of the child's personality.

PLAN FOR HELP

The child is in school for only a fraction of the day. On the basis of this limited contact, the teacher should not overestimate her potential influence on the youngster's emotional health. On the other hand, she should not take lightly the power of a positive school experience. Occasionally, the teacher will assume that a child from a problem home situation cannot be helped. If she starts with this premise, then she will be unable to contribute to the child's emotional growth.

While the child is in school, his degree of success in his relationships, activities, and control of his emotions relates significantly to the degree to which his needs are satisfied. Emotional development is furthered through the provision of experiences that satisfy his needs to belong, to be liked, to be approved, and to feel worthy. Guided participation in tasks, skills, and activities that meet with success leads to feelings of mastery. Clear, consistent guidelines for daily activity assure him of a safe field of operation and secure direction for what is going to happen. Guided opportunities to do for himself, to make the choices and solve the problems appropriate for his developmental level promote his feelings of independence.

A significant, but occasionally overlooked aspect of helping all children to grow emotionally is the atmosphere that prevails in the nursery-kindergarten. Positive emotions thrive in a warm, happy, relaxed environment; they wither in an atmosphere where fun and enjoyment are sacrificed in the interests of getting a series of jobs done.

It is commonly pointed out that "play is the work of children." The intended meaning suggests that when children are engaged in play, they learn about themselves and their world and how to cope more effectively with the things and events of their environment. In other words, play is not an idle way to pass time. In addition to its value in teaching the child about himself and his world, play functions for him just as for the adult. Play provides relaxation. The child learns that life is not always a serious business. Play is a time for the fanciful, the spontaneous, the light, the whimsical. It is a time to enjoy and explore fantasy. It may be a time of accomplishment, but it is also a time to do things simply for the fun of it.

During the preprimary period the balance between directed activities and play must be carefully maintained. Sufficient time devoted to play is of crucial significance because of the need to regenerate emotional energies. Without time-out, emotional stress develops. Play refreshes the feelings, renewing emotional vigor for living and growing.

For the child who indicates a negative cycle of emotional development, a concentrated program of help must be planned. In the following discussion describing such a program, reference is made to methods recommended in the manual, *Strategies for Teaching.*[5] Even though research for this manual focused on older age-groups, the strategies are applicable to the preprimary level.

The plan for help for the child who tends to show a pattern of negative reactions begins with efforts to change his self-image. Unable to evaluate his own worth and capabilities, the preprimary child is dependent upon significant adults to help him meet his needs and build his feelings of

---

[5] *Strategies for Teaching,* 2nd ed. Title III Project, Diagnostic Educational Grouping with Strategies in Teaching, in the Bucks County Public Schools in Pennsylvania, Bureau of Special Education, Pennsylvania Department of Education (March 1972).

self-esteem. He cannot do it alone. He probably will not progress emotionally without their supportive messages that he is worthy and capable.

The teacher must first develop a trusting relationship with the child. She spends time with him each day on a one-to-one basis. This supportive attention, if even for short periods, communicates to the child that he is worthy of someone's concern and opens the way for him to invest his trust. Until trust is established, efforts to improve the child's self-image will be in vain. He will not believe the teacher's positive view of him. The objective of the plan is to help develop realistic feelings of self-esteem.

Since the preprimary child tends to be concrete and literal, the teacher's simple, direct assurances, "I like you" or "I care about you" come through as sincere. Most children also respond to physical contact— touching by a caring adult. Helping a child to feel well-received may require a long period of consistent, day-by-day effort on the part of the teacher. When the child develops the confidence that comes from feeling worthy and liked, he no longer needs the teacher's support on such a concentrated basis. The strength begins to come from within. *Strategies for Teaching* recommends the supportive approach, but cautions that the child should eventually learn to realize rewards from within:

> The best reward is that you love him. This may be expressed in a physical way—a pat on the hand or a hug with the clinging children, but this should not be overdone. This can be given when the child needs it but encourage him to be satisfied with the reward of his own accomplishment. [6]

Encouraging the child to be satisfied with his own accomplishment often requires a revamping of attitudes toward participation in activities that lead to accomplishment. Children who devalue their abilities to do are scarcely ready to organize their tasks in ways that lead to success. In order to achieve, the emotionally troubled child needs structure, and the teacher must provide it for him. The manual recommends the following very structured approach to activities:

(a) Assign a task that will end in success.
(b) Set a definite short-term goal.
(c) Be pleased with small accomplishments.
(d) Break down tasks into steps.
(e) Choose areas of special interest whenever possible. [7]

A child's efforts are reinforced when he is praised. The use of praise is a sensitive motivational tool. *Deserved* praise spurs the child to strengthen

---

[6] *Strategies for Teaching,* p. 16.
[7] *Strategies for Teaching,* p. 15.

his efforts toward a goal. Indiscriminate praise is perceived by even very young children as a ruse that is soon tuned out and distrusted.

As the child begins to feel the confidence and security that comes with satisfying experiences, he tends to be less anxious. He is less vulnerable to potential threats to his well-being, and better able to tolerate denials and frustrations. He is in better command of himself and his emotions. He may need help, however, to change habitual responses to emotion-arousing situations. Therefore, the teacher provides activities for constructive outlets. Painting, working with clay and biscuit dough, and pounding serve to release pent-up feelings. There are times when children may display intense emotion, resulting in complete loss of control. The manual then advises to

> restrain them physically by hugging them firmly but not roughly. Losing control can be a frightening experience for a child even though it may stem from anger. Holding him provides a calming period to check the outburst and return to some stability.[8]

These recommended strategies form the basis for a plan to help the individual child to know success, build healthy feelings of self-esteem, and relieve the anxieties that tend to twist and warp his behavior. The preprimary period represents the optimal time to intervene. Emotional growth can be positively influenced by a plan of help carried out during these critical years.

Summary

Practically defined, an emotion is a feeling, an affective reaction experienced by the individual. A person's feelings influence his attitudes, his moods, his ability to cope with stress, and his motivation to learn and to do. In order to help the child grow emotionally, the teacher needs to understand the sequence of emotional development. By the preprimary period the child begins to develop characteristic ways of responding to life's situations.

A child's pattern of responding reflects how his needs have been satisfied. An emotional reaction is brought about by the satisfaction or frustration of a basic need. Early in life the following psychological needs develop: (1) the need for gregariousness, (2) the need for security, (3) the need for mastery, (4) the need for independence, and (5) the need for relaxation.

The child's emotional development is influenced by the way these needs are satisfied. In general, if he feels liked and approved, if he can

---

[8] *Strategies for Teaching,* p. 23.

master tasks and skills within reasonable limits, if he feels safe, if he can rely on himself, and if he is well-paced and knows how to relax, then he will tend to feel a pleasant emotional response toward living in his environment. And generally, if he feels rejected and unworthy, if he lacks accomplishments, if he lives with inconsistency, if he depends upon others to help him with tasks he should ordinarily take care of by himself, and if he is under continuing stress, his emotional reactions are more likely to be negative.

In identifying a child's characteristic ways of responding the teacher observes behaviors that reveal his attitudes, his moods, his level of self-control, and his signs of stress and fatigue. These behaviors are diagnostically significant only when they are so habitual that they are consistently characteristic of the child's personality.

In order to help all children to grow emotionally, the teacher provides experiences that will result in satisfaction of basic needs. She recognizes the importance of relaxation to regenerate emotional energies. The school environment reduces stress by maintaining a balance between directed activities and play. The teacher adopts special strategies to help the child whose emotions seem to be developing along negative lines. These strategies are based on the child's intensive one-to-one relationship with the teacher and focus on enhancing the child's self-image.

9

Diagnosing and Planning for Mental Development

Mental development is an all-inclusive term to describe the whole range of faculties related to the mind. A *faculty* is an ability, inherent or acquired, to perform a specific kind of behavior. Mental faculties, which include both thinking and feeling, provide the basis for perceiving, understanding, and retaining knowledge. Mental faculties also refer to the *use* of this knowledge in terms of reasoning and problem-solving.

Two terms used in association with mental development are *cognition* and *intelligence. Cognition* refers to *how* the mental faculties function, primarily to the processes by which a person acquires knowledge. The term *intelligence* reflects *how well* the mental faculties function. When a person behaves intelligently, he demonstrates the capacity to use all his mental powers to fullest advantage. Intelligence implies that judgments are based on thinking rather than on feeling.

Simply defined, *mental development* refers to the maturing of a person's faculties to acquire knowledge, to use reason, and to solve problems. In the past, little was known about how the mental faculties developed and how they functioned; consequently, the mental development of the young child was not of immediate concern to early childhood educators. Emphasis was on the child's physical, emotional, and social development in the preprimary years. With new knowledge of human development came a

growing interest in mental development. Concurrently, changing conditions in society contributed to the urgency of focusing on the mental dimension of growth during the early years.

Factors Influencing the Emphasis on Mental Development

Interest in the mental development of the young child emerged from diverse
sources. The observations of Jean Piaget opened new areas of knowledge
about how young children think and how they learn. Jerome Bruner pointed
out that any subject can be taught in some intellectually respectable way to
any child at any age.[1] Benjamin Bloom contended that environmental
stimulation has its greatest effect during the early period of rapid development.[2] Research to determine the effect of a lack of early stimulation revealed sobering results. Without an enriched environmental experience
during the initial growth years, birth to four years, the child suffers an in-
determinable loss in intellectual potential that cannot be recovered at a
later age.

In addition to the new information about human development,
international and domestic pressures, such as Sputnik and the space
race, the war on poverty and concern for the culturally deprived, spurred a
penetrating look at American education. There was speculation that education was neglecting a productive learning period, and that more efforts
to facilitate the mental development of the young child might cure the
educational ills existing at the higher levels. Inquiries into what measures
could be taken to make better use of intellectual resources led to a broad-
ened perspective of the nature of education. Fresh viewpoints about the
purpose of education, the educational process, and the characteristics of the
learner involved in the process provided new implications for early childhood education.

IMPLICATIONS FOR MENTAL DEVELOPMENT
OF THE YOUNG CHILD

These findings led to the conclusion that the child's mental growth is profoundly influenced before he ever officially enrolls in school. His education
begins at birth. The revelations about the importance of early mental development were timely in that recent technological and social changes are
placing increasing demands on the child. He not only has to deal with difficult concepts at a young age, but he must also learn to generate innovative

---

[1] Jerome S. Bruner, *The Process of Education* (New York: Random House, 1960), p. 12.

[2] Benjamin Bloom, *Stability and Change in Human Characteristics* (New York: John
Wiley & Sons, 1964), p. 194.

solutions to a widening range of new problems that confront him. To compete and keep pace in a fast-changing world, the child has to develop his mental powers to full capacity.

IMPLICATIONS FOR EARLY CHILDHOOD EDUCATION

Authorities agree that the early years represent the optimal time for mental development; consequently, educating the young child is too serious a business to be left to chance. But how should the job be done, and by whom? If education begins at birth, what is the role of the mother in this process? What does she need to know to be the child's first teacher? With more women of child-bearing age entering the labor market, what people or agencies are equipped to take over the responsibility of educating the children of working mothers? What should be the nature of early childhood programs? What should be the parent involvement in these programs?

The urgent need to upgrade the quality of early education has led to a proliferation of experimental techniques. These techniques are based on varying viewpoints about human development and learning. They also reflect different ideas concerning the ultimate purpose of early learning experiences. The techniques range from directive teaching situations to settings in which the child's learning occurs totally through discovery. Some programs focus on developing specific mental skills; others take into consideration the development of the whole child. Some nursery-kindergartens concentrate on intensive training in language and mathematics; the goal is to equip children with competencies basic to success in first grade. In many of these settings seat-bound children are instructed in a wide spectrum of formal learning activities, stressing abstract rather than concrete experiences.

THE DEVELOPMENTAL VIEWPOINT

According to the developmental viewpoint, education during the early years involves a far broader commitment than preparation for first grade. The competencies acquired during this period must not only prepare the child to meet standard and familiar situations, but equip him to deal with the unknown problems of an unpredictable tomorrow. Early learning experiences must be geared to help the child develop all his mental powers to their optimum potential.

Following the developmental model, planning for mental development begins with a diagnosis of what the individual child is ready to learn and to do. Since his mental faculties unfold along a continuum, a review of the developmental sequence provides a basis for understanding expected competencies of preprimary children. This sequence suggests guidelines for diagnosing and planning for the mental development of the individual child.

SEQUENCE OF MENTAL DEVELOPMENT

The child has a native need to reach out and to explore. He is curious to know what his world is like, how things feel, what they look like, what meanings they have for him. He strives to learn and is eager to please significant adults in his life as he acquires new knowledge and skills. The child acquires knowledge through discovery. He learns through his senses. He uses his eyes, ears, nose, and hands to interpret incoming impressions. A major exploratory method is to put things in his mouth. As he manipulates things in his environment, he learns many concepts that become a part of his stockpile of knowledge to be used in problem solving. Simple concepts are learned before more complex ideas and provide the basis for more difficult understandings. When the child creeps, then walks, his world is extended for exploring and experimenting. As he becomes more mobile, his experiences increase in number and complexity.

Concept Formation. In his early attempts to know, the child shows the tendency to *order* his world, to fit things and events with similar things and events, and to develop a framework for testing and making sense out of new information and experiences. He develops concepts (generalized ideas). The basic processes involved in developing concepts (conceptualization) are operative in rudimentary form. He *discriminates* (recognizes differences and similarities among stimuli); he *classifies* (groups objects or events according to one or more characteristics); he *generalizes* (relates similarities among different objects and events); he *memorizes* (holds an idea in his mind); he *sees cause and effect relationships* (sees an association between an event that produces change in another event or series of events). For example, all these processes are implicit when the child who has learned to nudge open an eye-level cabinet door in the kitchen and close it to hear the noise expects the same result when he opens *any* cabinet door. Upon seeing a cabinet, the child must recognize it as such, classify it as an object with a door that will open, relate the similarity between the kitchen cabinet at home and the one he sees, remember the response to the cabinet at home, and predict that slamming the door will have the effect of making a noise.

As the child encounters new things and events, he uses what information he has to solve problems. Effective *problem-solving* behavior involves the ability to discover and to apply appropriate responses to a situation. Concepts are revised and extended when they are inadequate to answer the question, clear up the confusion, or clarify the steps to a goal. Early in life the child frequently uses trial and error to solve his problems. He physically goes through the motions of alternative responses until he finds one that works. Later he tests the responses mentally. He begins to solve problems by reasoning. When he is able to plan out what he is going to do, his behavior becomes increasingly intentional.

By the preprimary period the child is dealing with many concepts. Some of his ideas are inaccurate and fragmented. His early tendency is to conceptualize on the basis of major or obvious similarities and differences. A wagon, a truck, and an automobile all have wheels and move; therefore, all three may fit the idea of "cars." Since he relies on physical attributes, he may be fooled by the appearance of objects. What looks longer or smaller or different *is* longer or smaller or different. As a result of these tendencies, misconceptions may develop.

As powers of vision and listening improve, sense impressions become more accurate. Functioning at increasingly refined levels, conceptualization processes enable the child to organize these impressions more precisely and comprehensively. With experience he learns that all the things he plays with, different though they may be, are "toys"; all the things he eats are "food"; all the things he wears are "clothes." He learns to retain more than one idea at a time; for example, not only does he learn the concept "three," but he learns that three remains three whether there are three big things like beach balls or three small things like buttons. Even though imagination liberates his thoughts to reach into the impossible, the unknown, and the unreal, he tries to separate the real from fantasy and evolve valid explanations for phenomena.[3] He tries to discover cause and effect relationships, as reflected by his perpetual "Why?"

Language Development. The conceptualization processes are closely interwoven with language development. *Language* is an arbitrary system of symbols and sounds. A fundamental assumption is that there is agreement about what the symbols and sounds represent. Early in his development the child begins to associate words with the things, events, and ideas that they represent. This enables him to manipulate his environment symbolically. Language reflects not only his background of experience, but also his mental processes.

Guidelines for Mental Development

A review of the developmental sequence brings to light critical assumptions about how *all* preprimary children know, reason, and solve

---

[3]Kenneth D. Wann, Miriam Selchen Dorn, and Elizabeth Ann Liddle, *Fostering Intellectual Development in Young Children* (New York: Teachers College Press, 1962), p. 15.

problems. These assumptions provide the rationale for the kinds of intellectual stimulation that are appropriate and meaningful in the early years. The following guidelines for mental development are drawn from these assumptions:

1. *Learning experiences should proceed from simple to complex.* A child's acquisition of knowledge and skills follows a progression from basic and simple to increasingly difficult and complex learnings. He must learn to recognize simple concepts before he can handle the more subtle distinctions of his environment. The child must know what numbers are: the concept of one, the concept of two—apart from memorization of numerals—before he can deal with combinations of numbers. He needs to develop a whole repertoire of basic competencies prior to handling the complex operations involved in reading.

2. *Learning experiences should proceed from concrete to abstract.* The child knows his world through direct sensory contact with tangible objects. Learning is not a passive process; the child is not a container into which knowledge is poured. From his earliest inquisitive exploration he acts on the environment to come to terms with it, understand it, order it. The more senses he brings to bear on the learning experience, the more strongly is the learning incorporated into his concept system. Not only does this assumption support the need for multisensory stimulation, but it also emphasizes the importance of experience with concrete objects. Before the child can acquire a firm sense of their representational meaning (words, signs, and symbols), he must see, hear, touch, smell, and taste the things in his environment. He must *see* the shapes of the animals in the zoo, *hear* the shrill sound of the siren, *touch* the roughness of wool, *smell* the fresh fragrance of honeysuckle, and *taste* the sweetness of honey. These experiences provide the basis for attaching meaning not only to the concrete objects, but also to the abstract symbols representing the objects.

3. *Learning experiences should emphasize problem-solving skills.* The child exhibits the characteristics essential for creative problem solving. He is curious, eager to learn, anxious to please. He wants to know why things happen, the real causes underlying phenomena. He is willing to experiment and try the unknown. Creative energies surge and seek expression. Involvement with fantasy gives flexibility to his thoughts. When solving problems, the child does not escape into make believe; he uses it to extend his understanding of the world. Creative fantasy adds another dimension to his thinking. These developmental characteristics make the preprimary years the optimal time for developing creative problem-solving skills.

4. *Learning experiences should begin where the child is developmentally.* Provision of appropriate and meaningful intellectual stimulation depends upon an awareness of the child's *total* developmental level. He must be physically, emotionally, mentally, and socially ready to acquire the learnings with ease. Introducing learnings for which the child is not ready exacts from him a disproportionate toll in growth energies. In order to deal with the fatigue following exertion, the child may develop compensatory behaviors that will prove detrimental later on.

In planning learning activities, it is imperative that the teacher identify where the child is in terms of knowledge acquisition and skill development. When she is unaware of his present competencies, she may expect performances for which the child is inadequately prepared. If the preliminary learnings are missing or fragmented, subsequent learnings tend to be superficial if they can be acquired at all. Learnings that are commensurate with a child's developmental level promote success. The success itself becomes a motivating factor in perpetuating further learning.

Identifying the Child's Level of Mental Development

The teacher identifies the child's level of mental development in terms of (1) his capacity to recognize likenesses and differences, (2) his general knowledge, (3) his problem-solving skills, (4) his mathematics concepts and skills, and (5) his language-arts skills. In order to observe the child and assess his development in these skills, the teacher structures the environment, enabling the child to reveal what he is able to do. The major headings of the Mental Inventory of the Master Readiness Record comprise these areas for observation.

RECOGNITION OF LIKENESSES AND DIFFERENCES

Skill in recognizing likenesses and differences depends upon vision, the capacity of the eye and brain to receive accurate sense impressions. This skill involves the processes of discrimination, classification, and generalization. Visual discrimination is basic to recognizing likenesses and differences.

Visual Discrimination. Visual discrimination refers to the capacity to distinguish likenesses and differences among stimuli impinging on the eyes. Early in the child's development his reactions to visual stimuli are at first general. He pays attention to main characteristics and ignores details.

The general to specific tendency is reflected in the *Copy Forms Exercise.* The child can first copy a circle. The next form he can execute is a cross (+), then the more complex square, and finally the diamond. Even though the circle may be wobbly and lopsided, an enclosed form qualifies as a satisfactory circle. A well-proportioned cross is not expected—a line bisected by another line at any angle is satisfactory. Two parallel vertical lines which are then crossed top and bottom by two horizontal lines is considered a satisfactory square. The preprimary child first makes an indistinct form that faintly resembles the diamond. Later, his form shows the more distinctive features of the diamond. He tends to copy a horizontal diamond before he executes a vertical one.[4]

To test, the teacher prepares a card, 9 by 12 inches, for each form. The form is drawn on the card leaving one-inch margins on either side; top and bottom margins will vary with the form. Large, bold forms with black lines one-half inch thick facilitate copying (see p. 129). The teacher places before the child a paper the size of the card and a crayon. He is given a fresh piece of paper for each form. She presents the unlabeled cards to the child one at a time and in order of complexity; circle, cross, square, diamond. After the child has looked at the card, the teacher directs: "Make one like this." Any size reproduction is acceptable. The child may have unlimited trials to copy (not trace) the forms, and they need not all be presented at one sitting. His final efforts are taken by the teacher to be placed in the child's individual folder.

The Copy Forms technique is of particular value because the acceptable copying of each of these geometric forms suggests progressive maturity in recognizing likenesses and differences. Inability to reproduce one or several forms may be rooted in problems other than immature visual discrimination; however, the child's level of success in copying does provide a clue to his level of maturity.

The child's skill in recognizing likenesses and differences is also revealed in his ability to *recognize colors,* a primitive category for organizing his world. His ability to *classify* objects is further evidence of this skill. Can he sort according to one likeness, or can he sort objects that are alike in more than one way (yellow hats, blue circles)? Has he advanced to the point where he can sort according to more sophisticated concepts (vegetables, fruits, vehicles, farm animals, zoo animals, animals with fur, animals with claws)? Recognition of likenesses and differences is also involved in *seriation;* i.e., ordering objects according to graduated size. Can he merely order by big and little, or can he put more than three different-sized objects in order? Proficiency in these preliminary skills, will help the child

---

[4]Frances L. Ilg and Louise Bates Ames, *School Readiness* (New York: Harper & Row Publishers, 1965), pp. 63–106.

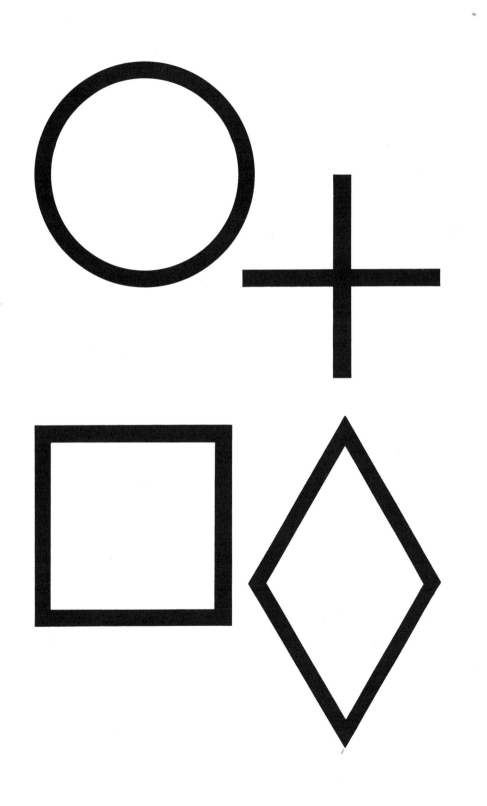

to recognize likenesses and differences among letters, words, and numerals.

GENERAL KNOWLEDGE

A child's general knowledge refers to the number of concepts that he understands. The general knowledge that a child exhibits not only reflects his background of experience, but his awareness of the world around him and his ability to retain information. Common concepts with which the child should be familiar involve parts of the body; members of his family; name, address, and telephone number; numbers one through five; primary colors; weather; pets; transportation; holidays and customs. Individual children may be familiar with a wide variety of concepts that range into extended and specialized areas. If the child is not familiar with the majority of common concepts, this finding may indicate meager background experience. Efforts to develop other mental faculties, such as problem solving, may not be productive until the basic concepts are meaningful to him.

PROBLEM-SOLVING SKILLS

Effective problem solving refers to the ability to discover or apply appropriate responses to a situation. Problem-solving skills involve all the conceptualization processes, especially the process of seeing cause and effect relationships. In identifying the child's maturity level, the teacher observes him as he attempts to solve the problems associated with all areas of his growth. How does he figure out how to hang up his coat? How does he resolve his fear of the hamster? How does he get the attention he needs? How does he get a coveted toy being used by another child? How does he make the toy work? How does he figure out how many juice cups are needed for four children at snack time? Does he *verbalize* the problem? Does he *rely on trial and error?* Does he *appeal to adults* to solve the problem before he tries to solve it himself? Is he *aware* of the world around him, sensitive to details? Is he *curious?* The more curious he is, the more likely he is to identify problems. He is more apt to be aware of conflicting stimuli in his environment.

The ease with which the child solves problems is related to his acquisition of creative-thinking skills. Creative-thinking skills are: (1) *originality,* the ability to generate new ideas; (2) *fluency,* the ability to generate a large number of ideas; (3) *flexibility,* the ability to discover different solutions to a problem; and (4) *elaboration,* the ability to extend an idea (the "what do you think would happen if" process). In assessing a child's mental development, the teacher estimates his ability to use creative-thinking skills in problem solving.

MATHEMATICS CONCEPTS AND SKILLS

Mathematics is an appropriate term to describe the young child's experience with numbers because it is more encompassing than those terms applying to specific areas of mathematics, such as arithmetic, algebra, etc. Arithmetic (computation of numbers), algebra (calculation of number relationships), geometry (measurement of area and space) are all found in the child's daily activities. Mathematics *concepts* presented in a sequential pattern are understood easily by the young child; however, if he does not internalize basic mathematical concepts before he attempts to attach the ideas to abstract symbols, he will have difficulty in mastering the mathematics skills later on in his development.

The concept of number, what *one* is, or how many objects represent the number *one,* must be understood before the relationship of numbers becomes meaningful to the child. Other concepts to be learned before the child deals with abstract symbols and ideas are computation, one-to-one

Understanding Number Concepts

correspondence, shape, and time. These concepts provide the foundations for the skills involved in manipulating numbers. The basic concepts are specifically listed in the Mental Inventory of the Master Readiness Record.

A child's understanding of these concepts is revealed during play activities as well as directed activities. As a child adds two plates for two more children who join in the dramatic play, he is demonstrating the concept of adding. As he shares his blocks with another child, he takes away a number of blocks from the number he has, thus using the concept of subtraction. As the play unfolds, the child internalizes the concepts of the computational skills, adding and subtracting. One-to-one correspondence is exhibited when he recognizes *one* chair for *one* child, *one* sock for *one* foot, *one* napkin per child for snack.

Everything in the environment has a shape, and every shape resembles or is derived from the basic shapes specifically listed in the Mental Inventory. The concept of shape precedes an understanding of relationships in space. Puzzles and block play are activities that reveal the child's understanding of spatial relationships.

How well the child grasps time concepts can be revealed in his understanding of the daily schedule, his home routines, and night and day. More mature concepts of time are revealed in his understanding of the days of the week, months, seasons, special holidays, and by his ability to comprehend time in waiting for what he wants. The skill of telling time by the clock is a later development that depends upon firm understanding of basic time concepts.

LANGUAGE-ARTS SKILLS

Language arts involve the communication skills of speaking, listening, writing, and reading. The preprimary period is the optimal time to develop speaking and listening skills. It is also the optimal time to develop *readiness* for writing and reading.

Speaking.   A child's spontaneous conversations reveal the maturity of his speech. In identifying his maturity level, the teacher must be aware of the sequence of language development. A child's early babbling in response to adult verbalizations helps him to learn the basic speech sounds. By the preprimary period he masters the basic vowel sounds and many of the consonant sounds. Templin has traced the sequence of the child's development in pronouncing consonant sounds. Seventy-five percent of the children studied were able to produce the following sounds: [5]

---

[5]Mildred C. Templin, *Certain Language Skills in Children,* Institute of Child Welfare Monograph Series, no. 26 (Minneapolis: University of Minnesota Press, 1957), p. 150.

3 years:	m,n,ng,p,f,h,w
3.5 years:	y
4 years:	k,b,d,g,r
4.5 years:	s,sh,ch
6 years:	t,th,v,l
7 years:	z,zh,j

By the beginning of the preprimary period, speech patterns (language usage) are forming. The child's language usage in terms of inflection, pronunciation, and expression reflect his culture and his maturity. He is learning *grammar* (rules of speech). It is not unusual for a child to say "I singing" or "I runned." With experience and guidance his grammar steadily improves.

Infantile pronunciation refers to the tendency to pronounce words in the way in which they were presumably spoken when the child first learned them. Depending upon their backgrounds, some children may retain virtually all of their original pronunciations during the preprimary period; others may use only a few of their earlier pronunciations and use them sparingly. Examples of common errors are *bwock* for *block*, *wite* for *right*, and *bubber* for *brother*. With experience and guidance the child's pronunciation acquires clarity.

During this period the child learns to control his voice. At first his voice may be so loud or so soft that his speech is almost unintelligible; he may vacillate between a screech and a soft murmur. As pointed out in Chapter 8, a whining, demanding, or strained tone of voice is a sign of stress and fatigue. Experience and guidance are also instrumental in the development of a modulated voice.

Observations of a child's speech over a period of time are necessary to determine whether grammatical constructions, infantile pronunciation, and quality of voice are characteristic patterns. Infantile speech or a screeching tone of voice, for example, may be a sign of immaturity or regressive behavior. If the child is anxious, he may revert to earlier speech patterns. The teacher needs to be alert to whether the speech patterns are a result of immaturity or lack of experience or guidance.

During this period the child becomes more precise in his speech. Initially he uses one word to refer to several distinct objects, events, or ideas. His sentences are short (three or four words), characterized by a preponderance of nouns. Later, his sentences are longer (six to eight words), more complex, and grammatically complete. He uses adverbs and adjectives with more frequency to qualify his ideas. He is increasingly verbal, experimenting with the mechanisms of language. Later, he becomes skillful in using language to solve problems and manipulate social situations. The social language—"please," "thank you"—is internalized.

As the child masters more concepts, his vocabulary expands. Development of *vocabulary*, i.e., stock of words used, depends upon a broad base of general experience. Only as the child understands the meanings of things and events of his experience can he fully and realistically relate to the meanings underlying abstract symbols. Meaningful speech, as well as reading and writing, is based on understanding concepts, not just vocabulary. Piaget points out, "Language reflects logic, and the mere acquisition of vocabulary will have little effect on his [the child's] thinking."[6]

During the preprimary period the *articulation* (speech production) skills develop rapidly and are established as habits. Early in his experience the child uses words without order; consequently, his thought expression tends to be garbled, distorted, and without sequence. "Sympathetic circularity" may develop; for example, overuse of "like," "you know," and similar terms to confirm ideas and demand understanding without fully expressing ideas.[7] With guidance and experience the child learns to express his ideas clearly, with more fluency and organization. Hesitations, stuttering, and repetition of words, characteristics of early speech, are less frequent.

Listening.   Listening is the faculty of the ears and brain to receive accurate sense impressions. As a child matures, he learns to listen. Most of the listening of preprimary children is *passive*. The child may be aware of sound, but the sound is not in focus; he hears, but does not listen. For example, passive listening occurs when a child watches television, but is engaged in another activity. A characteristic of the listening process is the ability to select what one wants to hear. He may elect not to listen. For example, a child may tune out environmental noise or too much direction from adults. Optimally children develop their skills in appreciative, attentive, and analytical listening during the preprimary years. *Appreciative* listening involves responding with feeling, for example, listening to a story to experience its effect. *Attentive* listening involves focusing, paying attention, for example, listening to directions that are given so as to follow them. *Analytical* listening involves thinking about what is heard and reacting to it; for example, listening to an argument or opinion so as to accept or reject it.

A child's listening skills are influenced by his *auditory discrimination* (capacity to distinguish among sounds). The ability to distinguish sounds is basic to pronunciation. Also, if a child does not hear the difference

---

[6] Millie Almy with Edward Chittenden and Paul Miller, *Young Children's Thinking* (New York: Teachers College, Columbia University, 1966), p. 75.

Celia Stendler Lavatelli, *Piaget's Theory Applied to an Early Childhood Curriculum*, A Center for Media Development Book (Boston: Amer. Sci. & Eng., 1970), p. 59.

between two words, he will have difficulty in distinguishing between their printed symbols. The more reliably the child sorts out sound sequences, the more accurately he discriminates and recognizes visual patterns.

The Word Reproduction Exercise (p. 136) was developed and its use tested for the specific purpose of helping the teacher identify how the child discriminates among sounds. The child's performance on this exercise reveals his development in distinguishing sounds. The words listed in Part I reflect the forty-four basic sounds identified in the Initial Teaching Alphabet (ITA) developed by Sir James Pitman to help children to read the conventional alphabet.[8] It must be recognized that a child's ability to cooperate in the Word Reproduction Exercise depends upon his attentive listening skills. To test the child on the Basic Words, the teacher pronounces the word distinctly and asks the child to repeat it. The teacher should allow as many trials as necessary for the child to produce the word. Success is indicated by production of the word within three trials. If the child can reproduce twenty-two words, he is judged minimally competent to discriminate basic sounds. Depending upon the child's success with the Basic Words, Part I, the teacher proceeds with Complex Words, Part II. The words included in this section are complex because they are multisyllabic or involve troublesome consonant blends. If the child can produce twelve of the complex words, he is judged minimally competent at this level. The child's level of competency in both sections of the exercise has specific implications for his plan of help.

Readiness for Writing and Reading.   Readiness for writing and reading depends upon the child's maturity levels in all areas of development. The physical, emotional, and mental growth sequences leading to these requisite levels of maturity have been cited throughout preceding chapters. Before the child is engaged in writing and reading skills, he should have achieved the specific skills and behaviors indicated in the Writing and Reading Readiness section of the Mental Inventory. Although emphasis in the early childhood curriculum is not on reading and writing, children should be helped to master the skills of recognizing and printing letters, numerals, their names, and words as they demonstrate readiness to acquire these skills with ease.

PLAN FOR HELP

In planning for the mental development of children, the adult's primary responsibility is to extend old concepts and to develop new concepts. This

---

[8] *The Story of ITA* (New York: ITA Publications, 1965).

WORD REPRODUCTION EXERCISE

Part I:

Directions: Ask the child to repeat each word after you. Check with an "X" the words he is able to produce within three trials. If he is unable to produce the word, check with an "O."

Part I: Basic Words

RACE _____		WIN _____
BELL _____		YET _____
CALL _____		ZERO _____
DOOR _____		PHASE _____
BEE _____		WHAT _____
FALL _____		CHIN _____
BEG _____		THREW _____
HAND _____		THEM _____
MY _____		SHIP _____
JELL _____		VISION _____
KIT _____		SING _____
LET _____		FATHER _____
MAT _____		CALL _____
NET _____		NAP _____
OPEN _____		LEG _____
PET _____		KILL _____
FIR _____		OX _____
RUN _____		JUMP _____
SPOT _____		LOOK _____
TRUE _____		MOON _____
USE _____		POUT _____
VOTE _____		BOIL _____

Part II: Complex Words

SISTER _____		EVERY _____
HAVE _____		BLOCKS _____
PIRATE _____		HOSPITAL _____
FISH _____		SOMETHING _____
THINGS _____		DRAW _____
INSIDE _____		VERY _____
WASHES _____		LITTLE _____
FINGER _____		THINK _____
POLLUTION _____		YESTERDAY _____
KISS _____		GROW _____
CREAM _____		SPACE _____

responsibility involves awareness and use of available opportunities for learning in the child's total experience. Concept development is not confined to the school environment; optimally the plan for help is extended into the home. Parents and teachers are in a close working relationship to help the child to know his environment, to use reason in dealing with his environment, and to solve the problems the environment presents.

In implementing the plan for help, parents and teachers discuss ways to foster the child's mental development at school and at home. A crucial recognition is that learning experiences are integrated throughout all the activities that make up the child's daily schedule. The most routine experience the child has may be a potential opportunity to reinforce and extend old concepts and develop new ones. For example, at snacktime (home or school) the adult (mother or teacher) helps the child to be aware of the *shape* of the cookie and the cup, the *color* of the juice, the *size* of the snacks. He can be guided to *classify* round cookies, square cookies, and animal-shaped cookies. Even though specific equipment can be used to teach specific things, the child's total environment, including home and nursery-kindergarten, is a rich and fertile source of learning. The world is the child's laboratory for experimenting, discovering, and testing hypotheses.

Extending Science Concepts

The plan for help for the individual child is derived from the teacher's observations in terms of his capacity to recognize likenesses and differences, his general knowledge, his problem-solving skills, his mathematics concepts and skills, and his language-arts skills. When the child first enters school, a tentative plan for help is based on observations made at the Diagnostic Interview. The teacher sets up the environment to enable the child to have experiences with intellectual skills. She observes his progress with these skills as he moves through the course of his daily activities. Also, she tests for particular items, for example, knowledge of color, visual and auditory discrimination. General knowledge is revealed during the evaluation period following a learning experience. After a trip to the zoo, for example, the teacher sets up activities to reveal concepts the child has derived from the experience.

Following the directions for observing and recording (Chapter 11), the teacher records the child's progress in intellectual competencies on the Mental Inventory of the Master Readiness Record. In reviewing this inventory, the teacher estimates the child's levels of maturity and evolves a plan for help based on his developmental profile.

Whenever possible, the teacher draws from the child's special interests in selecting materials and activities that are appropriate for his maturity and, at the same time, present challenges that stimulate his growth. Block play, for example, can be a basis for concept development and for enhancing all his conceptualization skills. Children derive security from playing with the materials related to their special interests. If concentration on one kind of activity goes on indefinitely, it is the teachers' responsibility to help the child extend his awareness of materials and activities in his environment. Mere involvement with the teacher in finding out about his environment gives the child a feeling of acceptance and warmth that builds security.

The following glimpse of activities related to specific skills is merely suggestive of the kinds of nursery-kindergarten experiences that promote development in the areas discussed. There are no rigid procedures to be followed with each child or groups of children. For example, an appropriate strategy to help the child develop auditory discrimination is to provide rhythm, marching, and clapping experiences. The variety of methods by which they may be done is a challenge to the imagination and skill of the teacher.

RECOGNIZING LIKENESSES AND DIFFERENCES

The plan for improving recognition of likenesses and differences is based on the child's maturity levels in the specific skills involved. Activities for improving visual discrimination are sorting objects or pictures of objects, assembling puzzles, copying patterns in bead-stringing, cutting around outlines, and tracing figures in templates (pattern or mold serving as a guide for tracing). If a child can copy a circle, but not a cross or square, he should be given objects and beads with bold, well-defined differences and puzzles with large obvious parts. If he can copy a cross and square, activities involving finer discriminations can be introduced. Cutting or tracing with bold, well-defined outlines requiring use of the large muscles should be encouraged prior to the child's mastery of the diamond.

In helping the child to learn colors, the teacher proceeds according to the guideline of simple to complex. She first helps the child to recognize true colors rather than variations of colors. For example, she introduces objects that are a true green rather than chartreuse or olive. When he has mastered true color, she proceeds to tints and hues. The record of color recognition has a special diagnostic implication. If the child has problems in discriminating greens and blues, this pattern should be watched as possibly indicative of color-blindness.

Classification and seriation activities begin at the child's level of skill development. Typical objects for sorting and seriating are buttons; beads; pieces of cloth; cooking equipment, such as measuring cups and mixing bowls; housekeeping equipment, such as toy dishes, pots and pans, and silverware; geometric shapes; blocks; balls; rings; and other children. If a child can sort objects according to one dimension, but not more than one, then he should be given simpler sorting activities until he gains proficiency with this basic skill. The same principle applies to seriation activities. When he gains proficiency, the teacher can introduce more complex activities.

In helping the child to recognize likenesses and differences, the teacher uses routine activities to stimulate awareness of the environment. For example, prior to taking a walk, she sets the stage for what is going to happen. She discusses with the group what they think they might see. Responses might be a "squirrel," a "tree," a "house," and a variety of other things—both real and imaginative. Anticipating the responses, the teacher has on hand pictures to emphasize the things that will be seen. During the walk, the delight the children feel in spotting the anticipated squirrel sharpens their awareness. The experience is reviewed at a followup discussion. The pictures help children to differentiate between the things they saw and those they did not see, and reinforce what they learned about those that were seen. This experience also helps the children to make distinctions between the real and the imaginary.

GENERAL KNOWLEDGE

Until the child has mastered the concepts referred to in the Mental Inventory, he will be unable to relate to usual nursery-kindergarten activities. If the child lacks knowledge of any of these concepts, he is helped by the teacher, who makes a special effort to teach the concepts.

Every experience the child has is a potential resource to extend old concepts and develop new ones. Since learning proceeds from concrete to abstract, the child learns concepts most effectively through real things. Participation in the cutting of a pumpkin for a Jack o' Lantern emphasizes size, shape, and texture. The child experiences how hard the surface is to cut. He feels the roundness of the pumpkin's contours, and discovers what is inside—the gaseous odor and the stringy web that holds the seeds. The seeds can be cooked, counted, painted, and eaten. Field trips are arranged to increase general knowledge. Children remember the redness of the engine at the firehouse, the hushed whispers at the library, and the aroma of a bakery. They also tend to remember the functions of these community places. Stories not only entertain; they inform. *The Three Little Pigs* emphasizes the relative durability of straw, twigs, and brick, and points out the value of building with materials that last. When they act out *Three Billy Goats Gruff,* children feel kinesthetically the relational concept of going *over* the bridge.

PROBLEM-SOLVING SKILLS

Children come to the nursery-kindergarten exhibiting varying degrees of curiosity. Since the ability to think creatively is rooted in curiosity, all children need experiences to stimulate their desire to know more about their environment. The teacher encourages curiosity by paying attention to the child's discoveries, and *by helping him to find answers to his questions,* rather than by merely answering them herself. The teacher can help children to apply skills in solving their individual problems. A child may be building a structure in the block corner. The wall keeps falling down. The teacher helps him to identify the problem and think through alternative solutions to secure the wall.

Curiosity is encouraged by group problem-solving sessions. A typical topic might be: What if there was no more gasoline? Children answer: "The car won't run"; "We can't go anyplace"; "I wear a sweater"; "The house is cold"; "We have a fire in the fireplace." Problems need not be hypothetical; they can derive from experiences close to the lives of the children. For example, the teacher might say, "We have one tricycle in the nursery-kindergarten and five children want to use it. What can we do?" As they learn to solve problems through direct experience, children become accustomed to thinking about alternatives.

MATHEMATICS CONCEPTS AND SKILLS

Learning mathematics is a sequential experience. Simple concepts are basic to more complex concepts. For example, a child needs to know what a number is before he sees the parts in relation to the whole, as in a fraction. The child must be firmly grounded in the concept 1–5 before he is involved with the concepts 1–10. He learns basic mathematics concepts through tangible objects—people, blocks, crayons, juice cups, tricycles, musical instruments, parts of the body, the calendar—the things that make up his daily experience. Such questions as "How many children are at the table?" and "How many crayons are left in the box when we take away two?" stimulate the child to count. Touching the objects when counting encourages accuracy. The child first learns through concrete objects (things he can hold and touch), then through semi-concrete objects (pictures of objects and drawings), and finally through symbols or numerals that represent the number of objects.

LANGUAGE-ARTS SKILLS

The most effective way the teacher helps the child to develop speaking and listening skills is by serving as a model. The child tends to pattern his speech after the pronunciation, grammar, tone of voice, and articulation skills of significant adults. If the teacher herself is a good listener and shows interest in what the child has to say, her example tends to be followed. Since children are not usually able to pick out the fine nuances of sound, adults should speak slowly and distinctly. Care should be taken not to use too many words.   Directions are given slowly and in logical sequence. Not only does adherence to these guidelines help the child's speech, but it also influences his listening. Using too many words and giving directions too often drives children to passive listening.

Children learn both language usage and articulation skills through talking. Some activities of the nursery-kindergarten specifically emphasize speaking skills—dramatic play, circle time, "Show-and-Tell," and problem-solving sessions. During other activities children should be encouraged to describe what they see, hear, touch, smell, and taste. They should be given opportunities to express their ideas. If an individual child shows a lag in speech development, arrangements are made to spend time talking with him each day on a one-to-one basis. These sessions should focus on his specific speech problems.

In order to encourage attentive listening skills, the teacher makes sure she has the child's attention before she gives directions or information that she expects the child to retain. When she has the child's attention, her voice is just loud enough to hear and understand the words. The children have to work to listen. Appreciative listening is promoted by creating a comfortable atmosphere, free of distraction, conducive to listening to the story or recording. Analytical listening is encouraged when the teacher turns the problem to the child with, "What do you think about this?"

Exercises that involve identification of characteristic sounds and the number, location, and organization of sounds help to develop auditory discrimination. A typical activity involves the children closing their eyes and identifying the following sounds: tapping on wood, tearing paper, clapping hands, closing a door. The sounds of whistles, sirens, horns, and ticking clocks provide variations. Popular activities are listening to recordings of sounds of animals, sounds of the city, and sounds of the farm. Whenever possible, children should simulate the sounds to experience them verbally. Rhythms, marching, and clapping help to develop awareness of timing.

All children profit by experiences in "pulling out" specific sounds from environmental noise. In order to identify the maturity levels of the individual child, the teacher uses the results of the Word Reproduction Exercise. If the child has not achieved minimal competency in the Basic Words section, then he needs a concentrated program in sound identification activities. Until he reaches minimal competency in the Complex Words section, he is probably not ready for concentrated work with the sounds of words. For example, a fairly mature mastery of consonant blends is necessary to be successful in sorting objects according to names that begin and end the same way.

PROMOTING ALL OF THE SKILLS

Many activities of the nursery-kindergarten can serve to promote all of the intellectual skills. Participation in baking cookies, for example, provides opportunities for learning in every area. The child is given experience in recognizing similarities and differences among the ingredients, for example, how some properties of flour are similar to and some are different from those of sugar. His general knowledge is extended as he sees the heat change the color, texture, size, shape, and state of matter. Sifting the flour, putting ingredients together in the proper order, and selecting the proper temperature for baking are all experiences in following directions. Mathematics concepts and skills are used in measuring the ingredients, dividing the dough, and counting the cookies. The child experiences time in terms of how long it takes the cookies to bake. His language-arts skills come into play. Not only must he be attentive to directions and analytical in solving problems, but he must expand his vocabulary to include new terms from science and mathematics. He has opportunity to describe the ingredients, the dough, and the final product—soft, hard, burned, crisp, soggy, sticky—and to articulate his ideas during the baking process.

It should be emphasized that learning sessions are not high-pressure activities emphasizing the abstract. Children learn through their everyday experiences with things. Directed activities are relaxed and fun and incorporate objects that children can warm up to and love. *The key to helping the child's mental development is to be aware of and focus on the multiple concepts and skills inherent in the routine.* Concentration on intellectual activities does not mean a neglect of physical, emotional, and social growth. The curriculum, and the child's individual plan for help, include activities that promote development in all areas.

Summary

Mental development refers to the maturing of a person's faculties to acquire knowledge, to use reasoning, and to solve problems. The current emphasis in early childhood education is on the mental dimension of growth. Political and social pressures, together with new information about human development, have directed attention to the preprimary child and how he learns. Research has led to the conclusion that the early years represent the optimal time for mental development.

Revelations about the importance of early mental development have led to a variety of preprimary programs that differ in purpose and method. According to the developmental model, the purpose of early learning experiences is to help the child develop all his mental faculties to their optimum potential. Planning for mental development depends upon an understanding of the developmental sequence.

Initially, the child learns about his world through his senses. Early in his experience he begins to order his world and develop concepts. As he matures, the basic conceptualization processes function in increasingly complex ways. He is able to evolve more realistic and comprehensive concepts. He begins to solve problems by reasoning. Concept formation influences and is influenced by language development.

The following guidelines for mental development are drawn from developmental assumptions about how preprimary children know, reason, and solve problems: (1) Learning experiences should proceed from simple to complex, (2) Learning experiences should proceed from concrete to abstract, (3) Learning experiences should emphasize problem-solving skills, and (4) Learning experiences should begin where the child is developmentally.

In order to identify the child's level of mental development, the teacher observes (1) his capacity to recognize likenesses and differences, (2) his general knowledge, (3) his problem-solving skills, (4) his mathematics concepts and skills, and (5) his language-arts skills, including speaking, listening, writing, and reading. The preprimary period is the optimal time to develop speaking and listening skills, and to develop *readiness* for writing and reading.

In evolving a plan for help, the primary responsibility of the adult is to extend old concepts and develop new ones. In carrying out this responsibility, parents and teachers work together to help the child benefit from all the available opportunities for learning in his total environment. The child's individual plan for help is based on the teacher's observations of his progress in the critical areas of competency.

The key to promoting mental development of the preprimary child is to be alert to and to focus on multiple concepts and skills inherent in routine experiences.

10

Diagnosing and Planning for Social Development

Social development represents increased capacity to establish and maintain relationships with other people. A *relationship* is formed when two or more people interact with one another. Relationships differ in depth and meaning; some are intimate and enduring, others are superficial. Whatever the scope and depth of the association, a relationship is successful when there is mutual satisfaction among the involved parties.

Successful relationships grow out of positive attitudes toward other people. In order to enter into a genuine give-and-take relationship, a child needs to learn to like people, to enjoy their company, and to care about them as human beings with needs, wants, ideas, and feelings. Only as he begins to appreciate and become sensitive to the "humanness" of others is he capable of establishing and maintaining successful relationships.

As the child develops this capacity to like, enjoy, and care about other people, he evolves increasingly mature ways to interact with them. Learning to get along with other people has its hard moments. It involves a series of conflicts between what the child wants and likes on the one hand, and what others want and like on the other hand. The child must at times compromise what he wants to do. The adjustments may be difficult, but the child basically wants to make them. As James Hymes writes,

> Every child, without exception, basically wants to be liked. He wants to be welcomed by his human society. He wants the skills that let him work side by side with people. No child has ever been born whose first choice was to be "hard to live with."[1]

The preprimary years represent the optimal time to learn what people are like, to develop positive attitudes towards them, and to acquire more effective ways to get along with them. Even though the home is the dominant socializing force in the life of the child, he is beginning to move beyond his family in forming relationships. He is experimenting with various behaviors and roles to test those that result in the most satisfying social adjustments. One of the major objectives of the nursery-kindergarten is to provide a laboratory for social experimentation. Not only does the child have opportunity to gain social experience, but he is guided toward more constructive ways to deal with both adults and other children. The nursery-kindergarten functions as a complementary socializing agency.

The term *socialization* refers to two interdependent processes: (1) how the child develops relationships with others and (2) how he develops a value system. Although the processes are closely related, each represents a somewhat different emphasis with regard to diagnosing and planning for social development. In terms of the child's social maturity, the teacher identifies how far he has progressed towards companionable behavior. She also estimates his progress in developing a value system.

Developing Relationships with Others

The child is not born a social creature. He develops his capacities to respond socially through interactions with other people. The early maternal-child relationship provides the foundation for his later ability to get along with others. Elkind describes Erikson's concept of a "sense of trust":

> The degree to which the child comes to trust the world, other people and himself, depends to a considerable extent upon the quality of the care he receives. The infant whose needs are met when they arise, whose discomforts are quickly removed, who is cuddled, fondled, played with and talked to, develops a sense of the world as a safe place to be and of people as helpful and dependable. When, however, the care is inconsistent, inadequate, and rejecting, it fosters a basic mistrust, an attitude of fear

---

[1]James L. Hymes, Jr., "Introduction," in *Discipline*, Bulletin 99 of the Association for Childhood Education International (Washington, D.C.: the Association, 1957), p. 2.

and suspicion on the part of the infant toward the world in general and people in particular.[2]

The child develops a specific attachment to his mother that builds to a peak during the second year. At this time even a short separation will elicit anxiety. As he acquires independence, he loosens the tie to his mother and begins to become an individual in his own right.

Early in his development the child tends to be *egocentric.* The self is the center of the world, and self-interest validates all actions. Having little or no regard for the interests, beliefs, or attitudes of others, the child is incapable of *empathy,* i.e., the capacity to experience the feelings, thoughts, and attitudes of another person. Cohen and Stern describe this characteristic:

> It is perhaps hard to believe, but nevertheless true, that young children at first look at one another as they do at objects and materials—as something to touch, to smell, and maybe to taste! So much is this so, that a little two-year old pours sand on another's head and then stares in amazement at his distress, or calmly pushes someone down the stairs if he is in the way, or pokes a finger into a youngster's eye to see what makes it shine. This sounds like the cruelest savagery but it is really nothing more than evidence for the fact that there is a time in the life of every human being when he does not understand that other people have feelings like his own.[3]

The child's speech reflects his egocentricism. "I," "me," and "mine" are used almost exclusively over "you" and "yours." His needs are imperative and he will communicate them with urgency. If needs are not involved, his conversations are not necessarily give-and-take exchanges. He is unconcerned about whether anyone is listening to him or understanding him. This lack of reciprocal speech is evidenced in the following dialogue:

"My mommy is sick," began the first little girl.
"Look at my new shoes," was the response of the other.

During the preprimary period the child gradually moves away from this orientation to self and begins to become companionable. His behavior is increasingly *sociocentric;* i.e., he is able to adopt an objective viewpoint about persons, places, and things. With this recognition he shows increased ability to view his actions from the stance of others. He begins to

---

[2]David Elkind, "Erik Erikson's Eight Stages of Man," *The New York Times Magazine* (April 5, 1970), p. 84.

[3]Dorothy H. Cohen and Virginia Stern, *Observing and Recording the Behavior of Young Children* (New York: Teachers College Press, 1958), p. 43.

cooperate, first with adults, then with peers. However, this transition from egocentric to sociocentric behavior is only beginning during the pre-primary years. The trend unfolds along a continuum that has its origins early in the life of the child and reaches a climax in adolescence.

Identifying the Child's Maturity in Developing Relationships

The child's progress in developing relationships with others is revealed by how he relates both to peers and adults. Sections I and II of the Social Inventory of the Master Readiness Record comprise these areas for observation.

RELATIONSHIPS WITH PEERS

The child's maturity in developing relationships with peers is evidenced in his spontaneous play behavior and his selection of playmates.

Play Behavior.   Reflecting the sequence of egocentrism to sociocentrism, play behavior follows a pattern. Initially the child plays alone (solitary play), then he plays beside other children (parallel play), and finally he plays with other children (cooperative play). When solitary play is predominant, the child interacts with his toys rather than with other children. He is seemingly unaware that other children are present. Encroachments on his play territory or toys are apt to trigger an angry defense of his rights or property. He may appeal to the adult to preserve or restore his possessions. At this developmental level the child is unable to empathize.

As he matures, the child is increasingly aware of other children and seeks the security of their closeness. Engrossed with his own activities, he plays beside other children. He shows a concern with the problem of how he fits into the social world. He tries to secure his position by demanding to be first and by boasting about his family, his accomplishments, and his possessions. Even though he shows increased interest in other children, he has not yet developed the capacity to consider their feelings.

With experience and guidance, the child begins to play with other children. Initially, he is primarily interested in the activity of the group, not in the individual playmates. Gradually he derives a sense of satisfaction from playing with others, and he begins to care about them as individuals. When he shows concern about a playmate's absence from school or requests to sit next to a particular child, he is demonstrating increasingly sociocentric behavior.

Cooperative play introduces new problems for the child in terms of how he fits into the social world. In their early efforts to play together, children tend to be bossy. They give commands, but may lack the skills to motivate others to follow. It is not unusual for all members of the play-group to envision themselves in charge. Each may issue a different set of directions, and each functions as if the others had followed. This bossi-ness is a vestige of egocentrism. Leadership suggests more than mere dominance of the group. True leadership emerges when a child develops the skills to initiate activities and to bring others willingly along with his ideas. When the child demonstrates leadership qualities, or willingness to follow a leader, he is exhibiting a more mature understanding of the group and his role within it. The child needs to learn to be both a leader and a follower. Both roles are basic to adequate socialization.

Play Behavior

In estimating the child's social maturity on the basis of play behavior, the teacher observes him over a period of time in a variety of situations. When the child enters school, he may experience adjustment problems. Children who have had limited opportunity to interact with peers may play alone for some weeks until they become used to the situation. Even children who have had considerable experience with peers in another setting may respond to a strange group of children by first playing alone, then playing beside, and finally playing with other children.

After the adjustment period, the child typically vacillates between solitary, parallel, and cooperative play. He may play with other children for several days, then suddenly revert to earlier forms of play behavior. One reason for this reversion is fatigue. Social interaction expends energy. The child needs time alone to restore his vigor and equilibrium. Also, some solitary play is not only to be expected, but encouraged. It is only when solitary and parallel play predominate that these behaviors are diagnostically significant.

Selection of Playmates. Other behaviors that are significant in assessing the child's social development are revealed in his selection of playmates. Initially a child's relationships with playmates tend to be mechanical. Other children are merely elements in a group activity that interests him. His playmates tend to change with his activities. In his beginning contacts, a child may interact with large numbers of children.

With experience the child becomes more selective in his playmates. He learns that some children make an activity stimulating and fun. He tends to gravitate toward those with skills and interests similar to his own. Gradually he begins to seek out particular playmates and spend more time with them. The playmates rather than the activities assume importance. In the beginning stages special playmates may be of either sex. Later, children tend to choose playmates of the same sex.

During the preprimary period it is not unusual for children to invent *imaginary playmates.* A companion of the child's own creation is a source of support. There is comfort in a make-believe friend who accepts him unconditionally, tolerates his aggressive feelings, and follows his commands. The invention of an imaginary playmate is a forerunner to cooperative play. Fantasy interaction gives the child the opportunity to try out various roles and to test the concept of "playmate."

RELATIONSHIPS WITH ADULTS

All of the child's relationships depend, in large part, upon the kind of relationship he has had with his mother. In order to identify the nature of this relationship, the teacher should review the Parent-Child Relationship section in the Diagnostic Interview Form.

The child brings to the nursery-kindergarten the feelings and behaviors acquired in the home. For example, the child who has been encouraged to do for himself and to solve the problems appropriate for his developmental level tends to be more independent of significant adults outside the home. He is more likely to be ready to move outside himself and to begin to interact with peers. Furthermore, independent children tend to be accepted more readily by their peers. On the other hand, the child who has been rewarded for seeking help with tasks and who has been denied the opportunity to solve his own problems tends to be dependent, and he transfers this dependency to adults outside the home. Dependent children who cling to the teacher and rely on her to solve their problems tend to be shunned or ignored by other children.

Parent-Child-Teacher Relationship. Although the preprimary child has ideally made significant strides toward independence, he is not yet independent enough to develop a meaningful relationship with another adult without parental support. Related to his need for the backing of his parents is his primary motive to achieve adult approval for what he does and even for how he feels about his experiences in other settings and with other people. The child feels comfortable in the school and in his relationship with the teacher when parents and teacher are partners in promoting his development.

The importance of rapport among parent, child, and teacher has been emphasized in Chapter 4 describing the Diagnostic Interview. If for some reason this rapport does not develop, problems may result. If the child perceives conflict between parent and teacher, he feels discomfort. Caught between significant adults who may be making contradictory demands, he is frustrated. He may act out by rebelling in home or in school (or in some cases, both settings), particularly if the conflict is so severe that he feels he can please neither parent nor teacher. Or he may try to please both of them, conforming to the requirements of home while at home and of school while at school. Another solution is to play one adult against the other.

Evidence of the child's problem is his silence about the teacher and what goes on in school when he is home, and his lack of reference to home and family when he is in school. Further evidence is the invention of an imaginary playmate or sibling on whom he projects his own behavior. He can report, without impugnity, what someone else has done.

Whatever defense the child employs to neutralize his anxious middle-figure role, his growth energies are polarized by two opposing forces. Caught in a tense parent-child-teacher relationship, his efforts are drained in nonproductive directions.

Implications for Learning. The child's progress in developing relationships influences his readiness for various learning experiences. If he is functioning at the earlier levels of social development, this immaturity will interfere with his capacity to acquire reading and writing skills with ease. Vacillation between egocentric and sociocentric behavior is normal and expected during the preprimary period; however, the child should evidence definitive trends toward developing positive relationships with peers and adults before he is engaged in learning to read and write.

Developing a Value System

The development of a value system is involved in the socialization process. A *value* is the estimate of the worth of an idea or concept. As the child has experience with various concepts, he classifies them according to their importance to him. The resulting system of values serves as a guide to his behavior.

Early in his development the child begins to learn his parents' values. He learns through their responses, their attitudes, their tones of voice, their total interaction with him. He also learns values through the limits his parents set for him. In helping the child to meet his needs in a socially acceptable way, parents make and enforce rules of conduct. These rules reflect their values.

In the beginning the child responds to the rules, not to the values they represent. If he is told to pick up his toys, he does so to obey, not because he values neatness. He cooperates because he is concerned with his parent's love and approval, and he is strongly motivated to please them. When parental requests run counter to what he wants, he may protest and resist; however, basically the child wants limits. He comes to understand values through limits. If limits do not exist, he tests situations until he finds out what is expected of him.

By the preprimary years the child has usually acquired faint beginnings of social values. He has learned that he lives in a community of other people. In order to be approved and accepted, certain things are expected of him. He begins to show signs of give-and-take behavior. This period brings about important changes in how he internalizes values. He not only learns approved behavior through limits, but also through imitation of significant adults.

The child tends to identify with his parents. He begins to think, feel, and behave as though their characteristics belong to him (identification process). Through this process, he incorporates his parents' values into his behavior. As he internalizes parental values, his behavior begins to be controlled from within. When he violates a rule, derived from a parental value, his conscience bothers him. He anticipates discomfort in the form of guilt feelings. If the child does not have a strong parental model with whom to identify, this lack reflects in his conscience development. He experiences more problems in developing self-control.

The child's concept development influences his values. In forming concepts, the young child may develop ideas that are incomplete due to lack of sufficient experience, or inaccurate due to misconceptions. These incomplete or inaccurate concepts may lead the child to socially unacceptable behavior. For example, unable to hold onto more than one idea at a time, he may believe that an act is right because the motive is right. He may take the cookies from one child to give to another child who has none. He is focused on sharing, a commendable motive. The fact that he is sharing the property of somebody else does not figure in his thinking.

The child may also have difficulty in classifying behaviors. It is confusing for him that socially approved behaviors vary from one situation to the next. When he makes a face at his brother, nobody seems to notice; yet, he is taken to task for making the same face at a visiting adult. He has trouble resolving the incongruity of being praised for seeking help at home and expected to do for himself at nursery school. Confusing concepts make it difficult to sort out and classify values. The preprimary years are the optimal time not only for internalizing values, but also for extending and refining concepts about socially acceptable behavior.

Identifying the Child's Progress in Developing a Value System

The child's progress in developing a value system is reflected in his ability to cooperate and in his problem-solving skills. Sections III and IV of the Social Inventory of the Master Readiness Record comprise these areas for observation. In diagnosing the child's social progress, the teacher uses data from both the Social Inventory and the Emotional Inventory. Unmet psychological needs are frequently evidenced in socially immature behavior; therefore, the child's pattern of emotional development is a significant component in assessing his social maturity.

COOPERATION

By the preprimary period most children are aware that living with other people is a give-and-take situation. In order for the child to exist happily in his social community, certain behaviors are expected of him. Living productively with a group of people requires some degree of conformity. *Cooperation* refers to the child's willingness to work together with other people for the welfare of the group.

Cooperative behavior includes conforming to the general expectations of the nursery-kindergarten. The child reveals his ability to fit in with group activity by *adjusting to routines, following directions,* and *focusing attention in groups.* Inability to accept the expectations and limits of nursery-kindergarten may result from lack of experience. Children who have lived without limits or limits that have not been enforced have more difficulty adjusting to these minimal requirements.

The child's ability to conceptualize social values is evidenced in his knowledge of rules. Acting on a rule of the nursery-kindergarten without the direction of the teacher is probable indication that the child has internalized the standard. When he puts the puzzles away without being told to do so, he is acting on inner direction. Verbalization of the rule indicates that he is not just reacting from habit. He may say, "We put the puzzles in here when we're done." Ability to generalize rules from one situation to another reflects maturity. If the child can translate the rule relating to puzzles to the crayons or blocks, he is seeing similarities among events. The rule is no longer specific to the one situation in which it was learned, but can be used in a variety of similar situations. Ability to generalize rules is evidence of a developing value system.

Spontaneous play with peers also reflects the child's maturity in terms of developing a value system. In the process of learning social values, children characteristically vacillate between egocentric, possessive behavior and more sociocentric, sharing behavior. If a child shows a pattern of being *possessive* of his toys and vocal about what he considers to be his share of the materials, this may indicate a lack of understanding of give and take. A tendency to *share*, on the other hand, indicates a willingness to yield to others and to cooperate. Sharing without being told may be evidence that a basic social value has been internalized by the child and is directing his behavior.

SKILLS IN PROBLEM SOLVING

A child's ability to operate in terms of social values is revealed in his problem-solving skills. Typical social problems include how to leave his mother, how to get the attention he needs, how to involve himself in play, and how to take care of his needs and wants and still cooperate. Interactions with other children provide many situations that require the child to discover or apply a response. Figuring out the response to use depends, to a large extent, on his understanding of cause and effect. If his problem is how to get a coveted toy from another child, he may be interested only in the end result of getting what he wants. The consequences of his actions in regard to his relationship with the other child may be of little or no value to him. His solution may be to cry, to appeal to the teacher, to grab the toy, or take the toy when the other child is not looking. A more socially mature child may evidence concern for the influence of his response on the relationship. He may recognize that wanting something from somebody else involves giving something in return. He may bargain. He may reason with the other child and persuade him to give up the toy willingly. He may also solve his problem by recognizing that another toy will do just as well.

PLAN FOR HELP

A child learns to develop successful relationships with other people and develop a value system through experience. As previously mentioned, one of the major objectives of the nursery-kindergarten is to provide a laboratory for social learning.

DEVELOPING RELATIONSHIPS WITH OTHERS

Some children have had extensive opportunities to socialize prior to entrance into nursery-kindergarten. Other children have had minimal contact with people outside the home. Because of their varied background experience, there may be wide differences among children in terms of their social progress.

The child's individual plan for help depends on where he is developmentally. The child who engages primarily in solitary play and who is dependent on the teacher needs a different plan for help from that of the more socially oriented child. The teacher assumes a central and directive role with more immature children. It is through cooperating with her that the child learns to relate to other children. After he begins to feel secure in his social interactions with the teacher, the child may be led into interactions with another child, then gradually with a number of children. These interactions should center on mutually enjoyable activities. The teacher may stimulate these relationships by making a casual suggestion, or by assuming a temporary role in the activity. For example, if two children demonstrate interest in block play, the teacher can engage them in constructing something with her. At first these interactive sessions are short (five to ten minutes) and involve only one activity. As the child becomes accustomed to this form of play, he can be engaged for a longer period. Less mature children may be encouraged to participate in larger group activities; however, they should not be coaxed. Forced participation tends to set up a resistance that is hard to overcome.

When the child is primarily engaged in parallel play, interactive sessions are arranged involving not only a mutually enjoyable activity, but the specific children who tend to play close together. The teacher may initiate the activity, but withdraw from a directive role when the children become absorbed. The child who has started to derive enjoyment from playing with other children needs guidance to extend his social experience. The teacher helps him to modify his imperious demands and make suggestions in ways that motivate others to go along with him. She

Teacher Helping Cooperative Play

encourages the child to contribute to play by assuming a needed role. If the children are playing bakery, he can be the delivery man rather than the baker, a role presently assumed by another child.

She may organize activities in which each child has opportunity both to lead and to follow. She encourages children to consider the range of things to do and to initiate activities of their own choosing. The teacher sets the stage for the children to develop their own rules for play.

DEVELOPING A VALUE SYSTEM

Helping the child to develop a value system represents a positive approach to discipline. The term *discipline* carries so many negative associations that its true meaning is often overlooked. The old idea of discipline as a correctional system—a set of rules with matching penalties—to forestall spoiling the child tends to turn away caring teachers. Harris reflects humanistically,

> These terms "spoiling" a child or "breaking" a child have always seemed to me so crude and cruel when applied to human beings that surely they were invented by some wicked fairy-tale stepmother who lived in a dark, dank tower somewhere on the moors! [4]

Simply defined, *discipline* means the guiding of behavior. Positive discipline involves more than an effort to help the child learn rules of con-

---

[4] Thomas A. Harris, M.D., *I'm OK–You're OK, A Practical Guide to Transactional Analysis* (New York: Harper & Row, Publishers, 1967), p. 153.

duct. It involves helping him to understand the purpose of the rules and the implications of the rules. Obedience to rules without understanding may tend to reflect superficial ways of conforming. Rules are essential to cooperative living, but to be effective they must be internalized by the child. Even when the child is told that he may *not* do something, it is important to tell him what he may do instead; i.e., "You may *not* paint the chair, but you *may* paint the cardboard box."

Emphasis on developing a value system is a more effective approach to preparing the child for progressive self-guidance. Values are the "why" of human behavior. When the child examines ideas and estimates their worth, he is building a system of reasons for his choices. A sound, stable value system makes the child more flexible and adaptable. Values, unlike rules, serve as guides to behavior anywhere, anytime.

The child develops a value system through experience. He learns indirectly from the consequences of his acts, particularly from the reactions of other people. He learns incidently through his own feelings of warmth or hurt, satisfaction or disappointment. He also learns about values through direct examination and discussion. Group problem-solving sessions can increase awareness of values. A typical session might be concerned with the problem of running in the nursery-kindergarten. Children discuss: What happens if everybody runs? Responses may include, "We'll bump," or "We'll knock the chairs over." Discussing what might happen promotes understanding of social values. When the value is accepted as his own, a child tends to act upon it and controls his own behavior. The child who is conscious only of an imposed rule about running may respond, "We're not supposed to." The welfare of other people and respect for property have not become more important to the child than the external enforcement of the rule. When the child accepts the rule as his own, he does not run in school because he does not want to hurt someone or disrupt the physical environment.

The child develops a value system through limits. Setting limits is primarily the responsibility of the teacher; however, she makes every effort to involve the children in making the rules and limits that concern them. If they have taken a part in setting the limit, children are more apt to accept it as their own, internalize it, and recognize the value underlying it. Not only do children learn to set limits for themselves, but also the value of limits, by the way the teacher assumes the responsibility. They learn that limits can be positive rather than negative guidelines. The approach, "Don't leave the puzzles on the table when you're finished" differs in emphasis from "When we're finished we put the puzzles in the puzzle box." The positive direction not only communicates a line of action that tends to be followed, but provides a basis for acceptable behavior in other situations.

When the teacher has to give specific guidance to individual children, she reproves the behavior, never the child; for example, "It's wrong to take Andy's ball" rather than "You're wrong to take Andy's ball." Since preprimary children tend to be concrete and literal, they are more apt to respond to reproval accompanied by an expression of the teacher's feelings; for example, "I like you, Randy, but I can't let you tear up Bobby's papers." Randy learns a rule of conduct, but more importantly, he experiences the value of accepting other people even though they do things he may not like. He also experiences that the teacher values him as a person even though he does things she doesn't like.

A fundamental principle in disciplining children is to recognize that they are human beings with feelings. It is all too easy to lose sight of this fact because the young child is only beginning his developmental career. As a result of his neophyte status, he is often viewed as incapable of input in guiding his own affairs. He may be talked down to, looked down upon, and made to feel psychologically as well as physically small. Discussions about him go on in his presence as if he were incapable of hearing and evaluating. Answers to his questions may suggest that he is being presumptuous to intrude in topics that belong to older people. He is not credited with understanding all kinds of situations that, in effect, he is attempting to interpret. If this adult attitude toward him prevails, the child senses that he must somehow be inferior, and his behavior tends to reflect this low evaluation.

The most important value is the child's estimate of his own worth. Helping the child to develop positive relationships with others and to develop a value system to guide his behavior begins with respect for him as a person, the basis for a healthy self-image.

Summary

Social development represents increased capacity to establish and maintain relationships with people. The preprimary period is the optimal time to gain social experience, to develop positive attitudes toward other people, and to evolve more mature ways to interact with them. The term *socialization* refers to two related processes: (1) how the child develops relationships with others and (2) how he develops a value system.

Reflecting the sequence from egocentric to more sociocentric behavior, the child's progress in developing relationships is revealed by how he relates to his peers. Initially the child plays alone, then plays beside other children, and finally plays with other children. In his beginning contacts his relationships with playmates are mechanical. He interacts with large numbers of children. Later, he singles out special playmates. For many children, imaginary playmates serve as a source of support.

The child's social maturity is revealed in his relationships with adults. The mother-child relationship serves as a foundation and largely determines how he will relate to others. Perceived conflict between mother and teacher is a source of anxiety for the child and may create adjustment problems.

Early in his development the child begins to establish a value system. Values, estimates of the worth of ideas, are systematized in order of importance and serve to guide behavior. The child first learns his parents' values by their interaction with him, by the limits they set, and by his identification with them. The preprimary years represent the optimal time for classifying and internalizing values, and for refining concepts about socially approved behavior. The child's progress in developing a value system is reflected in his cooperation, in his willingness to work together for the welfare of the group, and in his skills in problem solving.

The child's plan for help in developing relationships with other people depends upon his social maturity. In the early stages the teacher assumes a central and directive role in guiding his interactions. She helps the more socially mature child to extend his social experience and skills. Helping the child to develop a value system represents a positive approach to discipline. Defined as guiding behavior, *discipline* is more than an emphasis on rules of conduct. Guiding behavior includes helping children to acquire values to serve as a guide for their own behavior and as a basis for self-discipline. The child learns values through experience, through limits, and through the model of the teacher in setting limits.

11

The Master
Readiness Record

Introduction

The Master Readiness Record derives from the philosophy of working with children expressed throughout the preceding chapters; it can be appreciated and used to full advantage only in the context of the total book. Based on the developmental viewpoint, this philosophy assumes that each child is different with his own pattern of needs. In order to help each child to develop to his optimum potential, instruction must be individualized. The Master Readiness Record represents a collection of basic items that helps the teacher to identify the child's individual differences. Effective use of the record depends upon the following commitments:

1. Belief in the developmental viewpoint
2. Belief in the uniqueness of each child
3. Belief in the "whole child"
4. Belief in individual differences
5. Belief in the value of individualized instruction for *all* children, regardless of their rank along the developmental continuum.

The Master Readiness Record centralizes information about the individual child on one form. Providing a growing picture of the child's development, the record is organized according to the physical, emotional, mental, and social areas of growth. Geared to the "whole child," the instrument is set up to facilitate diagnoses of readiness based on the child's total development.

The record is keyed to help the teacher identify emerging maturity levels. When developments are noted, it is possible to trace out the child's readiness profile, including areas of slackened rate that need special attention and encouragement. On the basis of the profile, appropriate activities are planned to develop readiness in given areas. The record expedites this planning.

One of the primary purposes of the record is to streamline the teacher's system of collecting information and keeping it up to date. It provides direction for observation, inquiry, and gathering of information. Condensation of the information into a single form simplifies review and analysis. With written effort reduced to a minimum, the teacher has more time not only to observe but to work creatively with children in carrying out their individual plans for help.

Description of the Master Readiness Record

The Master Readiness Record (see pp. 171–89) consists of four sections: (1) Physical Inventory, (2) Emotional Inventory, (3) Mental Inventory, and (4) Social Inventory. Each inventory is organized according to developmental areas associated with the particular growth system. The developmental areas are included because of their diagnostic importance in determining readiness. Under each heading for a developmental area are listed specific behaviors that evidence progress in the given area. Reflecting readiness factors described in previous chapters, the inventories focus on behaviors that can be observed and recorded.

Readiness evolves from both maturation and experience. In some cases record entries indicate degree of developmental accomplishment. For example, in Section I of the Mental Inventory are items referring to copying forms. Ability to copy increasingly complex forms indicates progressive accomplishment. In the Physical Inventory an item in Section III refers to the reversal error. The presence or absence of this tendency to reverse letters, numerals, or words is a diagnostic sign suggesting level of maturity. Other entries reveal conditions that evidence level of maturity based on the child's experience. The item "understands relationships of number" in Section IV of the Mental Inventory reveals the child's mathematics vocabulary which is based on his experience.

In certain cases, the skills and behaviors a child has not mastered are as significant in assessing readiness as those he has mastered. For example, it is important to recognize that a specific child does not maintain balance in running. This fact may imply that more intensive observation of the child's running is needed to see if imbalance is a pattern. In terms of mental development, the child's inability to recognize colors has implications for his plan for help. The teacher knows where to begin in helping him develop color knowledge. When the child's inability to perform is diagnostically important, both the learning of a behavior and the lack of it are reflected in the inventory.

The inventories are designed to permit recordings about a behavior at four successive times. Four slots beside each behavior provide space for recording information about the behavior at any given time. At the top of each vertical column are spaces to date the entries made at a given time and to indicate the source of the information. Sequential entries over a period of time evidence the child's progress as well as his lags or regressions in terms of specific behavior. Dated entries make it possible to identify the time of onset of a behavior, the approximate time an immature behavior fades out, and the beginnings of a developmental trend. Patterns of behavior become apparent. In many cases a review of the record indicates when a problem was first noticed in the behavior of the child. Usually four spaces are sufficient for the number of observations that can reasonably be made during the course of a year. Although there may be instances when an observation requires the recording of an isolated behavior (for example, a sign of stress or fatigue), usually a series of behaviors in one developmental area are observed and recorded at one time. If there is reason to note the occurrence of a specific behavior at closer intervals over a period of time, a duplicate of the page of the inventory on which the behavior is listed can be inserted.

Each inventory contains a section with the heading, "Special Problems." Special problems refer to any unusual development not accounted for in the inventory. It is impossible to itemize every characteristic of an individual's behavior; therefore, provision is made to record items not listed. Also, notations about extreme deviations requiring special investigation or attention are recorded in this section.

Directions for Using the Master Readiness Record

Effective use of the Master Readiness Record depends upon thorough knowledge and understanding of the developmental areas, the specific behaviors, and the diagnostic meanings of the behaviors. The teacher's primary step in using the instrument is to familiarize herself with the behaviors and their implications for readiness. Knowing the record helps her to provide a program that gives all children opportunity to reveal and to develop readiness in the defined areas. Knowing the record helps the teacher to see children differently. Guiding observation, the inventories list the critical behaviors to be watched for in her daily interaction with a child. Knowing the record puts the teacher on the alert to recognize and note developmental indicators appearing in other records about a child. Increasing awareness of significant information, knowing the record directs the data-collection process.

COLLECTING INFORMATION FOR RECORD

Information about a child's behavior is collected from a variety of sources. "Feeder" records and direct observation are two of the information sources from which the teacher draws.

"Feeder" Records. The "feeder" records are devices for collecting information about specific aspects of the child's development. Some feeder records are designed to help the teacher collect information about the child's developmental history, his home environment, and his current adjustments to nursery-kindergarten. Examples of these feeder records are the Background Information Form, including the Health Record, the Diagnostic Interview Form, and the Summary Parent-Teacher Conference Form. Other feeder records provide specific data about a limited area of development, such as visual or auditory discrimination, fine motor coordination, or tendency to reverse letters, numerals, or words. Examples of these records are the results of such exercises as Copy Forms and the Word Reproduction Exercise, art products, and samples of printing. Reports from resource persons to whom the child has been referred represent still another type of feeder record. Whatever source casts additional light on the child's development or fills out his behavioral picture qualifies as a feeder record.

Transferring data from these records to the Master Readiness Record facilitates evaluation. *All the information about a child is potentially important*; however, the sheer bulk of unsifted material is unwieldy and time-consuming to peruse. Selected data reduce clutter and are easier to use. Diagnostic judgments may be based on summaries of pertinent data indicated on the Master Readiness Record, but if necessary, the feeder records are available for further investigation. Feeder records are maintained in the individual folder of the child.

Observation. Observation is the primary source of most objective data about chidren. It follows that well-developed observation skills are mandatory for early childhood teachers. Those who guide young children must sharpen their powers of observation to be attuned to behaviors that reveal readiness to learn and to do. Simply defined, *observation* is attentive noting. The teacher pays attention to the child to note how he is progressing with reference to specific skills and behaviors.

Observation is a continuous process. The teacher is always alert to behavior whenever or wherever it occurs. She must be ready for the unpredictable. For example, there is no way to foretell when a child may divulge the existence of an imaginary playmate. If this behavior occurs, the teacher must be attentive to note it and record it. As a continuous process, the observation task cannot be allocated to a certain time of day when the teacher can be relatively detached from the child. She must be geared to note attentively from the time the children enter the school until they leave.

The school environment and program of activities enable the child to reveal what he can do. The teacher observes him as he moves spontaneously through the course of his daily activities. If a child does not reveal what he can do with regard to a specific behavior, an activity is arranged to elicit the behavior. For example, the child may not hop in the course of his daily routines. The teacher plans an activity involving hopping to observe this motor accomplishment.

Even though the teacher is on the alert to note the behavior of each child as it unfolds, she may elect to observe specific behaviors of a particular child. For example, if a child evidences unusual behavior in any area, he may be observed on an intensive basis to see if intervention is necessary.

In most instances of observation, it is unnecessary to write a running record of the child's behavior as in the case of anecdotal records. The observer merely *checks* the behavior on the Master Readiness Record. In instances where more detailed information is needed, however, anecdotal records may be used to collect this information. The behaviors listed in the inventories provide directions for observing and for recording the anecdotes. After the incident is recorded, the behavior is identified in terms of the standard language of the Master Readiness Record. This standard language facilitates transfer of information to the inventories.

In gathering specific information, the teacher may observe particular behaviors of children at a given time. While working with children on a project, she might note the eye-hand coordination of two or three children. Or she might observe the creative thinking skills of one or two children during a problem-solving session. During balance-beam activities she would naturally be attentive to the balance exhibited by the children. Or, the playmate selection of specific children may be noted during free play on successive days. Depending upon the nature of the specific behaviors, the teacher gauges the number of children she can observe with accuracy.

Since children tend to behave differently in different circumstances and at different times of day, observations of specific behaviors should be made in a variety of situations throughout the course of the day. Social behavior, for example, may take on a new dimension when the child is in the less restrictive setting of the playground. The child who is active and assertive early in the day may wind down to a slower tempo later on. Recordings of his energy level based only on observations made in the earlier period would yield a distorted picture. Arrangements should be made to observe a child's physical, emotional, mental, and social behaviors in the various situations in which they are expressed.

RECORDING INFORMATION

Information about a specific behavior is entered on the Master Readiness Record by a tally mark in the slot next to the behavior. The entry is dated at the top of the column, and the source (e.g., preentrance record, observation) is noted. Data from the preentrance records are entered before school opens. Information from other records are noted as they are available.

If possible, behavioral incidents or sequences are recorded on the Master Readiness Record as they are observed. If on-the-spot recording is impossible, then the observation is noted at the earliest opportunity, preferably within the school day but certainly within the school week. Recent behaviors are more vividly remembered. If the teacher delays too long in recording, intervening activities will dull the recall of what happened.

It is possible for some behaviors to be noted and tallied more than one time in the course of an observation. The child may exhibit that he understands a number concept, recognizes a shape, or has mastered some skill more than once during a time period. Occasionally consistency (or inconsistency) of a behavior during a time period has significance. If, for example, lateral dominance is being observed, the child may use his right hand to reach for a piece of paper, to crayon, and to cut around an outline. In this case, three tallies would be entered in the slot next to "uses right hand." If he continues to use his right hand during subsequent observations, all of these tallies support the tentative judgment that dominance may be established. The tallies form a horizontal pattern that may confirm or deny the teacher's impression of his handedness.

Using the Record for Developmental Diagnosis

The Master Readiness Record facilitates diagnosis. A diagnosis is made when a judgment is applied to the information. In making a diagnostic judgment about the developmental status of the child, the teacher observes the following procedure:

1. Collect the data.
2. Summarize the pertinent data.
3. Evaluate the data.
4. Make the diagnosis.
5. State the diagnosis in objective terms.

Collect the Data.   The Master Readiness Record directs the data-collection process by listing the critical behaviors to be identified in the feeder records or through observation. Before the child enters school, data from the Health Record and the Diagnostic Interview Form are transferred to the Master Readiness Record. These readiness data form the basis for a tentative plan for help.

As soon as the child enters school, efforts are made to collect data about where he is developmentally so that a plan for help based on more substantial information can be put in motion. Since observation is a continuous process, data for the record are collected continuously.

Summarize the Pertinent Data.   One of the purposes of the Master Readiness Record is to summarize the data. When pertinent data about a developmental area are culled from a variety of sources, centralized on one form, and the entries organized under one heading, the information is in summary form ready to be evaluated.

Evaluate the Data.   Periodically the data on the record are reviewed and evaluated. Evaluation involves estimating the value of the information in clarifying the specific situation or problem. In evaluating the data, the teacher examines the information to determine developmental meanings, to estimate the progress of the child in various areas, and to evolve or update the plan for help. Each child's record should be reviewed at least once a month, and more frequently if necessary. By the end of the first month of school, sufficient data should be collected about each developmental area to warrant an evaluation.

With relation to some areas, developmental meanings are obvious. When specific behaviors are noted, the child's readiness profile comes into focus. Under Motor Coordination, for example, if the child can perform all the behaviors listed under "alternating laterality," but not those listed under "integrated laterality," his maturity level in this area is apparent. If he does or does not know his colors or shapes or common concepts, the meanings of these behaviors are obvious.

In other cases, developmental meanings become clear only in terms of emerging patterns. The child's maturity levels in emotional and social development, as well as vision, hearing, right-left orientation, problem-solving skills, and language-arts skills can only be determined by observing him over a period of time. At the initial evaluation of the record the teacher can sometimes identify a suggested pattern by a vertical review of the inventories. The teacher glances down the columns to see if related behaviors assume a vertical pattern. For example, according to the Emotional Inventory, recordings on a child might indicate hostile behavior, a sullen mood, inability to control emotions, and incidents of hitting and defacing property. In other cases, the pattern may cross the inventories. There may be recordings that a child clings to the teacher, asks for help with physical needs that he can take care of himself, shows a predominance of solitary play, and exhibits a resistant attitude.

When the teacher identifies a vertical pattern that suggests the need for special attention, she observes the behaviors closely for a two-week period. If the majority of behaviors are consistently repeated, forming a horizontal pattern, she can tentatively conclude that special attention is needed. It must be noted that a recording of any vision or hearing symptom or any change in complexion or energy level signals the need for close observation for the two-week period.

Make the Diagnosis. In cases where developmental meanings are obvious, diagnostic judgments tend to be clear. In terms of Motor Coordination, the teacher makes a judgment about the child's maturity level; for example, "He is functioning at the alternating laterality level." If the developmental meaning becomes clear only through a pattern, then the teacher waits until closer observation confirms a suspected pattern before applying a judgment to the information. Diagnoses might be: "Seems to show an immature pattern of emotional development" or "Seems to exhibit dependency needs." There will be a separate diagnosis for each developmental area indicated in the record.

State the Diagnosis in Objective Terms. The statement of the diagnosis must be supported by objective terms derived from the inventories. For example, the diagnosis would be stated as follows: "Seems to show an immature pattern of emotional development, as evidenced by a hostile attitude, sullen mood, inability to control emotions, and incidents of hitting and defacing property." The number of times he exhibited the attitude, mood, and inability to control his emotions also is noted.

USING THE RECORD TO DIAGNOSE ATYPICAL BEHAVIOR

If the child exhibits atypical behavior, his Master Readiness Record is examined to find an explanation for the problem. In general, the teacher follows the same steps in the procedure for diagnosis. Information has been routinely collected for the record. All the inventories are reviewed for information that might cast light on the irregularity. In order to facilitate evaluation, these data are culled from the inventories and summarized.

The pattern may stand out vividly; the data may suggest a continuing trend. In some cases, the behavior may not be consistent with all the other information about the child. The incidence may be only an episode, reflecting a passing event. As pointed out, dated entries make it possible to trace when a behavior originated.

USING THE RECORD TO EVOLVE
A PLAN FOR HELP

In terms of her diagnoses the teacher can identify the kinds of general help the child needs to develop readiness, and she can point to the areas requiring special emphasis. If the child is functioning at the alternating laterality level motorically, his plan for help will include activities appropriate for that developmental level. If he does not know the common concepts of number or color, for example, his plan for help includes provision for immediate opportunity to learn these concepts. If diagnosis is from a pattern of behaviors, as in the case of apparently immature emotional development, a specific plan is initiated to strengthen the child's self-image. If he is diagnosed as dependent, then his plan for help may suggest sensitive weaning toward greater independence.

Using the Record for Progress Reports

The Master Readiness Record is not only a helpful resource in guiding the child's daily experience, but also a basis for progress reports. It is often necessary to report a child's total developmental progress, or a limited area of developmental progress, to a resource person to whom the child has been referred. Dated entries about when a symptom first began to show up in a child's behavior and the frequency of its incidence may be of value to a specialist examining the child.

Periodically, information about a child's progress is reported to parents, to other teachers, and to the administrators. These reports are strengthened when statements can be clarified and validated by concrete data. There are occasions when the information on the Master Readiness Record is summarized in written form to give to teachers or to administrators. Providing the basis for discussion at the parent-teacher conferences, the record serves as a progress record. It helps the teacher to interpret the child's development to the parent and to evolve a cooperative plan for help.

When the child completes the nursery-kindergarten program, a summary of his progress based on the cumulative information in the Master

Readiness Record serves as a permanent record as well as a reference to the school to which the child transfers or to the receiving teacher if he remains in the same school system. In the Mental Inventory is a Reading and Writing Readiness Summary that can be duplicated for inclusion with the permanent record. This summary reveals the child's level of readiness to be engaged in formal instruction in these skills. He may be ready for formal instruction prior to completion of the nursery-kindergarten program. If so, this instruction has been included in his plan for help. If he has not reached this level of readiness, the receiving teacher has concrete direction about where to begin in working with him.

The Value of the Record in Helping the Individual Child

Maintenance of a Master Readiness Record on each child assures that *all* children, not just the exceptional few, are observed and receive the attention and help they need. The teacher's regular reference to the record of each child may reveal areas of scanty recordings, reflecting limited observation. These gaps alert the teacher to the danger of labeling without sufficient information. They also remind her to distribute her attention more evenly among the children. There are many youngsters who appear to be progressing at an expected rate. They seem to thrive with minimal attention; however, "differences" may become apparent if their behavior is noted attentively. When noticed early and given appropriate treatment, these minor irregularities may be arrested before they mature into major problems later on in life. As pointed out throughout the text, the earlier problems are identified, the more responsive they are to treatment and correction. A sensitive measure, the Master Readiness Record focuses on what is special about each child. Early intervention helps him to develop his strengths to their optimum potential and to minimize the influence of his limitations.

PEMS NURSERY-KINDERGARTEN

MASTER READINESS RECORD

Physical Inventory   Child's Name _____

School Year 19 ____ to 19 ____

	date:	date:	date:	date:
	source:	source:	source:	source:

I. HEALTH

Complexion:
  Pale
  Healthy
  Flushed
Energy level:
  Vigorous
  Active
  Listless
Vision:
  Symptoms
    Eyes crossed
    Eyes turning in or out
    Watering eyes
    Reddened eyes
    Encrusted eyelids
    Burning or itching of eyes
    Blurring of vision at
      any time
  Behaviors
    Thrusting head forward or
      backward while looking
      at distant objects
    Frowning or scowling
      during near work
    Tendency to touch and
      finger constantly
    Turning or tilting of
      head to use one
      side only
    Tendency to rub eyes

Professional Examination   Date: _____

                                          Findings: _____

Child's Name_____
School Year 19____to 19____

	date:	date:	date:	date:
	source:	source:	source:	source:

I. HEALTH (con't)
  Hearing:
    Symptoms
      Earaches
      Abnormal speech (omissions, substitutions, or distortions of sounds)
      Abnormal ear structure
    Behaviors
      Misunderstands directions
      Asks to have statements repeated
      Shows indifference to sound (including what people say)
      Holds head at peculiar angle to listen
      Rubs ear with fingers
      Speaks in monotone
      Speaks consistently in too loud a voice
      Speaks periodically in too loud a voice
      Shows difficulty in locating sound sources
      Shows difficulty in telling difference between sounds
      Does not maintain balance

Professional Examination   Date:_____

Findings:_____

Illnesses

Date of Absence	Date of Return	Cause
_____	_____	_____
_____	_____	_____
_____	_____	_____
_____	_____	_____
_____	_____	_____
_____	_____	_____
_____	_____	_____

I.   HEALTH (con't)
     Height and Weight:

	Height	Weight		Height	Weight
September	_____	_____	January	_____	_____
October	_____	_____	February	_____	_____
November	_____	_____	March	_____	_____
December	_____	_____	April	_____	_____
			May	_____	_____

     Existing Conditions:_____

     _____

     Precautionary Measures: _____

     _____

     Special Problems: _____

     _____

	date:	date:	date:	date:
II. MOTOR COORDINATION	source:	source:	source:	source:
Bilateral level:				
Child maintains balance in jumping				
Child is able to do Angels in the Snow Jumping Jacks				
Child does not maintain balance in jumping				
Child is not able to do Angels in the Snow Jumping Jacks				
Alternating laterality:				
Child maintains balance in walking				
running				
climbing				
ascending and descending stairs				

	date:	date:	date:	date:
II. MOTOR COORDINATION (con't)	source:	source:	source:	source:
hopping on				
right foot				
left foot				
walking				
on balance beam				
Child does not maintain balance in				
walking				
running				
climbing				
ascending and descending stairs				
hopping on				
right foot				
left foot				
walking on balance beam				
Integrated laterality:				
Child can				
skip				
coordinate				
thumb and index finger to hold an implement				
eye and hand				
Child cannot				
skip				
coordinate				
thumb and index finger to hold an implement				
eye and hand				
III. RIGHT-LEFT ORIENTATION				
Lateral dominance (Handedness):				
Child uses				
right hand				
left hand				
Reversal error:				
Child reverses				
letters				
words				
numbers				

III. RIGHT-LEFT ORIENTATION (con't)

	date:	date:	date:	date:
Recognition of right and left:	source:	source:	source:	source:
Child recognizes				
parts of his body				
parts of another's body				
position of objects				
Child does not recognize				
parts of his body				
parts of another's body				
position of objects				

IV. SKILLS (e.g., Tricycling, ball-throwing)

_____

_____

                    date: date: date: date:

                    source: source: source: source:

V. SELF-HELP
    Without help child can
      zipper
      button
      snap
      buckle
      tie
      dress himself
      pull on boots
      take care of
        bathroom needs
      wash hands
      swing
      pour from pitcher
        into cup or glass
      take care of
        possessions
    Without help child cannot
      zipper
      button
      snap

Child's Name _____

School Year 19____ to 19____

	date:	date:	date:	date:
	source:	source:	source:	source:

V. SELF-HELP (con't)
    buckle
    tie
    dress himself
    pull on boots
    take care of
      bathroom needs
    wash hands
    swing
    pour from pitcher
      into cup or glass
    take care of possessions

VI. SPECIAL PROBLEMS

_____

_____

VII. SPECIAL INTERESTS AND COMPETENCIES_____

_____

_____

PEMS NURSERY-KINDERGARTEN

MASTER READINESS RECORD

Emotional Inventory   Child's Name_____

School Year 19____ to 19____

	date:	date:	date:	date:
	source:	source:	source:	source:
I. ATTITUDES Child shows				
enthusiastic behavior				
receptive behavior				
responsive behavior				
indifferent behavior				
resigned behavior				
resistant behavior				
hostile behavior				
II. MOODS Child appears				
serene				
even				
troubled				
sullen				
III. SELF-CONTROL				
Regulates emotions				
Does not regulate emotions				
Shows ability to focus mentally				
Shows distractibility				
IV. SIGNS OF STRESS AND FATIGUE				
Bites nails				
Crosses eyes				
Picks nose				
Cries				
Kicks				
Stamps feet				
Bullies other children				
Destroys property				
Talks in a loud voice				
Responds irritably				
Hits				
Bites				

	date:	date:	date:	date:
	source:	source:	source:	source:

IV. SIGNS OF STRESS
AND FATIGUE (Con't)
Sucks thumb
Daydreams
Accuses others
Regresses to former
state (wetting, infantile
pronunciation, drinking
from bottle)
Shows strained expression
Shows masked expression
Shows rigid posture
Speaks in whining tone
Speaks in demanding
tone
Speaks in strained tone

V. SPECIAL PROBLEMS

_____

_____

_____

_____

MASTER READINESS RECORD

Mental Inventory   Child's Name_____

School Year 19____ to 19____

	date:	date:	date:	date:
I. CAPACITY TO RECOGNIZE LIKENESSES AND DIFFERENCES	source:	source:	source:	source:
The child can copy				
a circle				
a cross				
a square				
a diamond				
The child cannot copy				
a circle				
a cross				
a square				
a diamond				
He recognizes colors				
red				
yellow				
blue				
green				
purple				
orange				
He does not recognize				
red				
yellow				
blue				
green				
purple				
orange				
He can sort (classify) things that are alike				
in one way (circles)				
in two ways (yellow circles)				
in more than two ways				
He can categorize				
vegetables				
vehicles				
farm animals				
zoo animals				

Mental Inventory (con't)   Child's Name_____
                        School Year 19___ to 19___

	date:	date:	date:	date:
I. CAPACITY TO RECOGNIZE LIKENESSES, ETC. (con't)	source:	source:	source:	source:
animals with fur				
animals without fur				
He can seriate (order) by identifying big and little				
putting three or more different sized objects in order				
II. GENERAL KNOWLEDGE Child can identify				
parts of his body				
members of his family				
Child knows his full name				
address				
phone number				
primary colors				
secondary colors				
concepts of 1–5 (referring to objects)				
concepts 5-10 (referring to objects)				
names for different kinds of weather (rain, snow, cloudy, sunny)				
Can discuss pets				
transportation				
holidays and customs				
Exhibits enriched background experiences				
Exhibits meager background experiences				
Generalizes from experience				
Memorizes (Retains information)				

Child's Name_____

School Year 19_____to 19_____

	date:	date:	date:	date:
	source:	source:	source:	source:

III. PROBLEM SOLVING

Follows directions
Maintains mental focus
Appeals to adults to
   solve problems
Relies on trial and error
   to solve problems
Uses trial and error to
   solve problems
Shows ability to stay
   with a task
Uses reason to solve
   problems
Can identify problems
Verbalizes problems
Exhibits organization in
   solving problems
Sees cause and effect re-
   lationships
Exhibits curiosity
Generates new ideas
Can find different ways
   to solve problems
Can change direction in
   solving problems (with
   new information)
Can extend an idea

IV. MATHEMATICS CONCEPTS
AND SKILLS
Recognizes shape of
   circle
   square
   triangle
   rectangle
Does not recognize
   circle
   square
   triangle
   rectangle

	date:	date:	date:	date:
IV. MATHEMATICS CONCEPTS AND SKILLS (con't)	source:	source:	source:	source:
Recognizes concepts 1–5 (referring to objects)				
concepts 5–10 (referring to objects)				
numerals 1–5				
5–10				
10---				
Counts by 1's				
by 5's				
by 10's				
Understands relationships of number:				
more than				
less than				
combinations to make "5"				
combinations to make "10"				
Understands concepts of computation:				
subtraction (take away from objects)				
addition (add to objects)				
parts of a whole:				
1/2 (half of object), 2 parts				
1/4 (quarter of object), 4 parts				
equal (same number of objects)				
Recognizes one-to-one correspondence				
Understands concept of time:				
day-night				
schedule of the day				
month				
week				
year				
clock (tells time)				
Sees spatial relationships (puzzles)				

Child's Name _____
School Year 19 ____ to 19 ____

	date:	date:	date:	date:
	source:	source:	source:	source:

V. LANGUAGE ARTS

Speech:
- Does not speak clearly
- Does not communicate ideas clearly
- Uses few words
- Does not speak in complete sentences
- Shows hesitations, stuttering, repetition of words
- Uses large number of words
- Speaks in complete sentences
- Uses adjectives and adverbs to extend ideas
- Uses complex sentences
- Relates ideas and events in sequence
- Speaks clearly
- Communicates ideas clearly

Pronunciation:
- Pronounces vowel sounds
- Pronounces consonants
  m,n,ng,p,f,h,w
  y,k,b,d,g,r
  s,sh,ch
  t,th,v,l
  z,zh,j
- Exhibits control in voice
- Does not exhibit control in voice

Listening Skills:
- Understands directions
- Relates events accurately
- Relates stories with accuracy
- Thinks about information he hears
- Enjoys listening to a story, record, or poem
- Relates a story in sequence

183

School Year 19____to 19____

	date:	date:	date:	date:
V. LANGUAGE ARTS (con't)	source:	source:	source:	source:
Holds on to his own idea while listening to another person speak				
Listens to others				
Word Reproduction Exercise:				
Achieved minimal competency (22) in Basic Words				
Did not achieve minimal competency in Basic Words				
Achieved minimal competency (12) in Complex Words				
Did not achieve minimal competency in Complex Words				

VI. SPECIAL INTERESTS AND COMPETENCIES _____

_____

READING AND WRITING READINESS
SUMMARY

	date:	date:	date:	date:
I. PHYSICAL	source:	source:	source:	source:
Has achieved integrated laterality				
Has achieved right-left orientation				
Has infrequent reversal errors				
Is free from signs of visual fatigue				
Discriminates sounds in the environment				
II. EMOTIONAL				
Has achieved self-control				
Has receptive attitude				
III. MENTAL				
Recognizes primary and secondary colors				
Copies a diamond				

	date:	date:	date:	date:
III. MENTAL (con't)	source:	source:	source:	source:
Puts three or more objects in order				
Classifies objects in more than one way				
Maintains mental focus				
Follows directions				
Has mastered broad base of common concepts (experience)				
Exhibits basic rules of grammar				
Articulates sounds with clarity				
Pronounces 12 Complex Words in Word Reproduction Exercise				
Controls voice				
Shows clarity of expression				
Is free from hesitations, stuttering and repetition of words				
Speaks in complete sentences				
Uses language to solve problems				
Exhibits creative-thinking skills				
IV. SOCIAL				
Shows trends toward cooperative play				
Adjusts to routine				
Follows directions				
V. ACCOMPLISHED READING AND WRITING SKILLS				
Recognizes uppercase letters by sight				
by sound				
Recognizes lowercase letters by sight				
by sound				

185

Child's Name _____

School Year 19____ to 19____

	date:	date:	date:	date:
V. ACCOMPLISHED READING AND WRITING SKILLS (con't)	source:	source:	source:	source:
Recognizes first name				
Recognizes whole name				
Recognizes other words				
Word analysis:				
Recognizes initial consonants and blends				
Recognizes final consonants and blends				
Recognizes special word parts (in - fin, bin)				
Writing:				
Prints uppercase letters				
Prints lowercase letters				
Prints first name				
Prints whole name				
Prints other words				

VI. SPECIAL PROBLEMS: _____

_____

_____

_____

PEMS NURSERY-KINDERGARTEN

MASTER READINESS RECORD

Social Inventory   Child's Name _____

School Year 19_____to 19 _____

	date:	date:	date:	date:
I. RELATIONSHIP WITH PEERS	source:	source:	source:	source:
Play Behavior:				
Plays alone				
Plays beside other children				
Plays with other children				
Wants to be first				
Boasts				
Shows bossiness				
Quarrels				
Takes the lead				
Follows (assumes supportive role)				
Initiates activity				
Finds ways of entering group play				
Plays with same toy daily				
Flits from one toy to another				
Selection of Playmates:				
Plays with several children				
Plays with one child (singles out one child)				
Has same sex playmate(s)				
Has opposite sex play-mate(s)				
Has imaginary playmate(s)				
II. RELATIONSHIP WITH ADULTS				
Parent:				
Comfortable				
Strained				
Hostile				
Indifferent				
Teacher:				
Comfortable				
Strained				

	date:	date:	date:	date:
	source:	source:	source:	source:

II. RELATIONSHIP WITH
  ADULTS (con't)

Hostile				
Indifferent				
Dependent on adults				
Clings to adults				
Independent of adults				

III. COOPERATION

Accepts correction				
Does not accept correction				
Adjusts to routine				
Does not adjust to routine				
Cooperates with suggested activities				
Does not cooperate with suggested activities				
Follows rules when told				
Does not follow rules when told				
Verbalizes rules				
Generalizes rules				
Manipulates situations through coy or seductive behavior				
Exhibits sharing behavior				
Exhibits possessive behavior				

IV. GROUPS

Focuses attention in groups				
Exhibits inattentiveness				

V. SKILLS IN PROBLEM
  SOLVING

Cries				
Seeks help from teacher				
Grabs				
Takes toy when other child is not looking				

Social Inventory (con't)   Child's Name_____
                        School Year 19_____to 19_____

	date:	date:	date:	date:
V. SKILLS IN PROBLEM SOLVING (con't)	source:	source:	source:	source:
Bargains				
Reasons or talks other child out of toy				
Resigns himself to substitute toy				
Finds ways to enter group play				

VI. SPECIAL PROBLEMS

_____

_____

_____

VII. SPECIAL INTERESTS AND COMPETENCIES_____

_____

_____

Allan's Master Readiness Record

This section continues the story of Allan Norwood's career in the PEMS Nursery-Kindergarten. The Diagnostic Interview with Allan and his mother took place on May 25th. At that time Allan appeared to be ready for nursery school experience. Miss Murray, Director of PEMS Nursery-Kindergarten, and Mrs. Norwood agreed that the school was a suitable placement for him. The admission decision was to accept Allan without reservation.

Prior to the opening of school in September, Miss Murray routinely transferred pertinent information from the feeder records, the Diagnostic Interview Form and the Background Information Form, to Allan's Master Readiness Record (see pp. 203–21). In terms of physical development, for example, the Diagnostic Interview Form indicated that Allan was "pale," "ran rhythmically" (maintained balance in running), and "climbed with alternating feet" (maintained balance in climbing). This information was entered in the first column of the Master Readiness Record with the date "5/25" and the source as "Diag. int." (Diagnostic Interview).

Information about Allan's fine motor development was recorded next to "coordinates thumb and index finger to hold an implement" and "coordinates eye and hand." Under Self-Help, Special Problems, Miss Murray noted, "Dress—requires assistance" and "Parent gives help early." She also examined the following notations in the Recommendations section of the Diagnostic Interview Form:

A. Special interest   Trucks, *Winnie the Pooh,* ball play
B. Parent involvement   Early involvement
C. Plan for help   Examine Health Record for explanation
                           of frailty.
                           Build on special interests—will have
                           particular need for familiar objects
                           and activites.
                           Will probably feel abandoned in school—
                           advise staff not to coax him to partici-
                           pate in activities and routines. Allow
                           him to come on his own terms.
                           Assign to Miss Murray.

Reviewing the data on the Background Information Form, Miss Murray entered the information about Allan's tonsillectomy under Health, Special Problems. She also noted that he was "allergic to straw-berries," and according to the Health Record, was a "highly allergic child." Both vision and hearing had been checked in August and found to be normal. Mrs. Norwood had notified the school of the checkups and findings. All the preentrance records were scanned for information about Allan's emotional, mental, and social development and entries were made accordingly on the appropriate inventories of the Master Readiness Record.

On the basis of the preentrace information Miss Murray evolved a tentative plan for help for Allan. This plan not only served as a guideline to ease Allan's transition from home to school, but provided a basis for helping him until more refined information could be collected.

Plan for Help   Allan Norwood

1. Assign to Miss murray.

2. Assure plenty of rest and relaxation until status of health is clarified. Advise staff not to pressure Allan into physical activity.

3. Observe amount and kind of help necessary for care of physical needs. Assign aide to be available to help if necessary.

4. Have trucks, *Winnie the Pooh,* and traffic scene puzzle available. Be ready to guide Allan to these activities on day of entrance.

5. Involve more than one staff member or another child in one-to-one relationship sessions to extend Allan's social involvement.

6. Assign Miss Holland (assistant teacher) to maintain anecdotal recordings regarding emotional and social development to verify impression that Allan may need special help to adjust to social relationships in school.

7. Invite Mrs. Norwood to help with field trip to apple orchard in September.

8. Advise staff not to coax Allan to participate in group activities and projects. Let him adjust to school surroundings through individual activities and interactions with adults. Staff should be alert to his inclinations to participate in the group and be ready to assist him if necessary.

When Allan entered the school, the plan for help was put in motion. The room, equipment, and materials were arranged so that Allan and the other children could become engaged in various activities and show what they could do physically, emotionally, mentally, and socially. The balance beam was set up and ready for use. Balls were available for play on the playground. The indoor jungle gym was ready for climbing and sliding. Concentration toys that would provide experiences with shapes, graduated sizes, and number concepts were easily accessible. The easel was arranged so that four children could paint at one time. The workbench was assigned to an assistant teacher for supervision. Materials and tools were ready for hammering and sawing. The library corner invited individual browzing in familiar storybooks. *Winnie the Pooh* stood in the middle of the shelf.

COLLECTING AND RECORDING DATA FOR THE PHYSICAL INVENTORY

On September 6th the aide assigned to observe the amount and kind of care Allan would require for his physical needs reported that he needed help with several itmes. She checked that Allan could "take care of bathroom needs," "wash hands," and "swing." He could not "zipper," "button," "snap," "tie," "dress himself," or "take care of possessions without help." She added that he could take care of most of these self-care skills if he tried. Miss Murray advised that the aide continue to provide supportive help, for example, by buttoning his overall straps with him. He would be asked to button one strap while she buttoned the other, gradually challenging him to button both straps by himself. She could make the button and snap frames available for him to play with in order to extend his experience in routine self-care skills.

Miss Murray entered the self-care information on the Physical Inventory with the date "9/6" and the source "obs" (observation). Under Special Problems she noted: "Accustomed to help. Self-care problem probably due to lack of experience rather than maturation. Suggest to mother that he wear boxer pants." On the the basis of the aide's report on October 6th, entries in the second column showed that Allan had mastered the skills of buttoning, snapping, buckling, and dressing himself. He still could not zipper or tie, and he needed reminding and directed assistance to take care of his possessions.

Mrs. Norwood had agreed to accompany the group for the field trip to the apple orchard on September 13th. At this time Miss Murray inquired about the outcome of the tonsillectomy. Badly infected tonsils had apparently accounted for Allan's underweight. Since the operation, his appetite that continued to improve. The doctor had assured Mrs. Norwood that he would be fully recovered long before school opened. She reported that Allan still seemed to wear out quickly and needed plenty of rest.

On September 29th Miss Holland observed the gross motor co-ordination of Allan and two other children during playground activity. At first Allan did not participate; he remained by her side. Miss Holland engaged him in ball play, noting that he maintained balance in walking and running after the ball. Later, Allan responded to her suggestion to try the sliding board. He scrambled up the steps, slid down, and ran to the steps. He climbed to the top of the steps, then suddenly descended half-way and jumped to the ground, shouting "Look." Later, in order to check the hopping and skipping ability of the children under observation, Miss Holland organized the game, "Simon Says."

Following the activity, Miss Holland checked in the Physical Inventory that Allan "maintained balance in walking," "running," "climbing," "ascending and descending stairs," and "jumping." Since he could manage only two hops on either foot, she checked that he could not maintain balance in hopping on either his right or left foot. His attempted skip was a galloping movement so "cannot skip" was checked. She also noted under Health a "healthy" complexion and an "active" energy level.

On October 7th fifteen children were taken to the gym for creative movement activities. The warm-up session included activities in which children could demonstrate bilateral motor abilities, specifically "Angels in the Snow" and "Jumping Jacks." Miss Murray, Miss Holland, and an aide were each responsible to observe and record the coordinations of five specific children, respectively. Miss Holland noted that Allan quickly learned "Angels in the Snow," but could not seem to master the more complex coordinations of "Jumping Jacks." Even though he could jump, his arm-hand movements were not coordinated with his jumps.

During circle time on September 12th Miss Murray started the "All About You" unit. Following a developmental sequence in helping children to learn about themselves, this activity was scheduled over a period of time. The aspect of the unit taught on this particular day was planned early in the year to help teachers determine where each child was in terms of knowledge of his own body and of right-left orientation. In the context of broader concept learning the children were asked to name the number and functions of parts of the body. They were asked to point to their right hands, touch their left ears, etc., then point to a peer's right hand, touch his left ear, etc. The children were also asked to determine whether objects held up by Miss Murray were on her right or left side. Miss Holland was assigned to observe and record the responses of Allan and three other children. Sitting next to Miss Holland, Allan was willing to participate with her, but not with the other children. He could recognize his own right and left arms, legs, eyes, and ears, but tended to name the right and left sides of her body as opposite his own. His naming of the position of objects in space with Miss Murray as the reference point was generally inaccurate.

On October 16th Miss Murray organized an art activity with Allan and another child. The objective of the activity was three-fold: to determine the general knowledge of the children, to assess their skill in drawing and printing, and to extend Allan's social involvement by engaging him in a project in which she assumed a central and directive role. Miss Murray, Allan, and Bobby went to the shelf where the crayon boxes were kept. She asked the children if they could find their own boxes. Allan recognized his name on a box. Using 15-by-18 inch paper, Allan and Bobby were engaged in drawing the members of their families. Allan identified his drawings as his "mommy," "daddy," "Winnie," and "Tag." During the course of his drawing he used his right hand three times to pick up crayons and draw and his left hand two times. When they finished their drawings, Miss Murray asked the children to print their names at the top of the papers. Allan printed his name in large irregular letters, widely spaced. He reversed the "N."

COLLECTING AND RECORDING DATA ON THE MENTAL INVENTORY

Following the tentative plan for help, Miss Murray arranged to be available to work with Allan on an individual basis during the first weeks. Her primary objective was to provide the security of a familiar adult to ease his transition into the new environment. Coincidently she could use their time together to determine where he was in terms of mental development.

On September 18th she engaged Allan in a diagnostic exercise to elicit information about his capacity to recognize likenesses and differences, his mathematics concepts, and his language-arts skills. The

materials for the exercise included his box of crayons and a
mimeographed sheet of paper depicting outlines of a large circle and a
smaller square, a large triangle and a smaller rectangle.

"These are all called 'shapes' and each has a special name," explained Miss Murray. Pointing to the circle, she asked, "What do you
think is the name of this shape?"

"That's a cir- cir- circle," answered Allan, then volunteered, "That's
a 'quaoh (square), and that's a twiang'le (triangle) and wectang'le
(rectangle)."

That's right," said Miss Murray. "How many shapes are on the
page?"

One, two, fwee (three), foah (four)," counted Allan.

"Which is the bigger shape, this one or this one? she asked, pointing
to the circle, then the square.

"The cir- cir- circle."

In order to find out about his color knowledge, Miss Murray asked,
"Can you find a blue crayon?"

"This is one," he said picking out the crayon. "It's a pwetty (pretty)
color like the sky."

"Color the circle," she directed to verify his knowledge of the shape
and also to determine his willingness to cooperate and follow directions.

Allan began to color the circle, then stopped. "It's wuff (rough)," he
exclaimed. "It doesn't wun (run) smoovly (smoothly)." Examining the
crayon, he said, "It's bwoke (broke)."

"See if you can find a green crayon." Allan picked one out of the box,
and colored the circle. Following Miss Murray's directions, Allan identified a red crayon with which he filled in the square and a yellow one with
which he filled in the triangle. In order to see whether he could identify his
favorite color by word and selection, she asked him to choose it to fill in
the last shape. He chose a purple crayon. "What color is it?" she asked.

"Pu'ple," he replied.

After the session, Miss Murray checked in the Mental Inventory that
Allan recognized red, yellow, blue, green, and purple. He could identify
objects as big and little. Under General Knowledge she recorded that he
knew the primary colors and concepts of numbers one through five. In
view of his relating blue to the color of the sky, she checked that he generalized from experience and memorized. Under Mathematics Concepts
and Skills, he recognized consistently a circle, a square, a triangle, and a
rectangle, recognized concepts one through five, and counted by ones. He
followed all her directions.

Under Language-Arts, Allan's progress was revealed in his spontaneous comments and answers to Miss Murray's questions. Even though
he tended to show hesitations and speak unclearly, he used a large number

of words, spoke in complete sentences, used adjectives and adverbs to extend ideas, used complex sentences, and communicated ideas clearly. He had difficulty in pronouncing the consonants and consonant blends r, sq, th. He spoke in a controlled voice, understood directions, and listened to Miss Murray.

On September 21st Miss Murray engaged Allan in the Copy Forms Exercise (see p. 211). He could copy from models an acceptable circle, cross, and square; however, his attempt to copy a diamond was unsuccessful. At the same session she showed him a new dump truck with a mechanism for elevating the rear part of the truck to empty the contents. When she asked Allan if he could figure out how the dump truck worked, he identified and verbalized the problem. "This has to go up so things spill out." He examined the truck carefully, turned it over, touched the mechanism, then suddenly pulled the lever that elevated the rear part. Miss Murray checked "uses reason to solve problems," "can identify-problems," "exhibits organization in solving problems," "sees cause and effect relationships," "exhibits curiosity." She tallied the same items under Language Arts as on September 18th.

On October 16th Miss Murray worked with Allan and Bobby in an art activity, drawing the members of their families. During this project Allan indicated that he knew the members of his family, his full name, address, and phone number. He could discuss his pets, Winnie and Tag, and transportation, trucks and cars. He knew that Halloween was two weeks away, and he was going to wear a costume his mother was making—"a spath (space) man."

On October 17th Miss Murray gave Allan the Word Reproduction Exercise (see p. 215) to assess his auditory discrimination. He could successfully reproduce twenty-eight of the words in Part I, Basic Sounds, suggesting minimal competency in discriminating basic sounds. He could only reproduce seven of the words in Part II, Complex Words, suggesting that he had not achieved minimal competency in distinguishing more complex sounds.

COLLECTING AND RECORDING INFORMATION ON THE EMOTIONAL AND SOCIAL INVENTORIES

An evaluation of Allan's preentrance information had led Miss Murray to suspect that he might need special help to adjust to the social aspect of school experience. She had recognized that his mother had a tendency to keep him young and that he had had limited opportunity to interact with peers. In order to acquire early and thorough information about Allan's emotional and social development, she had decided to use anecdotal records. The following anecdotal records were obtained by Miss Holland who had been assigned to observe and record Allan's social and emotional behavior to verify and sharpen the impression of his needs in these areas:

Name: Allan—age 4

Date: September 27

Time of beginning: 1:30 PM

Time of ending: 2:00 PM

Setting: Room Four

Activity: Free play

Incident	*Behavior*
Allan was playing by himself, pushing a toy truck back and forth. Every two minutes he looked up, glanced around at the other children, sucking his thumb. Cheryl sat down beside him and showed him her string painting, "Look at my leaf!" She thrust the paper under Allan's nose. He turned away, saying, "No." As Cheryl bounced away he watched her, then continued to push his truck back and forth. He got up, cradling the truck, and edged near the table where Miss Murray and three children were string painting. Miss Murray said, "Look at the picture of a spider."	Plays alone Sucks thumb Resistant behavior
Allan asked, "They don't really hurt, do they?"	Curious
Miss Murray explained that some do and asked, "Would you like to make one?"	
Allan said, "No" and went to the book corner. He pretended to read *Sparky*. He looked up every two minutes and glanced around the room, sucking his thumb.	Sucks thumb Troubled mood

Date: October 2nd

Time of beginning: 3:00 PM

Time of ending: 3:30 PM

Setting: Playground

Incident	*Behavior*
Allan was playing with three other boys in the sandbox, yet not really talking to them. He filled a dump truck with sand, then dumped it. "Gimme," said Bobby. Allan turned his back, shaking his head and cradling the truck. Bobby	Plays beside other children Plays with same toy daily Possessive (of truck)

Incident	*Behavior*

tried to pull the truck away. "No, don't," cried
Allan. Bobby yanked the truck from him. Allan
ran to Miss Murray, crying, "He took it!" While   Depends on adult
Miss Murray retrieved the truck and soothed him,   Seeks help from teacher
he sucked his thumb saying, "I don't like him."   Sucks thumb
He continued to play with the truck until it was
time to go in. He took the truck into school. When
told to leave it out in the sandbox, he said, "I   Resistant behavior
goin' to take it home." When the teacher ex-   Does not follow rules
plained why he could not and asked him to leave   when told
it, he took it into school anyway.   Troubled mood

Date: October 4th

Time of beginning: 2:00 PM

Time of ending: 2:30 PM

Setting: Room Four

Activity: Circle—music

Incident	*Behavior*

Allan sat quietly, not getting into line to be a   Resistant behavior
train or soldier. Each child was asked to name his   Does not adjust to routines
favorite song. Allan answered, "I forget." He did   Does not cooperate with
not participate in the singing of "Beautiful Sun-   suggested activities
day." He spotted me on the bench, ran over, and   Inattentive in groups
sat close to me. I put my arm around him and   Comfortable with teacher
asked. "Don't you like to sing?"   Depends on adult
  "No," he answered, "I hate it."   Troubled mood

Date: October 6th

Time of beginning: 2:30 PM

Time of ending: 3:00 PM

Setting: Room Four

Activity: Snack time

Incident	*Behavior*

Allan ran up to me and said, "Look teacher,   Depends on adult
aren't my hands clean?" As I put the cookies   (for approval)
out, he counted all the cookies on the table.   Counts to ten
Before prayer, he broke his cookies in half,   Understands concept of
counted the four parts, and began to cram them   four parts of object
into his mouth. I told him to wait but he munched   Does not follow rules
on cookies during prayer. He swallowed his juice   when told
and stood by my chair, sucking his thumb. "Did   Resistant behavior

Incident	*Behavior*
you know my truck bwoke?" he asked. I told him	
to bring it to me. He pointed to Andy, "He bwoke	Accuses (Andy)
it!"	
"No, I didn't," said Andy.	Quarrels (with Andy)
"I saw you. You did!" accused Allan.	
"I did not," Andy protested.	
Allan walked to the block corner, sucking his	Sucks thumb
thumb.	Troubled mood

Date: October 9th

Time of beginning: 1:00 PM

Time of ending: 1:15 PM

Setting: Room Four

Activity: Arrival

Incident	*Behavior*
Allan ran to me and said, "Will you help	Seeks help from teacher
me?" yanking at his zipper. He carried a paper	
bag. I asked about the contents. He smiled and	Enthusiastic behavior
whispered, "I bwought a book an' a wecord from	Even mood
home 'cause teacher said I could."	
Julie asked, "What's in there?"	
"A wecord an' a book. Do you wanna see?"	Shares (possessions)
Mike looked on, and Allan showed all of us	
his book and record.	

Date: October 12th

Time of beginning: 1:30 PM

Time of ending: 2:00 PM

Setting: Room Four

Activity: Free play

Incident	*Behavior*
Allan was playing with water. He was pour-	Plays beside other children
ing water into glasses and bowls from one to	Receptive behavior
another and back again. He poured water over his	
sleeves. The teacher corrected him and he	Accepts correction
stopped. Julie unintentionally splashed water in	
his eyes. He yelled, "You dummy! I never goin' to	Responds irritably
play with you again." He poured water on her. He	
left the glasses and bowls in the water and went	
over to the block corner where Ricky and Bobby	Plays beside other children
were playing. He watched them building an air-	

Incident	*Behavior*
port, and played with a truck. Ricky started to take the truck, "Truck will carry the airplanes."	Possessive (of truck)
Allan said, "No," took the truck, and ran to me, whimpering. He stayed by my side until it was	Depends on adult
time to go to the gym. He sucked his thumb most	Sucks thumb
of the time. When I helped him zipper, he said,	Sees cause and effect
"Only halfway 'cause it's not so cold out."	relationships

Evaluating the Information to Revise the Plan for Help

Late in October there were sufficient entries in Allan's Master Readiness Record to warrant an evaluation and refine or revise the plan for help. In evaluating the record, Miss Murray examined the information to determine developmental meanings and estimate Allan's progress in the various areas. Aware that developmental meanings often become clear only in terms of emerging patterns, she made her diagnoses on the basis of patterns that the data were beginning to form. She then considered the implications of these judgments in terms of Allan's plan for help.

In evaluating the Physical Inventory, Miss Murray noted that there were limited entries under Health. On one occasion Miss Holland had recorded a "healthy" complexion and an "active" energy level. Mrs. Norwood had reported that he seemed to wear out quickly and needed plenty of rest. Miss Murray diagnosed that Allan's health trends were still uncertain; therefore, his plan for help should continue to include plenty of rest and relaxation. He should not be pressured into activities. Complexion and energy level should be watched closely. She also noted that the item "highly allergic child" on the preentrance Health Record needed to be investigated at the parent-teacher interview.

In evaluating Allan's level of motor coordination, Miss Murray noted that he could not do "Jumping Jacks." He could maintain balance in all the leg skills at the alternating laterality level, except for hopping. His inability to do "Jumping Jacks," hop, and skip led her to diagnose that Allan was functioning at the level of alternating laterality; therefore, his plan for help should include activities to develop the large muscles. Since he had not achieved the level of integrated laterality, close, fine work (printing, workbooks) should be introduced sparingly. His plan for help should emphasize activities to strengthen the large muscles and gradually develop the fine muscles.

In terms of right-left orientation, Allan's use of both his right and left hands indicated that handedness had not been established. This information, along with his reversal of "N" and his inability to recognize the parts of another's body and the position of objects, led to the diagnosis that he had not yet developed internal awareness of right and left; consequently, his plan for help should include experiences that would help him to feel how the two sides of his body function—balance-beam activities, experience with relational concepts, left-to-right sequencing activities with concrete objects.

Miss Murray noted that Allan had learned certain self-care skills in a short time, confirming her judgment that his self-care problem was probably due to lack of experience rather than insufficient maturation. Further support of this diagnosis was the information relating to his ability to coordinate his thumb and index finger to hold an implement and to coordinate his hand and eye. On the basis of this diagnosis, his plan for help should include support of the use of his own powers to follow self-care tasks through to completion. She noted that the suggestion should be made to Mrs. Norwood that Allan wear boxer pants rather than the overalls he could not yet manage.

In terms of Allan's Emotional Inventory, Miss Murray recognized that it was too early in his school experience to make a diagnosis. She had anticipated that problems in making the transition from home to school might reflect in this area. Beginning observations revealed a definite pattern of a resistant attitude, a troubled mood, and thumb-sucking. More recent observations included faint indications that the early pattern was a sign of temporary stress in a new situation. He was beginning to show a more positive attitude and even mood. His plan for help should include continued observations in anecdotal record form for at least another month to see if improvement sustained. Trucks and other familiar objects should continue to be available for Allan's use; however, in view of his security with staff members, Miss Murray judged that it was time to help him become aware of other materials and equipment in the school.

An overview of Allan's Mental Inventory indicated that he excelled in this area. The items checked in all of the sections formed a beginning pattern of advanced mental development. More careful scrutiny revealed that Allan's visual discrimination tested at an expected level of maturity. He could manage discrimination activities with refined differences, but his inability to copy a diamond indicated that cutting or tracing with bold outlines requiring use of the large muscles should be encouraged. According to the Word Reproduction Exercise, Allan had not reached minimal competency in the Complex Words section. This finding suggested that he would continue to profit by a concentrated program in sound identification activities. Possibly reflecting this level of maturity in auditory discrimination, his speech was not clear. He needed help with the pronunciation of consonants and consonant blends.

In filling out the Reading and Writing Readiness Summary, Miss Murray noted that he had achieved the following requisite behaviors in terms of mental development: "Recognizes primary and secondary colors," "maintains mental focus," "has mastered broad base of common concepts (experience)," "controls voice," "speaks in complete sentences," and "exhibits creative-thinking skills." In terms of physical development, however, the only checkmark was beside "is free from signs of visual fatigue." He had not achieved any of the behaviors in either emotional or social development. Recognizing that readiness to read and write is a-function of *total* development, Miss Murray diagnosed that Allan was not ready for formal instruction in reading and writing. She did judge, however, that he was ready for readiness experiences of greater complexity. Activities should be selected that would coincidently emphasize the development of visual and auditory discrimination. Since Allan could recognize and print letters, he would profit by certain word analysis exercises; for example, recognizing parts of words that are alike. During these exercises word comprehension should be emphasized; for example, picking out pictures of objects symbolized by spoken or printed words or acting out the meaning of certain words. Both visual discrimination and letter knowledge could be enhanced through both play activities and structured experiences. In order to help his speech and auditory discrimination, opportunities should be provided for him to pronounce words. Teachers working with him should speak slowly, clearly, and distinctly.

In checking over the Social Inventory, Miss Murray recognized that, as in the case of emotional development, it was too early in the year to diagnose. Following a sufficient adjustment period, more observations in anecdotal record form would be necessary to see what behaviors were the reflection of a new experience and what behaviors tended to be characteristic of his social interactions. She noted, however, the patterns that *seemed* to be emerging. The number of occurrences that he played beside other children suggested that he was moving from solitary to parallel play. This indicated increasing awareness of other children and a beginning concern with how he fit into the social world. In terms of his plan for help, interactive sessions involving a mutually enjoyable activity among children who played near one another should be arranged. Teachers should be alert to guide Allan into interactive sessions with Ricky and Bobby who shared his interest in activities involving transportation play.

The items checked in the Relationship with Adults and Skills in Problem Solving sections indicated a beginning pattern of dependency on adults. This pattern was also suggested by his reactions to self-care noted in the Physical Inventory. In order to ease his transition into nursery-kindergarten, the continuing support of an adult had been recommended. The primary consideration in helping Allan had been to provide security in a new situation. Building on the trust established at the preentrance interview, Miss Murray had continued a close relationship with Allan, gradually extending his social involvement to other staff members. In view of the signs of lessened anxiety, as evidenced in the Emotional Inventory, and his tendency to move toward other children, Miss Murray judged that he was secure enough to be weaned toward greater independence. Teachers should encourage him to solve his own problems, even allow problems to go unsolved, rather than to solve them for him. The number of one-to-one relationship sessions should be gradually reduced.

Another pattern seemed to be forming in the Cooperation section. The number of tallies next to "does not adjust to routine," does not cooperate with suggested activities," "does not follow rules when told," and "possessive" suggested a pattern of difficulty in fitting in with the general expectations of the school. Allan needed help to come to terms with and understand limits. Miss Murray recommended that teachers should continue to avoid coaxing him to participate since forcing him against his will might still create resistance; however, she noted that he should be observed carefully for indications of willingness to join activities. One-to-one sessions or small-group interactive sessions with two or three children should include highly structured activities involving the need to follow directions, to observe limits, and to pay attention, followed by more relaxed, flexible activities. The structured activities should be brief in duration at first, then gradually lengthen as Allan extends his capacity to work within limits.

MASTER READINESS RECORD

Physical Inventory   Child's Name *Allan Norwood*

School Year 19_____ to 19_____

	date: 5/25	date: 9/29	date:	date:
	source: *Diag Int*	source: *Obs.*	source:	source:
I. Health				
Complexion:				
Pale				
Healthy		/		
Flushed				
Energy level:				
Vigorous				
Active		/		
Listless				
Vision:				
Symptoms				
Eyes crossed				
Eyes turning in or out				
Watering eyes				
Reddened eyes				
Encrusted eyelids				
Burning or itching of eyes				
Blurring of vision at any time				
Behaviors:				
Thrusting head forward or backward while looking at distant objects				
Frowning or scowling during near work				
Tendency to touch and finger constantly				
Turning or tilting of head to use one side only				
Tendency to rub eyes				

A.H.

Professional Examination   Date: _____ *8/16* _____

                              Findings: *Normal* _____

Child's Name *Allan Norwood*

School Year 19____to 19____

	date:	date:	date:	date:
	source:	source:	source:	source:
I Health (con't)				
Hearing:				
Symptoms				
Earaches				
Abnormal speech (omissions, substitutions, or distortions of sounds)				
Abnormal ear structure				
Behaviors				
Misunderstands directions				
Asks to have statements repeated				
Shows indifference to sound (including what people say)				
Holds head at peculiar angle to listen				
Rubs ear with fingers				
Speaks in monotone				
Speaks consistently in too loud a voice				
Speaks periodically in too loud a voice				
Shows difficulty in locating sound sources				
Shows difficulty in telling difference between sounds				
Does not maintain balance				

Professional Examination   Date:____ *8/28* ____

Findings: *Normal* ____

Illnesses

Date of Absence   Date of Return   Cause

_____   _____   _____

_____   _____   _____

_____   _____   _____

_____   _____   _____

_____   _____   _____

Physical Inventory (con't)   Child's Name *Allan Norwood*

I Health (con't)   School Year 19____ to 19____

Height and Weight:

	Height	Weight		Height	Weight
September	40"	35 lb.	January	____	____
October	40"	35½ lb.	February	____	____
November	____	____	March	____	____
December	____	____	April	____	____
			May	____	____

Existing Conditions: *Back Inf. Form - allergic to straw-berries. Health Record - "highly allergic child"*

Precautionary Measures: _____

Special Problems: *Back Inf. Form - Tonsillectomy in July. 9/13 Mrs. N. verified that infected tonsils had accounted for underweight. Appetite improving. Allan seems to wear out quickly and needs plenty of rest.*

	date: 5/25	date: 9/29	date: 10/7	date:
	source: *Diag Int.*	source: *Obs.*	source:	source:
II. MOTOR COORDINATION				
Bilateral level:				
Child maintains balance in jumping			/	
Child is able to do				
Angels in the Snow				
Jumping Jacks				
Child does not maintain balance in			/	
jumping				
Child is not able to do				
Angels in the Snow				
Jumping Jacks				
Alternating laterality:				
Child maintains balance in				
walking		//		
running	/	///		
climbing	/	/		
ascending and descending stairs		/		
hopping on				
right foot				
left foot				
walking on balance beam				
	A.H.	*A.H.*		

205

Child's Name *Allan Norwood*

School Year 19____ to 19____

	date: 5/25 source: *Diag. Int.*	date: 9/12 source: *Obs.*	date: 9/29 source: *Obs.*	date: 10/16 source: *Obs.*
II. MOTOR COORDINATION (con't)				
Child does not maintain balance in				
walking				
running				
climbing				
ascending and descending stairs				
hopping on				
right foot			//	
left foot			//	
walking on balance beam				
Integrated laterality:				
Child can				
skip				
coordinate				
thumb and index finger to hold an implement	/			/
eye and hand	/			/
Child cannot				
skip			/	
coordinate				
thumb and index finger to hold an implement				
eye and hand				
III. RIGHT-LEFT ORIENTATION				
Lateral dominance (Handedness):				
Child uses				
right hand				///
left hand				//
Reversal error:				
Child reverses				
letters				*N*
words				
numbers				
Recognition of right and left:				
Child recognizes				
parts of his body		/		
parts of another's body				
position of objects				
Child does not recognize				
parts of his body				
parts of another's body		/		
position of objects				
		a.H.	*a.H.*	*g.m.*

206

Physical Inventory (con't)   Child's Name _A. Norwood_

School Year 19____ to 19____

IV. SKILLS (e.g., Tricycling, ball-throwing)

5/25 Diag. Int. - throws ball with direction.

	date: **9/6**	date: **10/6**	date:	date:
V. SELF-HELP	source: **Obs.**	source: **Obs.**	source:	source:
Without help child can				
zipper				
button		/		
snap		/		
buckle		/		
tie				
dress himself		/		
pull on boots				
take care of bathroom needs	/	/		
wash hands	/	/		
swing	/	/		
pour from pitcher into cup or glass				
take care of possessions				
Without help child cannot				
zipper	/	/		
button	/			
snap	/			
buckle				
tie	/	/		
dress himself	/			
pull on boots				
take care of bathroom needs				
wash hands				
swing				
pour from pitcher into cup or glass				
take care of possessions	/ *gm.*	*g.m.*		

VI. SPECIAL PROBLEMS

Diag. Int. - Dress-requires assistance. Parent gives help early. 9/6-Accustomed to help. Self care problem probably due to lack of experience rather than maturation. Suggest to mother that he wear boxer pants.

VII. SPECIAL INTERESTS AND COMPETENCIES_____

_____

_____

MASTER READINESS RECORD

Emotional Inventory   Child's Name *Allan Norwood*

School Year 19____ to 19____

	date: 5/25	date: 9/27	date: 10/2	date: 10/4
	source: *Diag Ent*	source: *Anec. Rec.*	source: *Anec. Rec.*	source: *Anec. Rec.*
I. ATTITUDES Child shows				
enthusiastic behavior				
receptive behavior				
responsive behavior	/			
indifferent behavior				
resigned behavior				
resistant behavior		/	/	/
hostile behavior				
II. MOODS Child appears				
serene				
even				
troubled	/	/	/	/
sullen				
III. SELF-CONTROL Regulates emotions	/			
Does not regulate emotions				
Shows ability to focus mentally	/			
Shows distractibility				
IV. SIGNS OF STRESS AND FATIGUE Bites nails				
Crosses eyes				
Picks nose				
Cries				
Kicks				
Stamps feet				
Bullies other children				
Destroys property				
Talks in a loud voice				
Responds irritably				
Hits				
Bites				
Sucks thumb	/	//	/	
		A.H.	*A.H.*	*A.H.*

208

MASTER READINESS RECORD

Emotional Inventory   Child's Name _A. Norwood_

School Year 19____ to 19____

	date: 10/6	date: 10/9	date: 10/12	date:
	source: Anec. Rec	source: Anec. Rec	source: Anec. Rec	source:
I. ATTITUDES Child shows:				
enthusiastic behavior		/		
receptive behavior			/	
responsive behavior				
indifferent behavior				
resigned behavior				
resistant behavior	/			
hostile behavior				
II. MOODS Child appears:				
serene				
even		/		
troubled	/			
sullen				
III. SELF-CONTROL Regulates emotions				
Does not regulate emotions				
Shows ability to focus mentally				
Shows distractibility				
IV. SIGNS OF STRESS AND FATIGUE Bites nails				
Crosses eyes				
Picks nose				
Cries				
Kicks				
Stamps feet				
Bullies other children				
Destroys property				
Talks in a loud voice				
Responds irritably			/	
Hits				
Bites				
Sucks thumb	/		/	
	A.H.	A.H.	A.H.	

Emotional Inventory (con't)   Child's Name *Allan Norwood*

School Year 19____ to 19____

	date: 10/8	date:	date:	date:
IV. SIGNS OF STRESS AND FATIGUE (con't)	source:	source:	source:	source:
Daydreams	/			
Accuses others				
Regresses to former state (wetting, infantile pronunciation, drinking from bottle)				
Shows strained expression				
Shows masked expression				
Shows rigid posture				
Speaks in whining tone				
Speaks in demanding tone				
Speaks in strained tone				

A.H.

V. SPECIAL PROBLEMS

Diag. Int. - Will have particular need for familiar objects and activities. He may feel abandoned in school. Should not be coaxed to participate in activities and routines. Should be allowed to come on his own terms.

210

PEMS NURSERY-KINDERGARTEN

MASTER READINESS RECORD

Mental Inventory   Child's Name _Allan Norwood_

School Year 19____to 19____

I. CAPACITY TO RECOGNIZE LIKENESSES AND DIFFERENCES	date: 5/25 source: Diag int.	date: 9/18 source: Diag Exer	date: 9/21 source: Diag Exer	date: source:
The child can copy				
a circle			I	
a cross			I	
a square			I	
a diamond				
The child cannot copy				
a circle				
a cross				
a square				
a diamond			I	
He recognizes colors				
red	I	I		
yellow	I	I		
blue		I		
green	I	I		
purple		I		
orange				
He does not recognize				
red				
yellow				
blue				
green				
purple				
orange				
He can sort (classify) things that are alike				
in one way (circles)				
in two ways (yellow circles)				
in more than two ways				
He can categorize				
vegetables				
vehicles				
farm animals				
zoo animals				
animals with fur				
animals without fur				
		J.m.	J.m.	

Child's Name *Allan Norwood*

School Year 19____ to 19____

	date: 5/25	date: 9/18	date: 10/16	date:
	source: Diag int.	source: Diag Exer	source: Ab.	source:

I. CAPACITY TO RECOGNIZE LIKENESSES AND DIFFERENCES (con't)

	5/25	9/18	10/16	
He can seriate (order) by identifying big and little putting three or more different sized objects in order		l		

II. GENERAL KNOWLEDGE

	5/25	9/18	10/16	
Child can identify parts of his body members of his family			l	
Child knows his full name			l	
address			l	
phone number			l	
primary colors		l		
secondary colors				
concepts of 1–5 (referring to objects)		l		
concepts 5–10 (referring to objects)				
names for different kinds of weather (rain, snow, cloudy, sunny)				
Can discuss pets			l	
transportation			l	
holidays and customs			l	
Exhibits enriched background experiences	l			
Exhibits meager background experiences				
Generalizes from experience		l		
Memorizes (Retains information)		l	l	

J.m.   *J.m.*

Child's Name _Allan Norwood_

School Year 19____to 19____

	date: 5/25	date: 9/18	date: 9/21	date: 10/12
	source: Diag.Int	source: Diag.Exer	source: Obs	source: Anec. Rec.
III. PROBLEM SOLVING				
Follows directions	I	I		
Maintains mental focus	I			
Appeals to adults to solve problems				
Relies on trial and error to solve problems				
Uses trial and error to solve problems				
Shows ability to stay with a task				
Uses reason to solve problems			I	
Can identify problems			I	
Verbalizes problems			I	
Exhibits organization in solving problems			I	
Sees cause and effect relationships			I	/
Exhibits curiosity	I		I	
Generates new ideas				
Can find different ways to solve problems				
Can change direction in solving problems (with new information)	I			
Can extend an idea				

IV. MATHEMATICS CONCEPTS AND SKILLS				
Recognizes shape of				
circle		II		
square		II		
triangle		II		
rectangle		II		
Does not recognize				
circle				
square				
triangle				
rectangle				

J.M.   J.M.   A.H.

Child's Name *Allan Norwood*

School Year 19____ to 19____

IV. MATHEMATICS CONCEPTS AND SKILLS (con't)	date: 5/25	date: 9/18	date: 10/6	date:
	source: Diag Inst	source: Diag Eval	source: Anec Rec.	source:
Recognizes concepts 1–5 (referring to objects)	I	I		
concepts 5–10 (referring to objects)				
numerals 1–5				
5–10				
10---				
Counts by 1's	I	I	to 10	
by 5's				
by 10's				
Understands relationships of number:				
more than				
less than				
combinations to make "5"				
combinations to make "10"				
Understands concepts of computation:				
subtraction (take away from objects)				
addition (add to objects)				
parts of a whole:				
1/2 (half of object), 2 parts				
1/4 (quarter of object), 4 parts			/	
equal (same number of objects)				
Recognizes one-to-one correspondence				
Understands concept of time:				
day-night				
schedule of the day				
month				
week				
year				
clock (tells time)				
Sees spatial relationships (puzzles)				

J.M.   A.H.

Mental Inventory (con't)   Child's Name *Allan Norwood*

School Year 19____ to 19____

V. LANGUAGE ARTS

	date: 5/25 source: Diagnost	date: 9/18 source: Diag Conv	date: 9/21 source: Diag Conv	date: 10/17 source: Word Repro Ex
Speech:				
Does not speak clearly				
Does not communicate ideas clearly				
Uses few words				
Does not speak in complete sentences				
Shows hesitations, stuttering, repetition of words		✓	✓	
Uses large number of words	✓	✓	✓	
Speaks in complete sentences	✓	✓	✓	
Uses adjectives and adverbs to extend ideas		✓	✓	
Uses complex sentences		✓	✓	
Relates ideas and events in sequence				
Speaks clearly				
Communicates ideas clearly		✓	✓	
Pronunciation:				
Pronounces vowel sounds				
Pronounces consonants				
m,n,ng,p,f,h,w		✓	✓	
y,k,b,d,g,r				
s,sh,ch				
t,th,v,l				
z,zh,j				
Exhibits control in voice		✓	✓	
Does not exhibit control in voice				
Listening Skills:				
Understands directions		✓	✓	
Relates events accurately				
Relates stories with accuracy				
Thinks about information he hears				
Enjoys listening to a story, record, or poem				
Relates a story in sequence				
Holds on to his own idea while listening to another person speak				
Listens to others	✓	✓	✓	
Word Reproduction Exercise:				
Achieved minimal competency (22) in Basic Words				
Did not achieve minimal competency in Basic Words				✓
Achieved minimal competency (12) in Complex Words				
Did not achieve minimal competency in Complex Words		J.M.	J.M.	J.M. ✓

VI. SPECIAL INTERESTS AND COMPETENCIES *Diag Int — Trucks, Winnie the Pooh*
Back inf. form — machines used on farm (tractor, combine, trucks)

215

Child's Name _Allan Norwood_

School Year 19____ to 19____

READING AND WRITING READINESS SUMMARY

	date: 10/22	date:	date:	date:
	source: Master Read Rec	source:	source:	source:
I. PHYSICAL				
Has achieved integrated laterality				
Has achieved right-left orientation				
Has infrequent reversal errors				
Is free from signs of visual fatigue	I			
Discriminates sounds in the environment				
II. EMOTIONAL				
Has achieved self-control				
Has receptive attitude				
III. MENTAL				
Recognizes primary and secondary colors	I			
Copies a diamond				
Puts three or more objects in order				
Classifies objects in more than one way				
Maintains mental focus	I			
Follows directions	I			
Has mastered broad base of common concepts (experience)	I			
Exhibits basic rules of grammar				
Articulates sounds with clarity				
Pronounces 12 Complex Words in Word Reproduction Exercise				
Controls voice	I			
Shows clarity of expression	I			
Is free from hesitations, stuttering, and repetition of words				
Speaks in complete sentences	I			
Uses language to solve problems				
Exhibits creative thinking skills	I			

Child's Name _Allan Norwood_

School Year 19____ to 19____

READING AND WRITING READINESS SUMMARY
(con't)

	date: 10/16	date:	date:	date:
	source: Obs	source:	source:	source:
IV. SOCIAL				
Shows trends toward cooperative play				
Adjusts to routine				
Follows directions				
V. ACCOMPLISHED READING AND WRITING SKILLS				
Recognizes upper-case letters				
by sight				
by sound				
Recognizes lower-case letters				
by sight				
by sound				
Recognizes first name				
Recognizes whole name	I			
Recognizes other words				
Word analysis:				
Recognizes initial consonants and blends				
Recognizes final consonants and blends				
Recognizes special word parts (in, fin, bin)				
Writing:				
Prints upper-case letters				
Prints lower-case letters				
Prints first name	I			
Prints whole name				
Prints other words				

J.M.

VI. SPECIAL PROBLEMS: _____

_____

_____

_____

MASTER READINESS RECORD

Social Inventory　　　　　　　Child's Name _Allan Norwood_

School Year 19_____ to 19_____

	date: 5/25 source: Diag. Int	date: 9/27 source: Anec. Rec.	date: 10/2 source: Anec. Rec.	date: 10/4 source: Anec. Rec.
I. RELATIONSHIP WITH PEERS				
Play Behavior:				
Plays alone		/		
Plays beside other children			/	
Plays with other children				
Wants to be first				
Boasts				
Shows bossiness				
Quarrels				
Takes the lead				
Follows (assumes supportive role)				
Initiates activity				
Finds way of entering group play				
Plays with same toy daily			/	
Flits from one toy to another				
Selection of Playmates:				
Plays with several children				
Plays with one child				
(singles out one child)				
Has same sex playmate (s)				
Has opposite sex playmate (s)				
Has imaginary playmate (s)				
II. RELATIONSHIP WITH ADULTS				
Parent:				
Comfortable				
Strained	/			
Hostile				
Indifferent				
Teacher:				
Comfortable	/			/
Strained				
Hostile				
Indifferent				
Dependent on adults			/	/
Clings to adults				
Independent of adults				
	A.H.	A.H.	A.H.	

218

PEMS NURSERY-KINDERGARTEN

MASTER READINESS RECORD

Social Inventory   Child's Name _Allan Morwood_

School Year 19____ to 19____

	date: 10/6	date: 10/12	date:	date:
	source: _Nurs. Rec._	source: _Nurs. Rec._	source:	source:
I. RELATIONSHIP WITH PEERS				
Play Behavior:				
Plays alone				
Plays beside other children		//		
Plays with other children				
Wants to be first				
Boasts				
Shows bossiness				
Quarrels	/			
Takes the lead				
Follows (assumes supportive role)				
Initiates activity				
Finds ways of entering group play				
Plays with same toy daily				
Flits from one toy to another				
Selection of Playmates:				
Plays with several children				
Plays with one child				
(singles out one child)				
Has same sex playmate (s)				
Has opposite sex playmate (s)				
Has imaginary playmate (s)				
II. RELATIONSHIP WITH ADULTS				
Parent:				
Comfortable				
Strained				
Hostile				
Indifferent				
Teacher:				
Comfortable				
Strained				
Hostile				
Indifferent				
Dependent on adults	/	/		
Clings to adults				
Independent of adults				

_A.H._   _A.H._

219

Social Inventory (con't) Child's Name *Allan Norwood*

School Year 19___ to 19___

	date: 5/25 source: Diag. Int.	date: 10/2 source: Anec. Rec.	date: 10/4 source: Anec. Rec.	date: 10/6 source: Anec. Rec.
III. COOPERATION				
Accepts correction				
Does not accept correction				
Adjusts to routine				
Does not adjust to routine			/	
Cooperates with suggested activities	/			
Does not cooperate with suggested activities			/	
Follows rules when told	/			
Does not follow rules when told		/		/
Verbalizes rules				
Generalizes rules				
Manipulates situations through coy or seductive behavior				
Exhibits sharing behavior				
Exhibits possessive behavior		/		
IV. GROUPS				
Focuses attention in groups				
Inattentive			/	
V. SKILLS IN PROBLEM SOLVING				
Cries				
Seeks help from teacher		/		
Grabs				
Takes toy when other child is not looking				
Bargains				
Reasons or talks other child out of toy				
Resigns himself to substitute toy				
Finds ways to enter group play				
	A.H.	A.H.	A.H.	

VI. SPECIAL PROBLEMS

_____

_____

_____

_____

VII. SPECIAL INTERESTS AND COMPETENCIES *Back. Inf. Form—Mother perceives Allan as cooperative, shy, sensitive, happy and usually doing what is asked of him.*

Child's Name_____

School Year 19____to 19____

	date: 10/9	date: 10/12	date:	date:
III. COOPERATION	source: Anec.Rec.	source: Anec.Rec.	source:	source:
Accepts correction				
Does not accept correction				
Adjusts to routine				
Does not adjust to routine				
Cooperates with suggested activities				
Does not cooperate with suggested activities				
Follows rules when told				
Does not follow rules when told				
Verbalizes rules				
Generalizes rules				
Manipulates situations through coy or seductive behavior				
Exhibits sharing behavior	/			
Exhibits possessive behavior		/		
IV. GROUPS				
Focuses attention in groups				
Inattentive				
V. SKILLS IN PROBLEM SOLVING				
Cries				
Seeks help from teacher	/			
Grabs				
Takes toy when other child is not looking				
Bargains				
Reasons or talks other child out of toy				
Resigns himself to substitute toy				
Finds ways to enter group play				
	A.H.	A.H.		

VI. SPECIAL PROBLEMS

_____

_____

_____

_____

VII. SPECIAL INTERESTS AND COMPETENCIES_____

_____

_____

Summary

The major purposes of the Master Readiness Record are to: (1) systematize the collection of readiness information about the individual child, and (2) facilitate diagnoses of readiness based on the child's total development. The record is organized according to the physical, emotional, mental, and social dimensions of growth. Inventories representing each growth system consist of listings of specific behaviors that reflect readiness. Designed to permit recordings of information about each behavior at four successive times, the inventories allow space for dating the entry and citing its source.

In order to use the record effectively, the teacher needs to be thoroughly familiar with the developmental areas, the specific behaviors, and their developmental meanings in terms of readiness. The teacher collects the information about the child's behavior from feeder records and through direct observation.

Feeder records are devices for collecting information about specific aspects of development. Data from these records are transferred to the Master Readiness Record to facilitate evaluation. *Observation* is attentive noting in which the teacher is alert to behavior whenever and wherever it unfolds. She may elect to observe the behavior of a particular child to see if intervention is warranted, or she may attentively note certain children to gather specific data. When she observes behavior, she enters a tally mark in the pertinent slot as soon as possible after the incident occurs.

The record facilitates diagnosis of the child's developmental levels. In using the record for diagnosis, the teacher follows the steps in the procedure for diagnosis. The records help the teacher to identify patterns of behavior. The record can also be used to trace out possible causes of atypical behavior. On the basis of the diagnoses, appropriate activities can be planned.

Not only does the instrument provide the basis for progress reports to other teachers, administrators, and resource personnel, but it also serves as the progress record at the parent-teacher conference. The Permanent Record, the final summary of the child's progress, is derived from the Master Readiness Record. Conscientious use of the record of each child helps the teacher to devote attention to all children.

12

Progress and Permanent Records

Introduction

Periodically the information on the Master Readiness Record is reported to the parents at the parent-teacher conference. In this context, the record provides the basis for discussion of the child's progress. Since involvement of the parents is so vital to the child's school experience, it is important to maintain records of what transpires during these conferences. The Summary Parent-Teacher Conference form becomes a supplementary progress record.

The Permanent Record represents a final summary of the child's total experiences in nursery-kindergarten. Reflecting the child's growth in each developmental area, the Permanent Record is a condensation of the Master Readiness Record. The Permanent Record may be retained in the teacher's file for future reference. A copy of the record may be sent to the child's receiving teacher if he remains in the same school system, or to the school to which the child transfers.

Communicating information about the child to other concerned persons represents a major responsibility of the teacher. What information to report, and how to report it, are crucial issues that are a continuing source of concern to the teacher. Even though she reports information about the child to other teachers, the administration, and resource persons to whom the child is referred, the teacher's most sensitive problems tend to be focused in communicating information about the child to the parent and reporting pertinent information about the child to the receiving teacher or the school where he transfers. In both cases, adequate records facilitate the reporting task.

REPORTING TO THE PARENT

The success of the child's educational experience depends in large measure on the system of communication established between home and school. Effective handling of the preentrance procedure opens communication and sets the climate for a trusting, cooperative relationship between parent and teacher. Not only are the parents encouraged to visit the school and contact the teacher about the child, but there is also opportunity for parental participation in various school activities.

The Parent-Teacher Conference

Regardless of the number of informal meetings with parents, it is essential to arrange planned parent-teacher conferences. These conferences assure sufficient frequency of contact between parent and teacher to permit a mutual understanding. Periodic meetings facilitate an exchange of information about the progress of the child. Discussions between parent and teacher help to promote continuity between what goes on in the home and what goes on in the school. Occasionally, home and school may inadvertently work at cross purposes. The conference sheds light on the motives, plans, and concerns of both the parents and the teacher. This increased understanding makes it possible to work in close harmony for the best developmental interests of the child.

The conference takes its direction from the following objectives: (1) to determine the child's reactions to school, as revealed at home, (2) to interpret the child's progress, as noted at school, to the parent, (3) to reveal unique characteristics of the child, as identified by the parent, (4) to evolve a cooperative plan for help, and (5) to promote rapport among parent, child, and teacher. Reflecting these objectives, the Summary Parent-Teacher Conference form (see p. 225) provides an easy method to record the substance of the discussion.

ARRANGING THE CONFERENCE

The number of parent-teacher conferences scheduled during the course of the year depends upon the child's individual needs; however, there should

PEMS NURSERY-KINDERGARTEN

SUMMARY PARENT-TEACHER CONFERENCE

Parent_____ Teacher_____

Child's Name_____
Date_____Conference No._____

I. CHILD'S REACTION TO SCHOOL
fatigue____lack of appetite (for lunch or dinner)____pleasant____
home experiences influenced by school experiences_____ for
example:_____
Child's report of experiences at school: no mention_____
minimal comment_____ talkative_____ no mention of other
children_____other children mentioned_____
Special interests are: satisfied at school____thwarted at school__
Child has developed new special interests____i.e.,_____

II. GENERAL ATTITUDE OF CHILD
happy____contented____satisfied____resigned____resentful___

III. DISCUSSION OF PROGRESS FROM MASTER READINESS
RECORD
Unique characteristics of the child identified by the parent:
_____
_____
_____

Points of emphasis of the conference:_____
_____
_____
_____

IV. PARENT REACTION TO CHILD'S PROGRESS AT SCHOOL
pleased____ accepting____ anxious____ surprised____
resigned____ indifferent____

V. COOPERATIVE PLAN FOR HELP
Parent willing to extend training in the home____
Parent not willing to extend training in the home____
Proposed Plan:_____
_____
_____

be a minimum of two conferences annually. The first conference is usually arranged in the fall soon after the child enters school; the second conference takes place in the spring.

The teacher contacts the parents to arrange for a mutually convenient date and time. An ideal conference situation includes both parents, but usually only the mother is available to come. Whether the conference takes place during school hours or when school is not in session depends upon the employment and other commitments of the parent as well as the availability of staff to relieve the teacher for this purpose. If the time is compatible with the parent's schedule and staff is available, the conference may be arranged while school is in session. Not only do most children like to have their parents come to the school, but also the visit represents another opportunity for the parents to see the program in operation. Provision of firsthand observation of what goes on in the school is an important way to bring the parent into the educational process of the child.

Parent-Teacher Conference

If the conference cannot be arranged during school hours, then the appointment is set for a time when school is not in session. Telephone arrangements for the date and time of the conference are followed by a letter of confirmation (see p. 227). Taking the time to send this form letter forestalls a frequent source of misunderstanding.

PEMS NURSERY-KINDERGARTEN
4 Circle Drive
Coventry Crossing, Pa. 14850

(Date)

Dear Parents,

To confirm your conference date: your conference with_____
_____ has been scheduled for _____
at _____ in _____.

We will look forward to seeing you at that time. In case of an emergency that prevents you from keeping the appointment, please call the school, 218–5356.

Sincerely,

Janice Murray, Director

PREPARING FOR THE CONFERENCE

The teacher's thorough preparation for the conference not only expedites discussion, but generates the parent's confidence in the information the teacher gives. The Master Readiness Record serves as the progress record. Use of this record obviates the need for a special progress record to be filled out prior to the conference. In anticipation of the conference, the teacher reviews the child's Master Readiness Record to become thoroughly familiar with his progress and to refresh her memory about incidents and conditions that require investigation or emphasis during the conference. Since one of the functions of the first conference is to explain the purposes and procedures for maintaining and using the Master Readiness Record, the instrument is available for reference and use. The teacher also has materials on hand to support or clarify the child's progress. Typical materials are samples of the child's printing and his art products.

The teacher also reviews the items on the Summary Parent-Teacher Conference form in order to help her focus discussion. She is geared to listen for certain information. This form is not in evidence during the conference; the items are checked as soon as possible after the parent leaves.

THE CONFERENCE SETTING

The conference takes place in a part of the school facility that is relatively free from traffic and distraction. It is an area that the children respect as off-limits for them; for example, an office with the door closed. If the conference takes place during school time, it is realistic to expect some interruption; however, if the staff is aware of the importance of the interview, disruptions can be kept to a minimum.

THE CHILD'S REACTIONS TO SCHOOL

The teacher begins the conference by initiating a discussion of the child's reactions to the school as revealed in the home. This immediately draws the parent into the conference in a contributing way, tending to alleviate feelings of anxiety the parent may be experiencing. Moreover, parental concerns about the child are more apt to surface when the parent takes the lead to inform and to report. Special problems come to light as the parent discusses the child. By merely asking, "What are his reactions to nursery-kindergarten?" the teacher gives direction to the discussion.

In finding out about the child's reactions to school, the teacher needs practical information that may influence the plan for help. The fatigue the child experiences at home is a crucial consideration. The child is normally fatigued when he first enters school. In the beginning, facing new people and adjusting to a changed routine demands energies the child is not used to expending. If he continues to experience unusual fatigue after a month or six weeks of school, he may be evidencing insufficient relaxation during the school routine. Any change in the child's eating habits should be noted. Snacktime may be scheduled too close to lunch or dinner. Any home experience that is influenced by school experiences should be noted during this discussion.

As the conference evolves, the teacher listens for or asks for information regarding the child's relationships with playmates. If he refers positively to his playmates and the activities he shares with them, he is probably indicating a pleasant orientation toward his relationships with other children. If he reports that he dislikes or hates the other children, or if he responds to questions about playmates in an annoyed, or tense manner, he may be indicating disturbance in his associations that warrants closer observation. No mention of playmates may be a sign of immaturity; other children simply do not matter to him yet. Absence of comment may also mean disturbance or resentment if he has moved toward the level of cooperative play at school.

Both teacher and parents must be cautious about reading too much into what the child does not say about school or home. A typical response to parental or teacher inquiry about what a child did is "Nothing." Often a vague or noncommital response is the result of how the adult approaches the child. Asking what a child did at school or home is too big an order. The child finds it hard to sift out his experience and give a report. Questions that focus on a particular part of the day; for example, "What story did you hear today?" tend to be more productive. Also, questions that require more than a "yes" or "no" answer help the child express himself. For example, "Tell me about your picture" is a type of questioning that gives the child the opportunity to use his articulation skills to communicate information of interest to the parent.

Since the child's special interests represent part of his plan for help, especially as he makes the transition from home to school, his report of the way his interests are satisfied in the school setting assumes importance. If he reports that he is not allowed to play with what he wants, or that the other children always take his favorite toy, he may be indicating that his special interest needs have not been given enough consideration. As a result of school or other experiences, the child may have developed new special interests that can become incorporated into his plan for help.

GENERAL ATTITUDE OF THE CHILD

The parent may indicate directly that the child is happy, contented, satisfied, resigned, or resentful in his attitude toward school. In other cases, the teacher infers his attitude. For example, if the child is eager to go to school, talks freely about his playmates, and reports with enthusiasm about special school activities, then his behavior suggests a positive attitude. If he resists getting ready for school and complains that he dislikes the school, the teacher, or the activities, he is indicating a reaction that may range from resignation to resentment.

DISCUSSION OF PROGRESS FROM MASTER READINESS RECORD

The Master Readiness Record provides the basis for discussion of the child's progress at school. At the initial conference the teacher explains the record, reviewing its organization into developmental areas, the system for recording, and the procedure for interpreting the data. This orientation to the record not only enables the parent to understand the current progress report, but it also serves subsequent conferences.

The record provides a concrete method for articulating the program to the parent. The seemingly unrelated activities of the nursery-kindergarten assume order and purpose in the perspective of the record. Discussion of techniques to identify and develop readiness in specific areas inspires questions and guides parents in their efforts to help the child at home. Moreover, the face that such a complete record of the child's progress is maintained communicates concern and interest in the child as a unique individual.

Not only do parents have the right to know how their child is progressing, but it is also their prerogative to know the basis for the evaluation. A progress report without supporting data can sometimes create wonder and worry about how the teacher arrived at the conclusions. If the parent is familiar with the data as indicated on the record, the evaluation is more meaningful and can better serve to benefit both the parent and the child. As Gilkeson points out,

> The teacher's image of the child is often the first professional evaluation the parent has had. If the teacher sees the child as interesting, creative and happy, the parent can let go of some of her everpresent anxiety about how he is doing. The parent can begin or dare to see her child in this way too. This is a tremendous contribution to family development."[1]

The review of the record lays the groundwork for the discussion of the child's progress. Even though the teacher now takes the lead, emphasis is on the total progress of the child. The child is not only developing at school, but he is also developing in similar and sometimes different ways at home. How the child is progressing at home is significant complementary information. Beginning with the positive, the teacher briefly summarizes the items in each developmental area. As the teacher discusses the progress of the child, items may elicit confirming comments from the parents. When the parent questions an item, it is more productive to inquire about the parent's observation and how it differs from the one reflected in the record.

UNIQUE CHARACTERISTICS OF THE CHILD

Frequently discussion of the child's progress leads the parent to reveal some unique characteristics of the child. These characteristics can range from a colorful item of little consequence to a special problem. In the event of a problem, the parent's voluntary comment facilitates discussion. When the parent rather than the teacher introduces the problem, threat is lessened. The parent is more inclined to be open and objective in examining the problem and finding constructive ways to deal with it.

Any unusual information arising from the conference should be noted in the Summary Parent-Teacher Conference form. The item might refer to a unique characteristic which has just come to light and warrants special

---

[1] Elizabeth C. Gilkeson, *Teacher-Child-Parent Relationships*, no. 88 (New York: Bank Street College of Education Publications, 1955), p. 2.

attention. Other information might concern a parental insight into how to handle a situation more effectively.

PARENT REACTION TO CHILD'S PROGRESS AT SCHOOL

During the discussion the teacher notes the parent's reaction to the child's progress at school. Parents who are pleased and accept the child's progress tend to be realistic in their evaluation of the child. They are aware of what he is and what he can do and express general contentment with the progress he is making. Accepting parents are usually reasonable in their expectations of the child. On the other hand, some parents are so anxious about the child's progress that they may find it difficult to accept a realistic evaluation, either because they find it too positive or not positive enough. They may question extensively and show a need to examine all the implications of a piece of information. Anxious parents need more supportive evidence to come to clear terms with the report. To some parents the child's progress is a surprising revelation because the information is not consistent with their conception of the child. In this instance, supporting data can be helpful in clarifying the evaluation. A surprised response may possibly be indicative of a conflict that causes the child to behave differently at home and at school.

Once they understand the basis for the evaluation, most parents are satisfied. However, a few parents assume an attitude of resignation indicating veiled disappointment in the child. No matter what the child's accomplishments, he does not measure up to their expectations. There are also a few parents who are indifferent to the child's progress. They tend merely to go through the motions of the conference. Asking few questions, they may show impatience with detailed explanations. This indifference is further indication of the nature of the parent-child relationship. Since this relationship tends to be translated into the child's relationships with others, the teacher's recognition of this reaction increases her understanding of the child's behavior and attitudes.

COOPERATIVE PLAN FOR HELP

Throughout the discussion of the child's progress there are opportunities to describe the educational program and the individualized strategies based on the child's specific needs. The notion that education is a series of activities taking place exclusively during school hours can be dispelled. The need for all adults in the child's experience to extend old concepts and develop new ones can be emphasized.

In many cases the school experience supplements a rich home environment that more than meets the child's needs. In other cases parents are eager to learn specific ways to extend training into the home. Unfortunately, there are also cases in which the parent is unwilling or unable to meet the responsibility of providing home training for the child.

Developmental areas that need special attention are discussed in terms of a plan for help that can be carried out in both home and school. The plan may include special recommendations, such as the need for a special eye examination.

For Winnie
2 cups dry foc
1 cup canned f
1 cup water
For Tag
1 cup dry food
½ cup canned
½ cup water

DOG
x x x
FOOD
x x x

TAG   WINNIE

Extending Training in the Home

PROMOTING RAPPORT

A continuing responsibility of the teacher is to establish and promote rapport among parent, child, and teacher. During the preentrance diagnostic interview, the teacher makes a concerted effort to establish a trusting relationship. The same guidelines for developing rapport described in Chapter 4 apply to subsequent contacts with the parent. When these guidelines are followed, understanding between parent and teacher grows. The better the parent and teacher understand one another, the better the child is understood by both.

Understanding does not mean seeing eye to eye on every point. The teacher operates within the framework of her own background, training, and interest in children. The parents bring to the conference not only their ideas and ways of doing things, but also their problems, struggles, and uncertainties. Concern with the realities of living may influence their receptiveness to the teacher's report and recommendations. Occasionally the parents may not respond to the child's progress or to other information according to the teacher's expectations. For example, to parents who are trying to balance the responsibilities of running a home, raising a family and earning a living, the task of helping the child to learn number concepts at home may seem an additional burden not crucial enough to bear. They may retreat from suggestions about involvement that encroach on valuable time.

Comments by the teacher that a change on the part of the parents would improve the child's progress communicates lack of empathy and caring about the parent's attitudes, motives, and concerns. Any hint that the parent should be or do other than what he is being or doing comes through as a rebuke. These impressions may strain rapport to the point of a shutdown in communication. Recommendations for helping the child evolve from a mutual understanding of the child's needs, the rapport that has been established, and reasonable expectations of parental involvement in terms of their total responsibilities. Support of the parents, based on appreciation of their roles, is one of the fundamental principles underlying techniques for guiding young children.

The Permanent Record

It has been emphasized throughout the text that education is a continuous process. The growth sequences and learnings of any given period are rooted in what has gone before and influence the events of the future. The child brings to the nursery-kindergarten learnings from early formative years that affect his adjustment to the program. The preprimary teacher picks up the positive threads of previous learnings to weave a new and extended pattern of experience.

Nursery-kindergarten, as the first formal schooling the child receives, must always be viewed in the larger educational perspective. The influence of the child's early school years reaches far into his academic future. His attitudes toward learning and school take root in this beginning experience. Optimally, he has had the opportunities to acquire the learnings that prepare him to move on to the next level with ease and confidence. For a variety of reasons, however, he may not have progressed in one or more growth dimensions to the point where he can benefit from a more advanced level of educational experience. In view of individual differences, his progress is always evaluated in terms of the total developmental context.

In order to assure continuity of educational experience, a summary of the child's progress should be maintained in the school file for future reference. In addition to a summary of the child's progress, a summary of the child's total experiences should be maintained in the form of a Permanent Record. This permanent record should also be sent to the receiving teacher if the child remains in the same school system, or to the school to which he transfers.

PROBLEMS IN COMPLETING PERMANENT RECORDS

How to fill out the permanent record in a way that enhances rather than diminishes the child's later school experience is a critical educational problem. Some teachers avoid making any negative comments for fear that they may blight the academic and social future of the child. Their summaries emphasize only the positive. There are also techniques for describing behavior in a noninformative way.

Reporting behavior on the basis of insufficient information is an all too frequent tendency. The teacher may have impressions of where the child is developmentally. Her mental pictures of the child's behavioral patterns may or may not coincide with the facts. If she lacks objective data to back up her impressions, she fills out the record on the basis of her subjective evaluation. She may resort to labels to describe the child's behavior, and these labels frequently communicate different messages from those intended. Moreover, labels have a way of becoming permanently attached to the records of a child. It is not unusual for the stigma of a label to follow the child into his advanced educational years. Because of this tendency to record by labels, the academic careers of many children have been adversely affected. In a sense, some youngsters are defeated by their records before they are ever given a chance to prove themselves. These indignities have caused educators to raise searching questions about the potential value of permanent records.

PURPOSES OF THE PERMANENT RECORD

The Permanent Record (see pp. 236–38) described in the following section resolves some of the problems that have raised doubts about the merits of such a record when it is completed according to the recommended guidelines. The primary purpose of the record is to articulate the progress of the child to the receiving teacher and to do so in a manner that protects the dignity of the individual child. Presenting a cogent, objective picture of the child's development, the record provides the teacher with concrete directions for helping him.

Derived from objective data about the child's total development, the record emphasizes the child's individuality—not how he conforms to or deviates from the fictitious normative child. All children have both strengths and limitations; both need to be communicated. There may be comments that can be interpreted as negative; however, these comments are neutralized in the total context of the report. When comments are supported by evidence, there is no need to communicate by labels. The data transmit the image of behavior in terms that mean the same thing to everybody.

DESCRIPTION OF THE PERMANENT RECORD

The information for the Permanent Record is drawn from records available in the child's folder. The first page includes items calling for identifying data about the child and his family. These data are derived from the Background Information Form completed by the parents prior to the child's entrance into nursery-kindergarten. A copy of the child's Health Record completed by the parents as a part of the Background Information Form is included with the Permanent Record. The balance of the items are derived from the main headings on the Master Readiness Record. A final section is designated for recommendations. A sample copy of the Master Readiness Record may be sent to the teacher so that she may understand the basis for the information.

A section of the Mental Inventory of the Master Readiness Record, entitled "Reading and Writing Readiness Summary," is duplicated for enclosure with the Permanent Record. The summary lists critical behaviors reflecting levels of maturity that should be achieved in each dimension of growth before a child is engaged in formal instruction in reading and writing. Dated entries indicate the child's progress in terms of the items listed.

GUIDELINES FOR COMPLETING THE RECORD

In filling out the record, the teacher writes a *brief* summary of the child's progress in each of the listed areas. The following guidelines are observed:

1.   The summary should report *progress,* not just final achievement. If only the final developmental status of the child is reported in the record, there is no indication of how far he has advanced in nursery-kindergarten. Two children may have similar developmental profiles at the end of the program; in terms of where each began, one may have shown dramatic progress, the other may have advanced only minimally.

2.   The descriptive terms from the Master Readiness Record should be used. These terms provide a standard language that promotes objectivity. Most of the behaviors are listed in terms of action verbs. To record

PEMS NURSERY-KINDERGARTEN
4 Circle Drive
Coventry Crossing, Pa. 14850

PERMANENT RECORD

Child's Name_____ Date_____
      (last) (first) (middle)
Teacher_____ Director_____
                                   (or principal)

I. BACKGROUND INFORMATION

Child's Preferred Name_____
(first, middle, or nickname)

Address_____
       (number)   (street)   (city)   (state)   (zip)

Phone Number_____

Birth Date_____ Age_____
        (mo.) (da.) (yr.)

Sex: Male____female____

Father's Name_____
(or guardian)   (last)   (first)   (middle)

Occupation_____

Business Address _____
               (street)   (city)   (state)   (zip)

Business Phone_____

Mother's Name_____
(or guardian)   (last)   (first)   (middle)

Occupation_____

Business Address_____
              (street)   (city)   (state)   (zip)

Business Phone _____

Is father living?____ Is mother living?____ Divorced?____
                                          Separated?____

236

Legal custody of child_____

Child lives with_____

Other members of the family: (brothers, sisters, grandparents, etc.) living at home

NAME	AGE	RELATIONSHIP	INDICATE NAME USED BY CHILD

COMMENTS:_____

Find attached copy of child's Health Record that was filled out by parent at the beginning of the year.

II. Physical Inventory

    A. Health
        1. Complexion
        2. Energy level
        3. Vision
        4. Hearing
        5. Illness
        6. Height_____in   Weight_____lb
        7. Special problems_____

    B. Motor Coordination
    C. Right-Left Orientation
    D. Self-Help
    E. Special Problems_____

III. Emotional Inventory
    A. Attitude
    B. Mood
    C. Self-Control
    D. Signs of Stress and Fatigue
    E. Special Problems_____

IV. Mental Inventory

    A. General Knowledge
      1. Background experience
      2. Command of common concepts
      3. Ability to memorize (retain information)
    B. Problem Solving
      1. Ability to solve problems
      2. Creative-thinking skills
    C. Mathematic Concepts and Skills
      1. Recognizes basic shapes (circle, square, triangle, rectangle)
      2. Recognizes number concepts:
        1-5 _____ 5–10 _____ 10 _____
      3. Recognizes numerals:
        1-5 _____ 5-10 _____ 10 _____
      4. Counts 1 _____
        1-5 _____ 5-10 _____ 10 _____
      5. Understands concepts of computation:
        subtraction _____ addition _____ equal _____
        1-1 correspondence _____
    D. Language Arts
      1. Speaking:
        a. Vocabulary: rich _____ good _____ limited _____
        b. Articulation of sounds _____
        c. Articulation of ideas _____
      2. Listening:
        a. Understands directions _____
        b. Relates information _____

V. Social Inventory

    A. Relationship with Peers
    B. Relationship with Adults
    C. Cooperation
    D. Group Activity
    E. Skills in Solving Social Problems

VI. Recommendations

that a child follows directions and shares is more concrete and objective than merely to report that he is cooperative. The action verbs allow for greater specificity and facilitate clear communication.

An objective report of the child's progress to the receiving teacher or the school to which he transfers helps to assure continuity of educational experience. Without a complete report of where the child is developmentally, the receiving teacher must make quick, sometimes invalid judgments about what the child knows and what he can do. Until she has time to confirm these assumptions, she may expect too much or too little. Expectations that are not commensurate with the child's maturity levels may cause a developmental setback that could have been avoided by adequate information about his earlier experience.

The following sample recording from Allan Norwood's Permanent Record illustrates the preceding guidelines.

II.   Physical Inventory

A. Health

1. Complexion	Child was pale at first, but gradually acquired a healthy complexion.
2. Energy level	Tended to be vigorous and active
3. Vision	Professionally checked—normal
4. Hearing	Professionally checked—normal
5. Illness	Missed two days—colds
6. Height 41½ in.	Weight 39 lbs.
7. Special problems	Allergic to strawberries

B. Motor Coordination

When he entered was unable to maintain balance in hopping, but threw ball with direction. Now maintains balance in all gross motor skills. Cannot skip. Not proficient in thumb-index finger coordination.

C. Right-Left Orientation

Handedness not established. Shows tendency to reverse E, N, 7, and 9.

D. Self-help

When he entered needed considerable help to take care of needs Now requires help with back buttons and fasteners. Does not always keep track of possessions.

III.   Emotional Inventory

A. Attitude

When he entered tended to show a resistant attitude, but after a month began to show a receptive attitude consistently.

B. Mood

At first tended to show a tense mood, but after a month showed a consistently even mood.

C. Self-control

At first had difficulty in keeping his emotions under control, but showed increasing control. Maintains mental focus.

D. Signs of Stress and Fatigue

Frequent thumb-sucking when he entered. Now shows behavior infrequently.

240

E. Special Problems

None

IV. Mental Inventory

A. General Knowledge
  1. Background experience

  Has travelled extensively. Mother spends considerable time reading to him and helping him with skills.

  2. Command of common concepts

  Knew common concepts when he entered nursery-kindergarten

  3. Ability to memorize (retain information)

  Shows ability to memorize rhymes and songs; remembers directions and rules.

B. Problem Solving

  1. Ability to solve problems

  Has consistently shown organization in problem-solving; conceptualizes problems; tends to use reason.

  2. Creative-thinking skills

  Curiosity demonstrated when he entered has sustained. Shows increasing ability to generate new ideas and extend ideas.

C. Mathematics Concepts and Skills

  1. Recognizes basic shapes (circles, square, triangle, rectangle)
  Knew all above shapes when he entered
  2. Recognizes number concepts:
  1-5 _____   5-10_____   10 __X__
  Recognizes numerals:
  1-5 _____   5-10_____   10 __X__
  4. Counts 1–100
  5. Understands relationship of number:
  1-5 _____   5-10_____   10 __X__
  6. Understands concepts of computation:
  subtraction __X__ addition __X__ equal __X__
  1-1 correspondence __X__

    D.   Language Arts

       1. Speaking:

          a. Vocabulary: rich __X__ good_____ limited_____
          b. Articulation of sounds

            When he entered had difficulty with following con-
            sonants: r, th, sq
            Now has difficulty with: th, l

          c. Articulation of ideas

            Has consistently expressed ideas in sequence. At first
            showed frequent hesitations. Now shows few hesitations.

       2. Listening:

          a. Understands directions

            At first did not appear to understand directions.
            Now listens attentively.

          b. Relates information

            Consistently reliable in reporting.

V. Social Inventory

    A. Relationship with Peers

      When he entered tended to play alone. Now plays cooperatively
      some of the time. Tends to play with two other boys.

    B. Relationship with Adults

      At first tended to be dependent upon adults. After first month
      showed increasing independence.

    C. Cooperation

      At first did not participate in school routines, but gradually
      adjusted. Still shows occasional lack of acceptance of routine.
      At first tended to be possessive. Sharing now predominant.

    D. Group Activity

      When he entered did not participate in group activity, organized
      or informal. Participates on occasion. Prefers leadership role.
      Does not follow.

    E. Skills in solving social problems

      Uses reason to solve problems.

242

PERMANENT RECORD (con't)

VI. Recommendations

Allan can proceed on his own to learn. Needs little teacher stimulation and guidance. Can learn through discovery methods.

Tendency to overexertion needs to be watched. Requires frequent periods of relaxation and restful activities.

Summary

Communicating information about the child to the parents and to the receiving teacher or school to which the child transfers represents a major responsibility of the teacher. Periodic parent-teacher conferences facilitate an exchange of information about the progress of the child. The objectives of such conferences are (1) to determine the child's reactions to school, as revealed at home, (2) to interpret the child's progress, as noted at school, to the parent, (3) to reveal unique characteristics of the child, as identified by the parents, (4) to evolve a cooperative plan for help, and (5) to promote rapport among parent, child, and teacher.

Since the Master Readiness Record serves as the progress record, the teacher reviews it to become familiar with his progress. She also reviews the items on the Summary Parent-Teacher Conference form to help her to focus the discussion. At the conference the child's reactions to school in terms of fatigue, eating habits, relationships with playmates, special interests, and general attitude are discussed. Prior to interpreting the child's progress to the parents, the teacher orients the parents to the Master Readiness Record. The ensuing discussion emphasizes the total progress of the child, including his development at home as well as at school. On the basis of the discussion, parents and teacher evolve a cooperative plan for help for the child. The manner in which the teacher conducts the conference promotes rapport among parent, teacher, and child.

Because education should be a continuous process, a summary of the child's total experiences, in the form of a Permanent Record, is sent to the receiving teacher if the child remains in the same school system or to the school to which the child transfers. Some methods of completing a permanent record hinder rather than enhance a child's future educational experience. If the teacher lacks objective data, she may fill out the record on the basis of her subjective impressions. She may rely on labels to describe the child's behavior.

The proposed Permanent Record is designed to articulate the progress of the child to the receiving teacher in a way that protects the dignity of the individual child. The child's strengths and limitations are reported in the context of his total development. The record consists of a face page of identifying data about the child and his family, a copy of his Health Record, items derived from the major headings of the Master Readiness Record, and the Reading and Writing Readiness Summary from the Mental Inventory. In filling out the record, the teacher writes a brief summary of the child's progress in each of the listed areas. She observes the following guidelines: (1) The summary should report *progress*, not just final achievement; (2) Descriptive terms derived from the Master Readiness Record should be used in the summary. A complete and objective communication of the child's progress to the next level helps to assure continuity of his educational experience.

Glossary

Abnormal speech: omissions, substitutions, or distortions of sounds.

Alternating laterality: stage of neuromuscular development at which the child begins to use one side of the body without the involvement of the other side to accomplish a task.

Anxiety: anticipation of an unpleasant event; the feeling that follows upon the perception of danger, be it real or imagined.

Application form: official form used by the parents or guardian in making a formal request for enrollment in any program for the child.

Articulation: speech production skills; clarity in reproducing sounds such as vowels and consonants, as well as expression of ideas in logical sequence.

Attitude: one's prevailing feeling toward oneself or other people, or toward the things and events of one's environment.

Auditory discrimination: capacity to distinguish among sounds; ability to hear likenesses and differences among sounds.

Background Information Form: form completed by the parents prior to the child's entrance to school. Its purpose is to provide information about the child's immediate and extended family, his current and past health, and his mental, emotional, and social development.

Balance: equilibrium resulting from the distribution of energy used to control weight on both sides of the body.

Basic words: those words designated as basic in the Word Reproduction Exercise.

Bilaterality: stage of neuromuscular development at which the child uses both sides of his body equally and at the same time to accomplish a task.

Brochure: folder describing the school, the program, facilities, and staff. It communicates general information to the public and, particularly, to parents of prospective applicants.

Cause and effect relationship: association between a stimulus and response; association between an event that produces change in another event or series of events.

Classification: grouping objects or events according to one or more common characteristics.

Cognition: processes of mental functioning; primarily the process of taking information through the senses and conceptualizing.

Communication: exchange of information.

Communication-system: orderly way of exchanging information.

Complexion: color and texture of skin.

Complex words: those words designated as complex in the Word Reproduction Exercise.

Concept: generalized idea.

Conceptualization: use of the basic processes involved in developing concepts including discrimination, classification, generalization, memorization, and recognition of cause and effect relationships.

Cooperation: willingness to work together with other people for the welfare of the individual or the group.

Cooperative play: situation in which the child plays *with* other children (one child, or more).

Development: unfolding or changing of the child physically, emotionally, mentally, and socially.

Developmental continuum: continuous process of development regardless of the direction it takes.

Diagnosis: judgment applied to information.

Diagnostic interview: preentrance meeting arranged among parent(s), child, and teacher to determine the suitability of the program for the child.

Diagnostic Interview Form: guide for collecting and recording information, and summary of the information gathered at the Diagnostic Interview.

Directionality: ability to make judgments about the direction and position of objects outside one's own body.

Discipline: guiding of behavior.

Discrimination: recognition of differences and similarities among things and events in the environment.

Egocentrism: the tendency to see oneself as the center of the world; inability to comprehend or experience the feelings of others.

Elaboration: extension of an idea. (The ability to elaborate is a creative thinking skill.)

Emotion: a feeling; an affective reaction experienced by an individual.

Emotional development: increased capacity to experience and to express feelings.

Empathy: capacity to comprehend and experience the feelings, thoughts, and attitudes of another person.

Energy level: state of constant energy of the child (related to endurance, stamina).

Entry agreement: formal written expression of the contractual terms agreed upon by home and school.

Evaluation: estimation of the value of information used in clarifying a specific situation or problem.

Feeder records: any source of information collected about specific aspects of the child's development to be fed to the Master Readiness Record.

Fine motor coordination: control of small muscles.

Flexibility: the ability to discover different solutions to a problem. (A creative thinking skill).

Fluency: ability to generate a large number of ideas. (A creative thinking skill).

Four areas of growth: physical, emotional, mental, and social dimensions of growth.

Generalization: act or process of relating similarities among different objects and events in the environment.

Gross motor coordination: control of the large muscles.

Growth lag: period in growth when there appears to be little or no progress.

Growth sequence: order of physical, emotional, mental, and social growth that is followed by most children.

Growth spurt: growth period of accelerated progress.

Guidance: knowing and helping of the child both as an individual and as a member of a group.

Handedness: preferred use and superior functioning of one hand over the other.

Health: state of wholesome well-being.

Hearing: faculty of the ears to receive sound impressions.

Identification: process by which a child thinks, feels, and behaves as if the characteristics of another person belong to him.

Illness: presence of indisposition, disease, or defect that has a mild to severe effect on the child's learning and growing.

Infantile pronunciation: tendency to pronounce words in the way in which they were presumably spoken when the child first learned them.

Integrated laterality: stage of neuromuscular development at which one side of the body does one task while the other side of the body does another task.

Intelligence: measure of how well the mental faculties function.

Kinesthesia: sensation of movement in the muscles.

Label: capsule-form method to transmit a mental image of certain behavioral characteristics exhibited by the child.

Laboratory school: school program reflecting specific theory and methods.

Language: arbitrary system of symbols and sounds.

Language arts: communication skills of speaking, listening, writing, and reading.

Lateral dominance: preferred use and dominant functioning of one side of the body over the other.

Listening: capacity of the ears and brain to receive and interpret accurate sound impressions.

Master Readiness Record: summary of the available data about the individual child in the four areas of growth.

Mathematics: encompassing term including arithmetic (computation of numbers), algebra (calculation of relationships of numbers), and geometry (measurement of areas and space).

Maturation: process of biological changes that ripen a child's capacities to learn and to do.

Maturity: maximum level of developmental progress achieved by the child at a given time in any area of growth.

Memorization: holding of an idea in one's mind; the retention of information.

Mental development: maturing of a person's capacities to acquire knowledge, to use reason, and to solve problems.

Mental faculty: an ability, inherent or acquired, to perform a specific kind of behavior.

Monolaterality: tendency to rely on one side of the body to the extent that the other side is less active; one side of the body does not keep pace with the development of the favored side.

Mood: one's emotional state or outlook at a particular moment.

Motor coordination: body movement involving control of the voluntary muscles.

Number: refers to the concept of how many.

Numeral: refers to the symbol used to represent the number.

Nurturance: warm, caring, protective concern for the child.

Observation: attentive noting.

Originality: ability to generate new ideas. (A creative thinking skill).

Parallel play: situation in which child plays beside other children.

Parent involvement: parent participation in the educational experience of the child.

Permanent record: final summary of the child's total experiences in nursery-kindergarten, indicating his levels of maturity attained in the four areas of growth.

Physical development: increasing capacity of the body to learn and to do.

Preentrance records: sequence of communications between home and school to guide the enrollment procedure.

Preprimary years: ages two to six.

Primary colors: red, yellow, and blue.

Problem solving: discovering and applying appropriate responses to a situation.

Progress record: periodic summary of the child's progress at school and at home indicating the levels of maturity attained in the four areas of growth.

Readiness: level of total development that enables a child to learn a behavior, to comprehend a concept, or to perform in a given way with ease.

Records: forms, inventories, charts, summary sheets, and other materials which structure the collection and recording of data.

Record system: logical sequence of records for collection and use of information about the individual child.

Regression: reversion to more immature behavior.

Reversal error: tendency to mirror letters, words, and numbers in writing; symbols that are reproduced backwards or upside down. (The reversal error may be noted in reading. Symbols may be transposed in shape and order.)

Right-left orientation: ability to distinguish between the right and left sides of the body.

School philosophy: practical, cogent statement of the staff's beliefs about children, how they grow, and how they learn.

Secondary colors: orange, green, and purple.

Self-control: ability to regulate the emotions and behavior in proportion to the emotion-arousing situation.

Self-esteem: one's sense of worth for one's own sake, for one's own capabilities, and for oneself as a human being with unique qualities.

Self-image: one's perception of what others think one is.

Seriation: ordering of objects according to graduated sizes.

Sight: ability to see; the eye's response to light shining into it.

Signs of stress and fatigue: behaviors that express tensions, conflicts, and emotional fatigue.

Social development: increased capacity to establish and maintain relationships with other people and to acquire a value system.

Socialization: two interdependent processes involving the development of relationships with others and the development of a value system.

Sociocentrism: ability to adopt an objective viewpoint about persons, places, and things.

Solitary play: situation in which the child plays alone.

Special problems: as referred to in the Master Readiness Record, any unusual development not accounted for in the inventories.

Stress: fatigue that results from unrelenting strain or stimulation.

Sympathetic circularity: overuse of "like," "you know," and similar terms to confirm ideas and demand understanding without fully expressing ideas.

Template: pattern or mold serving as a guide for tracing.

Trial and error: method of physically going through the motions of alternative responses until one finds a solution that works.

Value: estimate of the worth of a concept.

Value system: set of values classified by order of importance that serves to guide one's behavior.

Vision: capacity of the eyes and brain to receive and interpret accurate sense impressions from an illuminated environment.

Visual discrimination: capacity to distinguish likenesses and differences among stimuli impinging on the eyes.

Selected Bibliography

Alexander, Theron. *Children and Adolescents.* New York: Atherton Press, 1969.

Almy, Millie, with Chittenden and Miller. *Young Children's Thinking.* New York: Teachers College Press, Columbia University, 1966.

Association for Childhood International. *Discipline,* Bulletin 99. Washington, D.C.: the Association, 1957.

Bloom, Benjamin. *Stability and Change in Human Characteristics.* New York: John Wiley & Sons, 1964.

Breckenridge, Marian E., and Murphy, Margaret Nesbitt. *Growth and Development of the Young Child.* 8th ed. Philadelphia, Pa.: W. B. Saunders Company, 1969.

Bruner, Jerome S. *The Process of Education.* New York: Random House, 1960.

Clarke, Paul A. *Child-Adolescent Psychology.* Columbus, Ohio: Charles E. Merrill Publishing Company, 1968.

Cohen, Dorothy H., and Stern, Virginia. *Observing and Recording the Behavior of Young Children.* New York: Teachers College Press, Columbia University, 1970.

Denzin, Norman K. "Childhood as a Conversation of Gestures." Paper read at the 1971 Annual Meetings of the American Sociological Association, Denver, Colorado.

Dittman, Laura L., ed. *Curriculum is What Happens.* Washington, D.C.: National Association for the Education of Young Children, 1970.

Ebersole, Marylou; Kephart, Newell C.; and Ebersole, James B. *Steps to Achievement for the Slow Learner.* Columbus, Ohio: Charles E. Merrill Publishing Company, 1968.

Foster, Josephine, and Headley, Elizabeth. *Education in the Kindergarten.* New York: American Book Company, 1966.

251

Freud, Anna. *Normality and Pathology in Childhood: Assessments of Development*. The Writings of Anna Freud, vol. 6. New York: International Universities Press, 1965.

Furth, Hans G. *Piaget for Teachers*. Englewood Cliffs, N.J.: Prentice-Hall, 1970.

Havighurst, Robert J. *Human Development and Education*. New York: David McKay Co., 1965.

Hurlock, Elizabeth B. *Child Development*. 4th ed. New York: McGraw-Hill Book Company 1964.

Ilg, Frances L., and Ames, Louise Bates. *School Readiness*. New York: Harper & Row Publishers, 1965.

Jenkins, Gladys; Shacter, Helen; and Bauer, William W. *These are Your Children*. Glenview, Ill.: Scott, Foresman and Company, 1966.

Kagan, Jerome. *Understanding Children*. New York: Harcourt, Brace, Jovanovich, 1971.

Kephart, Newell C. *The Slow Learner in the Classroom*. Columbus, Ohio: Charles E. Merrill Publishing Company, 1971.

Lavatelli, Celia. *Piaget's Theory Applied to an Early Childhood Curriculum*, A Center for Media Development Book. Boston: Amer. Sci. & Eng., 1970.

Leeper, Sarah H.; Dales, Ruth J.; Skipper, Doris S.; and Witherspoon, Ralph L. *Good Schools for Young Children*. New York: The Macmillan Company, 1968.

Lowe, Joe. *Prediction and Prevention of Underachievement at the Kindergarten and Primary Level*. Muncie, Ind.: Indiana Public School Study Council, Ball State Teachers College, 1964.

Lowenfeld, Victor, and Brittain, W. Lambert. *Creative and Mental Growth*. New York: The Macmillan Company, 1964.

Muller, Philippe. *The Tasks of Childhood*. New York: McGraw-Hill Book Company, 1969.

Mussen, Paul Henry; Conger, John Janeway; and Kagan, Jerome. *Child Development and Personality*. New York: Harper & Row Publishers, 1969.

Parker, Ronald. *The Preschool in Action*. Boston: Allyn & Bacon, 1972.

Smart, Russell C., and Smart, Mollie S. *Readings in Child Development and Relationships*. New York: The Macmillan Company, 1972.

Smith, Helen K., ed. *Perception and Reading*, vol. 12, part 4, Proceedings of the Twelfth Annual Convention, International Reading Association, Newark, Delaware, 1968.

Soar, Robert S., and Soar, Ruth M. "An Empirical Analysis of Selected Follow Through Programs: An Example of a Process Approach to Evaluation." In *Early Childhood Education*. The Seventy-First Yearbook of the National Society for the Study of Education, Part II, pp. 229–259. Chicago: University of Chicago Press, 1972.

Stank, Peggy L. "Kidi-Prep: A Kindergarten Diagnostic Prereading Program." Harrisburg, Pa.: Bureau of Educational Research, Pennsylvania Department of Education, 1973.

Stone, L. Joseph, and Church, Joseph. *Childhood and Adolescence.* New York: Random House, 1973.

Strategies for Teaching. 2nd ed. Title III Project, Diagnostic Educational Grouping with Strategies in Teaching, in the Bucks County Public Schools in Pennsylvania, Bureau of Special Education, Pennsylvania Department of Education, March 1972.

Wann, Kenneth D.; Dorn, Miriam Selchen; and Liddle. Elizabeth Ann, *Fostering Intellectual Development in Young Children.* New York: Teachers College Press, Columbia University, 1962.

Ward, Evangeline. *Early Childhood Education.* New York: F. A. Owen Publishing Co., 1968.

Weber, Evelyn. *Early Childhood Education: Perspectives on Change.* Worthington, Ohio: Charles A. Jones Publishing Company, 1970.

Index

Ability, diagnosing, 162–68
Abstract experiences:
  guidelines for mental development, 126
  implications for early childhood education, 123
  plan for help, 142–43
Abstractions:
  influence of right-left orientation, 100
  readiness to understand, 99
Academic program, 121–44
Acceptance, 54–55, 232–33
Activities. (*See also* Planned activities)
  for developing fine motor coordination, 98–99
  for developing gross motor coordination, 97–98
  for developing relationships with others, 155–56
  for developing right-left orientation, 102–3
  for developing a value system, 157
  for health, 93–94
  for helping emotional growth, 118–19
  for mental development, 135–43
Admissions decision, 55–57
Alternating laterality, 95
  importance in assessing readiness, 95
  plan for help, 97–98
Amblyopia, 92
Anecdotal records:
  case of Allan, 195–99
  when to use, 165
Anxiety, 113–14
  related to need satisfaction, 113–14

Application Form, 27, 29
  sample, 28
  a preentrance record, 19
Articulating progress:
  continuity of guidance, 4
  Progress and Permanent Records, 223–44
Assessment:
  case of Allan, 59–77
  Diagnostic Interview, 47–58
  guidance procedure, 5
  Master Readiness Record, 161–222
  progress, 223–44
  total experience, 233–43
Attitudes, 115
  Emotional Inventory, 177
Auditory discrimination, 134–35

Baby talk. (*See* Infantile pronunciation)
Background experience, 84–87
Background Information Form, 35–45
  Allan's completed form, 72–77
  a preentrance record, 19
  sample, 39–43
Balance, 95
Balance beam:
  assessing motor development, 95
  developing right-left orientation, 102
Basic Words, Word Reproduction Exercise, 135
Behavior, atypical, 16, 168–69
Behavioral patterns, identification of, 6.
  (*See also* Developmental patterns)
Bilaterality, 94–95

Bilaterality (cont.)
 "Angels in the Snow" activity, 95
 importance in assessing readiness, 95
 "Jumping Jacks" activity, 95
 plan for help, 97
Bloom, Benjamin, 81, 82, 122
Brochure, 21–27
 construction, 21
 content for PEMS Nursery-Kindergarten,
  23–26
 preentrance record, 19
Bruner, Jerome, 122

Case studies:
 Allan's Master Readiness Record,
  189–221
 Allan's Permanent Record, 234–43
 case of Allan, 59–77
 case of Eric, 11–16
Classification, 128–30, 138–39, 179–80
Cognition, 121
Cohen, Dorothy H., 147
Color blindness, 139
Communication, 19. (See also home-school
  communication)
 facilitating, 6
Communication system, 19
Complex words, Word Reproduction
  Exercise, 135
Complexion, 90–91
Concept formation, 124–25
Concept, 124
 developing, 124–25
 general knowledge, 30
Concrete experiences:
 guidelines for mental development, 126
 plan for help, 142–43
Confidentiality, 16–17
Conscience, 152
Consonant sounds, 132–33
Continuity of educational experience.
  (See Education, continuity of)
Cooperation, 153–54
 assessing maturity levels, 154
 Social Inventory, 188
Copy Forms Exercise, 128
Copy Forms Models, 129
Creative-thinking skills, 130–31
Curiosity, 126, 130
Curriculum, 21. (See also Plan for help)

Data collection. (See Information gathering)
Developmental continuum, 80
Developmental patterns, 80–82
 changing emphases in early childhood

Developmental patterns (cont.)
 education, 2
 general to specific responses, 80–81
 growth sequence, 80
 identifying the child's, 6
 implications for early childhood teacher,
  2
 implications for plan for help, 16
 related to individual child, 80
 revising the diagnosis, 11
 varied rates of growth, 81–82
Developmental profile:
 implications for guidance, 3
 procedure for diagnosis, 9
 revealed by Master Readiness Record,
  161–222
Developmental progress:
 case of Eric, 12
 revealed by Master Readiness Record,
  161–222
 using the records to determine, 8
Developmental viewpoint, 80–83
Diagnosis, 8
 plan for help, 16
 procedure for, 9–16
 from recorded materials, 8–16
 revision of, 11
 teacher's role in, 8
 using Master Readiness Record for,
  166–69
Diagnostic Interview, 47–58
 admission decision, 55–57
 creating the atmosphere, 54
 establishing rapport, 54–55
 follow-up letter. (See Follow-up letter)
 illustrated by case of Allan, 59–64
 knowing the child, 48–50
 knowing the parent, 50–52
 letter confirming appointment. (See
  Letter of confirmation)
 mutual decision making, 55–57
 objectives, 48
 parent involvement, 55
 understanding parent-child relationship,
  52–54
Diagnostic Interview Form, 29–30
 Allan's completed form, 68–71
 filling out Allan's form, 65–67
 a preentrance record, 19
 sample, 31–34
Directionality, 100
Disabilities, identifying, 5
Discipline, 156–58
 implementing, 156–58
Dominance. (See Lateral Dominance)

Early childhood education:
  changing emphases in, 1–2
  nature of, 1
  planned guidance, 4–5
  record system, 3
  significance of, 1–2, 80–83, 122–23
Early childhood teacher, 2
Education, continuity of, 4, 233–44
Egocentrism, 147
Elkind, David, 146–47
Emotion, 109–10
Emotional development:
  attitudes. (See Attitudes)
  behaviors reflecting pattern of, 115–16
  diagnosing and planning for, 109–12
  helping growth of all children, 116–17
  helping growth of individual, 117–19
  identifying child's pattern of, 114–16
  importance in total readiness, 109
  importance of play in. (See Play)
  influence of maturation in, 84
  methods from Strategies for Teaching.
    (See Strategies for teaching)
  moods. (See Moods)
  negative cycle of growth, 114
  optimal time. (See Optimal times)
  plan for help. (See Plan for help)
  positive cycle of growth, 114
  role of praise in, 116–19
  self-control. (See Self-control)
  sequence of, 110
  signs of stress and fatigue. (See Signs
    of stress and fatigue)
Emotional Inventory, Master Readiness
  Record:
  attitudes, 177
  moods, 177
  sample, 177–78
  self-control, 177
  signs of stress and fatigue, 177–78
Empathy, 147
Energy level, 90–91
Enrollment procedure, 19–77
Entry Agreement Form, 35
  a preentrance record, 19
  sample, 38
Environment, enriched, 85
Erikson, Eric, 146–47
Evaluation, 10
  information of Master Readiness Record.
    (See Master Readiness Record)
  procedure for diagnosis, 9–11
  revision of diagnosis, 11
  using the records for, 8
  values of record system for, 5

Experience. (See also Background
    experience)
  influence on maturation, 87
  influence on self-care, 105

Fatigue:
  effects on motor development, 96
  health habits, 94
  need for relaxation, 112
  regenerating energy, 150
  signs of, 116
"Feeder" records, 164
Fine motor coordination. (See Motor
    coordination)
Finger painting, 98
First day:
  for Allan, 67, 190–91
  recommendations for, 57
Follow-up letter, 30
  a preentrance record, 19
  sample, acceptance, 36
  sample, rejection, 37

General knowledge, 130
  mental inventory. (See Mental Inventory)
  plan for help. (See Plan for help)
Gilkeson, Elizabeth C., 230
Gross motor coordination. (See Motor
    coordination)
Group activity. (See Planned activities)
Growth lag, 82
Growth spurt, 82
Growth-systems, interdependence of, 2,
    82–83
Guidance, 2
  implications for early childhood, 2–3
  influence on self-care, 105–6
  promoting education as a continuous
    process, 4, 233–44
  record system, 3
Guidance assumptions:
  guidance is for all children, 4
  guidance is continuous, 4
  guidance is for the individual, 4
  guidance is planned, 4
  records based on, 6
Guided activities. (See Planned activities)
Guidelines for construction of brochure, 45
Guidelines for mental development, 125–27

Hamilton, David, 91–92
Handedness. (See Lateral Dominance)
Harris, Thomas A., 156
Havighurst, Robert, 87

Health, 90
  assessing physical condition, 90–94
  importance of relaxation. (*See* Relaxation)
  importance of rest period, 94
  developing sound habits, 94
  importance of teacher observation, 90
  Physical Inventory. (*See* Physical
    Inventory)
  plan for help. (*See* Plan for help)
  planning for individual differences,
    93–94
Health Record, 43
Hearing, 92
  identifying problems, 92
  professional examination (*See*
    Professional examination)
  resources for referral, 92
Height:
  importance of recording, 93
Helping strategies, 5. (*See also* Plan for help)
Hopping:
  assessing motor development, 95
Home-school communication:
  importance for information collecting, 19
  importance for preprimary level, 20
  preentrance records, 19–46
  progress and permanent records, 233–44
  values of record system, 6
Home-school relations:
  case of Allan, 59–77
  collaboration, 20
  conferences, 223–33
  confidence in program, 21
  continuity of guidance, 4
  Diagnostic interview, 47–58
  rapport, 20
Humanistic approach, 2
Hymes, James, 145–46
Hyperactive, l·1

Identification process, 152
Illnesses:
  importance of recording, 92–93
Independence:
  in self-care skills, 104–6
  need for. (*See* Needs, psychological)
Individual attention:
  guidance, 4
  using Master Readiness Record in, 170
  values of record system for, 6
  when to give, 67, 191–202
Individual child:
  guidance, 4
  helping by use of Master Readiness
    Record, 170

Individual child (cont.)
  implications for guidance, 2
  meaning of diagnosis, 8
  procedure for diagnosis of, 9, 11
  type of school, 27
  record system, 3
  values of record system, 6
Individual folder, 17, 128, 227, 233–34
Individualized plan for help. (*See also* Plan
    for help)
  after the diagnosis, 16
  planned guidance, 5
  procedure for diagnosis, 10
  revision of diagnosis, 11
Infantile pronunciation, 133
  case of Eric, 13
Information gathering:
  appropriate, 19–49
  implications for guidance, 3
  meaning of diagnosis, 8
  using the records, 7
  values of record system, 5
Initial Teaching Alphabet, ITA, 135
Integrated laterality, 95–96
  importance in assessing readiness, 96
Intelligence, 121
  optimal time for development, 82
Intellectual development. (*See also* Mental
    development)
  changing emphases in early childhood
    education, 1
Intervention:
  case of Eric, 16
Irregularity:
  diagnosing from Master Readiness
    Record, 168–69
  motor sequence, 96–97
  need for early identification, 82
  procedure for diagnosis, 9–10
  trends in identifying, 2
  using the records, 8

Judgment:
  in diagnosis, 16
  meaning of diagnosis, 8
  procedure for diagnosis, 9–11

Kindergarten Diagnostic Prereading
    Program (Kidi-Prep), 85–87
Kinesthesia, 98

Labeling:
  dangers of, 11, 17, 234
Language arts skills, 132–35. (*See also* Plan

Language arts skills (cont.)
  for help, Language development,
    Mental Inventory)
Language development, 125
Lateral dominance, 100
  implications for plan for help, 101–2
Leadership, 149
Learning disability, 11
Left-right sequencing:
  developing right-left orientation, 103
Letter of confirmation, 27, 29
  sample, 29
Likenesses and differences, 127–30. (See
  also Mental Inventory)
Limits:
  importance for security, 111
  plan for developing a value system,
    157–58
Listening, 92, 134–35

Master Readiness Record, 161–222
  Allan's Record, 202–21
  anecdotal records. (See Anecdotal
    records)
  collecting information for, 164–66
  diagnosing abilities, 162–68
  directions for using, 162–70
  discussing progress from. (See Parent-
    teacher conference)
  Emotional Inventory. (See Emotional
    Inventory)
  evaluating data, 167–68
  "feeder" records as source for. (See
    "Feeder" records)
  Mental Inventory. (See Mental Inventory)
  observation as source for. (See
    Observation)
  Physical Inventory. (See Physical
    Inventory)
  procedure for diagnosis, 9–10
  purposes, 162
  recording information on, 166
  sample, 171–89
  Social Inventory. (See Social Inventory)
  support for referrals, 169
  underlying philosophy, 161
  use in case of Allan, 189–221
  using for diagnosis, 166–69
  using to diagnose atypical behavior,
    168–69
  using to evolve a plan for help. (See Plan
    for help)
Master Readiness Record (cont.):
  using for progress reports, 169–70
  value in helping individual child, 170

Mathematics concepts and skills, 131–32.
  (See also Mental Inventory)
  a sequential experience, 131–32
Maturation, 83–84, 87
  influence on readiness, 83–84
  influence on self-care, 105–6
Maturity, 83
Maturity levels:
  identification of, 5
  procedure for diagnosis, 10
Mental development, 121
  activities, 135–43
  changing emphases in early childhood
    education, 2
  concept formation, 124–25
  developmental viewpoint, 123
  diagnosing and planning for, 121–44
  factors influencing emphasis, 122
  general knowledge, 130, 139–40, 180
  identifying child's level of, 127, 143
  implications for early childhood
    education, 123
  influence of maturation on, 84
  language, 125
  language-arts skills, 132–35
  mathematics concepts and skills, 131–32
  plan for help, 135–37
  problem-solving skills, 130–31
  recognizing likenesses and differences,
    127–30
  science concepts, 142–43
  sequence of development, 124–125
Mental Inventory, Master Readiness
  Record:
  general knowledge, 180
  language arts, 183–84
  mathematics concepts and skills, 181–82
  problem-solving, 181
  Reading and Writing Readiness
    Summary, 184–86
  recognizing likenesses and differences,
    179–80
  sample, 179–86
Models for developing speech:
  case of Eric, 12, 15, 16
  language arts, 141
Monolaterality, 96–97
Moods, 115–16
  Emotional Inventory, 177
Motor coordination, 94
  activities for development, 97–99
  alternating laterality, 95
  assessing readiness, 94–99
  bilaterality, 94–95
  case of Eric, 12

Motor coordination (cont.)
  influence on mental readiness, 99
  plan for help, 97–99
  plan for helping fine motor coordination,
    98–99
  plan for helping gross motor coordination,
    97–98
  Physical Inventory, 173–74
  sequence of development, 94–97
Motor development:
  effects of fatigue, 96–97
  irregularities in sequence, 96–97
Mutual decision making:
  case of Allan, 59–77
  Diagnostic Interview, 55–57

Nagging:
  influence on listening, 141
Needs, psychological, 110–12
  for gregariousness, 111
  for independence, 111–12
  influence on emotional growth, 110–11
  for love, 111
  for mastery, 111
  for relaxation, 112
  for security, 111
  related to anxiety, 113–14
  related to self-esteem, 112–14
Nursery-Kindergarten:
  enrollment procedure, 19–77
  selection for child, 55–57
Nurturance, 52–53

Objectives:
  PEMS Nursery-kindergarten, 24
  Diagnostic Interview, 48
  parent-teacher conference, 224
Observation, 165
  anecdotal records, 165
  behaviors of specific children, 165–66
  as a continuous process, 165
  how to perform, 164–66
  new way of seeing child, 6
Observing and recording:
  behavior, 3
  how to perform, 162–68
Optimal times, 82
  for developing positive relationships, 146
  for developing a value system, 153
  for intellectual stimulation, 1
  for mastering emotions, 110
  for promoting emotional growth, 119

Parallel play, 148
Parent-child-teacher relationship:
  initiating, 54–55
  relationship with adults, 151

Parent-teacher conference, 224–33
  arranging the conference, 224–26
  assessing parent reaction to
    child progress, 231
  case of Eric, 15
  conference setting, 228
  discussing child's reactions to school,
    228–29
  discussing general attitude of child, 229
  discussing progress from Master
    Readiness Record, 229–30
  discussing unique characteristics of
    child, 230–31
  evolving cooperative plan for help, 231–32
  letter of confirmation, 226
  sample, 227
  objectives of, 224
  preparing for conference, 227
  promoting rapport, 232–33
  Summary Parent-Teacher Conference,
    225
  values of record system, 5–6
Parental expectations:
  of child, 66, 231
  of school, 58
Pattern of information:
  case of Eric, 15–16
  identifying from Master Readiness
    Record, 167–68
  procedure for diagnosis, 10
Peer relationships. (See Social development)
PEMS Nursery-Kindergarten, 20
  brochure, 23–26
  history, 23
  philosophy, 20
Permanent records, 233–44
  Allan's record, 240–43
  guidelines for completing, 235–39
  problems in completing, 234
  purposes of, 234
  receivers of, 234
  sample, 236–38
  values of record system, 6
  what to pass on, 234–35
Physical development. (See also Health,
    Motor coordination, Right-left
    orientation, Self-care skills)
  diagnosing and planning for, 89–107
  importance in assessing readiness, 89–90
  importance in early identification
    of problems, 90
  influence of maturation on, 84
  teacher's responsibility, 89–90
Physical Inventory:
  health, 171–73
  motor coordination, 173–74
  right-left orientation, 174–75

Physical Inventory (cont.)
  sample, 171–76
  self-help, 175–76
Physician's report, 44
Piaget, Jean, 85, 122, 134
Philosophy, school, 21–22
  sample of, 21
Plan for help:
  classification, 138–39
  developing relationships with others,
    155–56
  developing a value system, 156–58
  emotional development, 116–19
  evolving at parent-teacher conference,
    231–32
  evolving from Master Readiness Record,
    169
  general knowledge, 139–40
  health, 93–94
  language-arts skills, 141
  likenesses and differences,
    recognizing, 138–39
  mathematics concepts and skills, 140
  mental development, 135–37
  motor coordination, 97–99
  problem-solving skills, 140
  promoting all skills, 142
  revised plan for Allan, 199–202
  right-left orientation, 101–3
  self-care skills, 106
  social development, 155–58
Planned activities. (See also Activities;
    Plan for help)
  influence on readiness, 85–87
  group, 25, 84–89, 153–54, 155–56
Play:
  importance of, 117
  in emotional development, 116–19
  in mental development, 135–43
  in physical development, 97–99, 101, 103
  in social development, 155–58
Play behavior:
  cooperative play defined, 148
  leadership, 149
  parallel play defined, 148
  sequence of development, 148–50
  solitary play defined, 148
Playmates:
  imaginary, 150
  selection of, 150
Praise, 116–19
Preentrance records:
  Application Form (See Application
    Form)
  Background Information Form (See
    Background Information Form)
  brochure. (See Brochure)

Preentrance records (cont.)
  case of Eric, 13–14
  content, 20
  Diagnostic Interview Form. (See
    Diagnostic Interview Form)
  Entry-Agreement. (See Entry Agreement)
  follow-up letter. (See Follow-up letter)
  importance of, 19–46
  letter of confirmation. (See Letter of
    confirmation)
  purpose of, 19
  values of record system, 5
Preprimary years, 1
Primary grades:
  record system, 3
Preventive guidance:
  importance of, 5
  planned guidance, 5
  using the records, 7
Primary school teacher:
  communication of progress to, 6
Problems:
  early identification of, 5, 15, 82
  helping. (See Plan for help)
  meaning of diagnosis, 8
  procedure for diagnosis, 9–11
  Mental Inventory, 181
Problem-solving skills, 130–31. (See also
    Creative-thinking skills)
  Plan for help, 140
  Social Inventory, 188–89
  solving social problems, 154–55
Procedure for diagnosis:
  Collect the data, 9, 12–13, 18
  Evaluate the data, 9–10, 14–15, 18
  Make the diagnosis, 9–10, 15–18
  related to Master Readiness Record, 9–10
  State the diagnosis in objective terms,
    9–11, 15, 18
  Summarize the pertinent data, 9–10.
    13–14, 18
  teacher's role, 8
Professional examination:
  hearing, 92
  preentrance, 44
  related to plan for help, 93
  result of diagnosis, 16
  vision, 92
Professional training:
  for using record system, 3
Progress records, 223–44
  based on Master Readiness Record,
    169–70, 229–30
  parent-teacher conference. (See Parent-
    teacher conference)
  reporting to the parent, 224–33
  Summary Parent-Teacher Conference,

Progress records (cont.)
  225
  teacher's responsibility in reporting,
    223–24
  value of record system, 6
Progress report:
  receivers of, 169–70
  reporting to parent, 228–30
Psychological needs. (*See* Needs,
    psychological)

Questioning skill, 228-29
Quarreling:
  relationship with peers, 187
  solitary play, 148

Rapport:
  establishing, 54–55
  developing home-school, 19–46
  during Diagnostic Interview, 54–55
Readiness, 79–88
  developmental concept of, 83–87
  emotional, 109–12
  importance of teacher-directed activity,
    84–87
  influence of experience on, 84–87
  influence of maturation on, 83–84
  mental 121–44
  nursery-kindergarten, 47–57, 59–78
  physical, 89–107
  reading, 99, 135, 169–70
  Reading and Writing Readiness
    Summary, 135
  records
    Diagnostic Interview Form, 31–34
    Emotional Inventory, 177–78
    Master Readiness Record, 171–89
    Mental Inventory, 179–86
    Physical Inventory, 171–76
    Social Inventory, 187–89
    values of record system, 5
  social, 145–59
  writing, 96, 135
Reading:
  basic competencies, 126
  influence of motor development on, 99
  parent expectations, 51
  readiness, 99, 135, 169–70
  results of "Kidi-Prep," 85–87
Reading and Writing Readiness Summary,
    184–86
Recognizing likenesses and differences:
  discussion of, 127–30
  Mental Inventory, 179–80
  visual discrimination, 127–30

Record-keeping:
  importance of, 7–8
  procedure, 3
Records, 3
  construction, 3
  continuity of guidance, 4
  Master Readiness Record. (*See* Master
    Readiness Record)
  permanent record. (*See* Permanent
    record)
  preentrance records. (*See* Preentrance
    records)
  progress records. (*See* Progress records)
  purpose, 3
  use of the records, 3, 7–18
Record system, 3
  confidentiality, 16–17
  individual guidance, 4
  planned guidance, 5
  understanding all children, 4
  precision tool for guidance, 3
  procedure for diagnosis, 9
  using the records, 7
  values of, 5–6
Referral:
  after the diagnosis, 16
  basis for recommendations, 6
  hearing, 92
  using Master Readiness Record. (*See*
    Master Readiness Record)
  vision, 92
Regression, 82
Relationship, 145
  developing with others, 146–52
  importance of early maternal-child, 111
  parent-child-teacher, 54–55, 151
  supportive of parent, 58
  with adults, 150–51, 187–88
  with peers, 148–50, 187
Relaxation:
  developing health habits, 94
  need for, 112. (*See also* Needs,
    psychological)
Resource agency:
  after the diagnosis, 16
  basis for recommendations to, 6
Rest period:
  health habits, 94
  importance for regenerating energy, 94,
    112, 150
Reversal error, 101
  identification of, 101
  implications for plan for help, 101–2
Right-left orientation, 99
  activities for development, 102–3

Right-left orientation (cont.)
    assessing maturity level, 100
    assessing readiness, 99–101
    developmental sequence, 99–101
    lateral dominance, 100
    Physical Inventory, 174–75
    plan for help, 101–3
    reversal error, 101

Self-care skills:
    assessing readiness, 103–6
    developmental sequence, 104–5
    factors influencing progress, 105–6
    independence, 104–6
    plan for help, 106
    self-responsibility, 105
Self-control:
    development of, 110
    Emotional Inventory, 177
    indications of maturity, 116
Self-esteem, 113
    developing, 112–14
    related to need satisfaction, 112–14
Self-image, 111, 115
    basis for, 158
    development of, 111
    helping individual emotional growth,
        117–18
    influence of physical development on, 103
    plan for developing value system, 158
    related to attitudes, 115
Seriation, 128, 130, 139
Signs of stress and fatigue, 116
    Emotional Inventory, 177–78
    identifying, 116
    plan for help 116–19
Social development, 145
    developing relationships with others,
        146–52
    developing a value system, 152–55
    diagnosing and planning for,
        145–59
    estimating maturity levels, 149–50
    importance in readiness, 151–52
    influence of maturation on, 84
    plan for help, 155–58
    play behavior. (See Play behavior)
    relationship with adults, 150–51
    relationship with peers, 148–50
    selection of playmates, 150
    sequence of development, 146–48
    skills in problem solving. (See Problem
        solving skills)
Social Inventory:
    cooperation, 188

Social Inventory (cont.)
    groups, 188
    relationship with adults, 187–88
    relationship with peers, 187
    sample, 187–89
    skills in problem solving, 188–89
Socialization, 146
Sociocentrism, 147
Speech:
    speaking, 132–34
    case of Eric, 12–16
Staff:
    assignment, 48
    members, confidentiality, 17
    PEMS Nursery-Kindergarten, 25
    and services, brochure, 26
Stern, Virginia, 147
Stimulation:
    influence on readiness, 85
Stress, 112
    atmosphere, 117
    behaviors, 116, 177–78
    influence on development, 112

"Teachable Moment," Havighurst, 87
Teaching strategies, 117–19
Templin, Mildred, 132
Total child:
    case of Eric, 15
    changing emphasis in early childhood
        education, 2
    procedure for diagnosis, 10
    understanding the, 5
Total development:
    influence on readiness, 82–83
Trust:
    developing, 55
    between home and school, 20
Trusting relationship:
    importance in emotional growth, 118

Understanding the child:
    case of Allan, 59–77
    Diagnostic Interview, 48–50
    importance of diagnosis in, 8–11
    from parent perspective, 228–31
    philosophy for, 4–6
    tool for, 2–6
Understanding the parent:
    appreciation of, 232–33
    case of Allan, 59–77
    Diagnostic Interview, 50–52
    tool for, 2–6

Uniqueness of each child:
  determining, 171–89
  recognizing, 4–6

Value, 152
  developing, 152–53, 156–58
Value system, 152
  assessing progress in development,
    153–55
  development of, 152–55
  plan for help, 156–58
  sequence of development, 152–53
Vision, 91
  amblyopia, 92
  assessing readiness, 91–92
  developmental visual problems, 91

Vision (cont.)
  professional examination, 92
  resources for referral, 92
  symptoms of problems, 91
Visual discrimination, 127. (*See also* Likenesses and differences)
Vowel sounds, 132

Weight:
  importance of recording, 93
Word Reproduction Exercise, 135
  case of Eric, 13, 14, 15
  sample form, 136

Yanoff, Jay M., 94–103